THE ROAD BACK TO CHRIST:

REFLECTIONS ON LENT, HOLY WEEK AND THE RESURRECTION

FR. STAVROS N. AKROTIRIANAKIS

Copyright © 2016 by Fr. Stavros N. Akrotirianakis

The Road Back to Christ:
Reflections on Lent, Holy Week and the Resurrection
by Fr. Stavros N. Akrotirianakis

Printed in the United States of America.

ISBN 9781498490184

All rights reserved solely by the author. The author guarantees all contents are original and do not infringe upon the legal rights of any other person or work. No part of this book may be reproduced in any form without the permission of the author. The views expressed in this book are not necessarily those of the publisher.

Unless otherwise noted, Scripture quotations taken from the Revised Standard Version (RSV). Copyright © 1946, 1952, and 1971 the Division of Christian Education of the National Council of the Churches of Christ in the United States of America. Used by permission. All rights reserved.

Cover icons of the Crucifixion and Resurrection, as well as the line drawing of the Prodigal Son, the Extreme Humility, Palm-Sunday-Last Supper-Entombment, the Resurrection and the Ascension—thru the hand of Fr. Anthony Salzman, www.imageandlikeness.com.

Liturgical translations of the various services utilized in this manuscript by Fr. Seraphim Dedes, ued with permission.

Liturgical translations of some of the Holy Week services taken from *Greek Orthodox Holy Week and Easter Services,* compiled and translated by Father George L. Papadeas, published by Patmos Press, South Daytona, FL, 1996 edition.

Quotations from the Divine Liturgy come from two sources: *The Divine Liturgy of St. John Chrysostom*, translated by the Faculty of Holy Cross Greek Orthodox School of Theology, Holy Cross Orthodox Press, Brookline, MA, 1985; and *The Divine Liturgy of Our Father Among the Saints Basil the Great*, translated by the Faculty of Holy Cross Greek Orthodox School of Theology, Holy Cross Orthodox Press, Brookline, MA, 1988. Used with permission.

www.xulonpress.com

In Memory of my Dad, Nicholas J. Akrotirianakis
In Honor of my Mom, Barbara Akrotirianakis

Table of Contents

The Format of This Book..xiii
A Chart of Key Dates..xiv
Acknowledgements... xv
Introduction—Opening the Gates xvii

PART ONE—THE LENTEN JOURNEY

Sunday of the Publican and the Pharisee—Time for a Check Up......................23
Monday of the Prodigal Son—He Whom Humbles Himself Will Be Exalted............25
Tuesday of the Prodigal Son—Your Body Belongs to the Lord 27
Wednesday of the Prodigal Son—He Came To Himself—The Critical Moment..........29
Thursday of the Prodigal Son—One Happy Father 31
Friday of the Prodigal Son—I Never Left! Not True 33
Saturday of the Prodigal Son—We're All Going to Answer 35
Sunday of the Prodigal Son—It Came Naturally to Them 37
Monday of Meatfare—Our Piety is Between Us and God.............................39
Tuesday of Meatfare—What Goes Around Comes Around............................41
Wednesday of Meatfare—And When You Fast 43
Thursday of Meatfare—Treasure in Heaven 46
Friday of Meatfare—God Crowns Effort 48
First Saturday of the Souls—We Don't Worship the Rules...........................50
Meatfare Sunday/Sunday of the Last Judgment—Faith Can Move Mountains 52
Monday of Cheesefare—Come and See What? 55
Tuesday of Cheesefare—Being a Good Friend..57
Wednesday of Cheesefare—Your Soul is the Most Valuable Thing You Have 59
Thursday of Cheesefare—He Had to Become Like Us in Every Way..................62
Friday of Cheesefare—Behold, I am the Handmaiden of the Lord 64
Second Saturday of the Souls—I Can *So* Relate to This 67
Cheesefare Sunday/Forgiveness Sunday—To Serve and Not To Be Served 69

PART TWO—THE JOURNEY TO THE CROSS

Monday of the First Week of Lent—Different Kinds of Healing 75
Tuesday of the First Week of Lent—Martha Actually Set a Great Example 78
Wednesday of the First Week of Lent—Having the Right Values 80
Thursday of the First Week of Lent—We Must Become Like Children.................... 82
Friday of the First Week of Lent—Come with Conviction, Not Just for the Signs 84
Third Saturday of the Souls—God Expects Us to Produce Fruit........................ 87
First Sunday of Lent/Sunday of Orthodoxy—Behold the Bridegroom Comes!
    And What Will He Find You Doing?.. 90
Monday of the Second Week of Lent—Are We in the End Times? Is Everyone
    Going to be Saved?... 92
Tuesday of the Second Week of Lent—All You Need to Remember are
    These Two Things... 95
Wednesday of the Second Week of Lent—What Is Your Foundation Made Of?.......... 97
Thursday of the Second Week of Lent—When You Need Comfort, Go Read a Psalm..... 97
Friday of the Second Week of Lent—The Story of Job 101
Saturday of the Second Week of Lent—Everyone Has Some Talent—God
    Expects Us to Use Them.. 104
Second Sunday of Lent/St. Gregory Palamas—Our Traditions Are Scripture-Based..... 107
Monday of the Third Week of Lent—We've Got to Get it Right in this Life 109
Tuesday of the Third Week of Lent—The Sin of Judas Was Not the Betrayal 112
Wednesday of the Third Week of Lent—The New Covenant 115
Thursday of the Third Week of Lent—Confession: The Manner By Which
    We Examine Ourselves 118
Friday of the Third Week of Lent—By THIS All Men Will Know That
    You Are My Disciples 121
Saturday of the Third Week of Lent—Let Not Your Hearts Be Troubled 123
Third Sunday of Lent/Veneration of the Holy Cross—The Vine and Branches:
    Abiding in God's Love.. 125
Monday of the Fourth Week of Lent—Your Faith Will Make You Some Enemies 128
Tuesday of the Fourth Week of Lent—Christ's Hope for Us............................ 131
Wednesday of the Fourth Week of Lent—Will You Stay When it Counts?................ 133
Thursday of the Fourth Week of Lent—The Importance of "Watching" 136
Friday of the Fourth Week of Lent—Leaning on God When You Are in Agony.......... 138
Saturday of the Fourth Week of Lent—Syncing Up the Flesh with the Spirit............ 141
Fourth Sunday of Lent/St. John of the Ladder—My Kingdom Is Not of This World..... 144
Monday of the Fifth Week of Lent—What is Truth?.................................. 147
Tuesday of the Fifth Week of Lent—Stop Passing the Buck............................ 150
Wednesday of the Fifth Week of Lent—Even Christ Had Help Carrying His Cross...... 153

Thursday of the Fifth Week of Lent—The Greatest Example of Forgiveness 155
Friday of the Fifth Week of Lent—Salvation is Possible Until the Very Last Moment,
    But Don't Wait. 157
Saturday of the Fifth Week of Lent—The Establishment of the Church. 159
Fifth Sunday of Lent/St. Mary of Egypt—What Will Your Last Words Be? 161
Monday of the Sixth Week of Lent—The Passover in the Old and New Testaments. 163
Tuesday of the Sixth Week of Lent—The Executioner of Christ Became a Saint 165
Wednesday of the Sixth Week of Lent—Will We Be Seekers? Attendees? Masters? 167
Thursday of the Sixth Week of Lent—The Fulfilling of a Journey. 173
Friday of the Sixth Week of Lent—Who is Going to Step Forward? 173

PART THREE—THE GREAT AND HOLY WEEK

Saturday of Lazarus—I AM the Resurrection and the Life 179
Palm Sunday—Fear Not Daughter of Zion, Your King is Coming on a DONKEY 182
Holy Monday—Stop Living an Old Testament Christianity. 184
Holy Tuesday—Wise or Foolish, Which are You? 187
Holy Wednesday—Holy Unction and Our Need for Spiritual Cleansing 190
Holy Thursday—Do THIS in REMEMBRANCE of Me. 193
Great and Holy Friday—Condemned by a Tree, Saved by the Tree 195
Holy Saturday—And God "Rested". 198

PART FOUR—THE JOY OF THE RESURRECTION

PASCHA—The Paschal Homily of St. John Chrysostom 203
Bright Monday—The Icon of the Resurrection. 205
Bright Tuesday—The Most Joyful Hymn 208
Bright Wednesday—The Resurrection, from the Gospel of Matthew 210
Bright Thursday—The Resurrection, from the Gospel of Mark 212
Bright Friday/Feast of the Life-Giving Fountain—The Resurrection, from the
    Gospel of Luke. 214
Bright Saturday—The Resurrection, from the Gospel of John. 216
Thomas Sunday—Have You Seen the Lord? Does it Make You Glad to See Him? 218
Monday of the 2nd Week of Pascha—The First Ordination 220
Tuesday of the 2nd Week of Pascha—One of Christ's Greatest Gifts to US. One of the
    Greatest Gifts You Can Give Yourself. 222
Wednesday of the 2nd Week of Pascha—Unless I See, I will not Believe 225
Thursday of the 2nd Week of Pascha—Jesus is My_____ and My _____ 228
Friday of the 2nd Week of Pascha—Believing without Seeing:
    Our Greatest Challenge 230
Saturday of the 2nd Week of Pascha—Being a Christian Requires a Soft Heart. 232

Second Sunday of Pascha/The Myrrh-Bearing Women—Mary Magdalene:
   Talk About a Turnaround 235
Monday of the 3rd Week of Pascha—The Resurrection Didn't Bring Joy to Everyone..... 237
Tuesday of the 3rd Week of Pascha—There Will Still Be Moments of Confusion 239
Wednesday of the 3rd Week of Pascha—Communion is How We Stoke the Fire 241
Thursday of 3rd Week of Pascha—Proof of the Resurrection 243
Friday of the 3rd Week of Pascha—Going Fishing? Now Is Not the Time to Let Up 246
Saturday of the 3rd Week of Pascha—We Are All Supposed to Become Fishermen 249
Third Sunday of Pascha/Sunday of the Paralytic—The Meaning of the Word "Love" 251
Monday of the 4th Week of Pascha—Peter Really Got it Right When it Counted........ 253
Tuesday of the 4th Week of Pascha—Don't Worry About the Other Guy................ 256
Wednesday of the 4th Week of Pascha/Feast of Mid-Pentecost—Let God Arise,
   and the Story of a Dear Friend Named Eva................................. 258
Thursday of the 4th Week of Pascha—Let's Go Back to the Beginning................. 261
Friday of the 4th Week of Pascha—Darkness Can Never Defeat the Light............... 263
Saturday of the 4th Week of Pascha—Are You Ready to "Testify" as a "Witness"? 266
Fourth Sunday of Pascha/Sunday of the Samaritan Woman—Everyone
   Has the Light 268
Monday of the 5th Week of Pascha—There is Power in Being a Child of God............ 270
Tuesday of the 5th Week of Pascha—The Story of the Nativity in Nine Words 272
Wednesday of the 5th Week of Pascha—Show Me Your Glory!........................ 274
Thursday of the 5th Week of Pascha—Grace Molds Us Gradually and Continually....... 277
Friday of the 5th Week of Pascha—Grace and Truth Supersede the Law................ 279
Saturday of the 5th Week of Pascha—His Plans Don't Necessarily Match Our Plans 281
Fifth Sunday of Pascha/Sunday of the Blind Man—What is a Commission? 283
Monday of the 6th Week of Pascha—We Are All Called to Be Disciples and Apostles 286
Tuesday of the 6th Week of Pascha—He Works with Us Even When We Doubt 288
Leave-Taking of Pascha—Recruiting Others is Part of the Deal........................ 290
Feast of the Ascension of our Lord—He Ascended in Glory........................... 293
Friday after the Ascension—So, what Now? 296
Saturday after the Ascension—Baptized by the Holy Spirit........................... 298
Sunday of the Holy Fathers of the First Ecumenical Council—Alive to God
   in Christ Jesus.. 300
Monday after the Ascension—John's End: The Purpose of the "Book".................. 302
Tuesday after the Ascension—The Most Important Thing in Life Is the Only
   Non-Seasonal Thing We Do 304
Wednesday after the Ascension—I Am with You Always! 306
Thursday after the Ascension—Don't Just Stand Around............................. 308
Leave-Taking of the Ascension—The Holy Spirit Comes Down as Fire
   on All People... 310

Saturday of the Souls Before Pentecost—How Many Languages Can You Speak? 312
Pentecost—A Little Pentecost at Every Liturgy 315

EPILOGUE-THE MISSION OF THE CHURCH

Feast of the Holy Spirit—Life in the Early Church 319
Tuesday after Pentecost—The Shortest Distance Between Two Points
   is a Straight Line. 322
Wednesday after Pentecost—Three Thousand Souls in One Day! 324
Thursday after Pentecost—The Purpose of the Church 326
Friday after Pentecost—"Common" is the Root of "Community" 328
Leave-Taking of Pentecost—Do What Pleases God. 331
Feast of All Saints—The End Goal for Everyone: Numbered Among the Saints 333

The Format of This Book

In the Orthodox Christian Church, the feast of the Resurrection is referred to as "Pascha," rather than "Easter." The date of Pascha is calculated each year so that it falls after the first Sunday after the first full moon of the spring equinox, provided that the feast of Passover has occurred. This results many times in a difference in the dates that the Resurrection is celebrated between the Orthodox Church and other Christian denominations. Roughly 20% of the time, both the Orthodox Church and the other churches celebrate the Resurrection on the same day. About 20% of the time, the date is five weeks off. The rest of the time, the date is one week off.

There is 19 Sunday (18 week) period of time each year in the Orthodox Church that surrounds the Feast of Pascha. The first three weeks, including four Sundays, are called the Triodion, or pre-Lenten period. The next forty days, which includes nearly six weeks and five Sundays, is called Great Lent. In the Orthodox Church, Great Lent begins on a Monday called Clean Monday, rather than Ash Wednesday, as it does in the other churches. Great Lent ends on a Friday.

Holy Week follows Great Lent and it begins on a day called "Saturday of Lazarus." Palm Sunday follows, along with Great and Holy Week.

The Feast of the Resurrection is called Pascha and it begins a forty-day period of celebration. After forty days, the church celebrates the Feast of the Ascension. Ten days later (fifty days after the Resurrection), the church celebrates the Feast of Pentecost. The Sunday after Pentecost is the Feast of All Saints. This ends this cycle of "movable feasts" (called this because their date moves every year), which surround the feast of Pascha.

The intention of this book is that it is to be read according to the Orthodox celebration of Lent, Holy Week, Pascha, and Pentecost in a given year. The accompanying chart gives the dates of Pascha from 2017-2050.

Where the chart says, "Triodion begins" that is the day that you should begin reading this book. There is one reflection for each day culminating in the feast of All Saints. If you are not an Orthodox Christian, there are two ways you can read this book. Either you can read it on the Orthodox calendar, or you can read it according to the date of Western Easter, which is also shown on the chart. Take the date of Western Easter and beginning reading 10 weeks prior to that date. If you read this book more than once, you'd read it according to the dates shown on the chart.

Key Dates of the Movable Feasts Associated with Pascha
2017-2050

	Triodion Begins	Great Lent Begins	Palm Sunday	Pascha	Western Easter	Ascension	All Saints
2017	Feb. 5	Feb. 27	April 9	April 16	April 16	May 25	June 11
2018	Jan. 28	Feb. 19	April 1	April 8	April 1	May 17	June 3
2019	Feb. 17	March 11	April 21	April 28	April 21	June 6	June 23
2020	Feb. 9	March 2	April 12	April 19	April 12	May 28	June 14
2021	Feb. 21	March 15	April 25	May 2	April 4	June 10	June 27
2022	Feb. 13	March 7	April 17	April 24	April 17	June 2	June 19
2023	Feb. 5	Feb. 27	April 9	April 16	April 9	May 25	June 11
2024	Feb. 25	March 18	April 28	May 5	March 31	June 13	June 30
2025	Feb. 9	March 3	April 13	April 20	April 20	May 29	June 15
2026	Feb. 1	Feb. 23	April 5	April 12	April 5	May 21	June 7
2027	Feb 21	March 15	April 25	May 2	March 28	June 10	June 27
2028	Feb 6	Feb. 28	April 9	April 16	April 16	May 25	June 11
2029	Jan. 28	Feb. 19	April 1	April 8	April 1	May 17	June 3
2030	Feb. 17	March 11	April 21	April 28	April 21	June 6	June 23
2031	Feb. 2	Feb. 24	April 6	April 13	April 13	May 22	June 8
2032	Feb. 22	March 15	April 25	May 2	March 28	June 10	June 27
2033	Feb. 13	March 7	April 17	April 24	April 17	June 2	June 19
2034	Jan. 29	Feb. 20	April 2	April 9	April 9	May 18	June 4
2035	Feb. 18	March 12	April 22	April 29	March 25	June 7	June 24
2036	Feb. 10	March 3	April 13	April 20	April 13	May 29	June 15
2037	Jan. 25	Feb. 16	March 29	April 5	April 5	May 14	May 31
2038	Feb. 14	March 6	April 18	April 25	April 25	June 3	June 21
2039	Feb. 6	Feb. 28	April 10	April 17	April 10	May 26	June 12
2040	Feb. 26	March 19	April 29	May 6	April 1	June 14	July 1
2041	Feb. 10	March 4	April 14	April 21	April 21	May 30	June 16
2042	Feb. 2	Feb. 24	April 6	April 13	April 6	May 22	June 8
2043	Feb. 22	March 16	April 26	May 3	March 29	June 11	June 28
2044	Feb. 14	March 7	April 17	April 24	April 17	June 2	June 19
2045	Jan. 29	Feb. 20	April 2	April 9	April 9	May 18	June 4
2046	Feb. 18	March 12	April 22	April 29	March 25	June 7	June 24
2047	Feb. 10	March 4	April 14	April 21	April 14	May 30	June 16
2048	Jan. 26	Feb. 17	March 29	April 5	April 5	May 14	May 31
2049	Feb. 14	March 8	April 18	April 25	April 18	June 3	June 20
2050	Feb. 6	Feb. 28	April 10	April 17	April 10	May 26	June 12

Acknowledgements

*I*n February 2015, a parishioner approached me with an idea about creating a *prayer team*—a group of parishioners who would commit to praying for the church and for me during the upcoming Lenten period on a daily basis. I have always enjoyed writing and decided that for the period of Lent in 2015, I would write a daily reflection and send it to whoever joined the prayer team. I had hoped that thirty people would join and the intention was to do this for forty days. Over 150 people joined the Prayer Team and as Lent came to an end, they asked me if I would continue the daily reflections, and so I did.

On the one-year anniversary of these daily writings, as Lent approached in 2016, I decided to create a unit of writings to carry through the 18 weeks of movable feasts connected to Pascha in the Orthodox Church. Encouraged by many to put these reflections in writing, I approached Xulon Press with this project. This is the second book that has come out of the daily reflections of the Prayer Team. The first is entitled *Let All Creation Rejoice: Reflections for Advent, the Nativity and Epiphany.*

I wish to thank those who have helped and encouraged me in this project:

His Eminence Metropolitan Alexios of Atlanta, the Greek Orthodox Bishop of the Metropolis of Atlanta, for his prayers and blessings;

To three mentors who inspired my love of Holy Week: His Eminence Metropolitan Methodios of Boston, Fr. John Zanetos (of blessed memory) and Fr. James T. Adams;

To the many parishioners of St. John the Baptist Greek Orthodox Church in Tampa, FL, for their support of the prayer team and encouragement to move forward with this project;

To all the members of the Prayer Team, for reading my reflections, for your prayers, and for your encouragement;

To the Orthodox Christian Network (OCN) for posting my writings;

To an anonymous donor who provided the funds to make this project a reality;

To Father Anthony Salzman at www.imageandlikeness.com for his permission to use one of his icons as the front cover of the book and as title pages for its five sections;

To Father Seraphim Dedes for his permission to use his translations of the liturgical services;

To the family of the late Fr. George Papadeas at Patmos Press for permission to use his translations of the liturgical services;

To Fr. Tony Vrame at the Holy Cross School of Theology Press for permission to use their translations of the liturgical services;

To Charlie Hambos, Aris Rogers and Catherine Mitseas, who offered helpful suggestions for the text and back cover;

To my Mom for her encouragement and help, and for encouraging me from a young age to develop my writing skills;

To my son, Nicholas, who already enjoys writing, for his unconditional love, and for the beautiful stories he tells;

To my wife, Lisa, for her support of my ministry, for the many sacrifices she makes for our family, and her encouragement to write.

Finally, and most especially, to the Lord, for the great blessing to serve as a Greek Orthodox priest, for giving me a talent to write, and a desire to share that gift through this project. I am thankful for the continued inspiration that He provides and this blessing He has given me to share my thoughts on His Passion and Resurrection.

Create in me a clean heart, o God, and put a new and right spirit within me.
—Psalm 51:10

INTRODUCTION

Opening the Gates

Indeed I count everything as loss because of the surpassing worth of knowing Christ Jesus my Lord. For His sake I have suffered the loss of all things, and count them as refuse, in order that I may gain Christ and be found in Him, not having a righteousness of my own, based on law, but that which is through faith in Christ, the righteousness from God that depends on faith; that I may know Him and the power of His Resurrection, and may share His sufferings, becoming like Him in His death, that if possible I may attain the Resurrection from the dead.
Philippians 3:8-11

Tomorrow we will enter into a nineteen-week period of feasts and fasts connected to the feast of Pascha, the Resurrection of our Lord Jesus Christ. This yearly journey combines preparation, introspection, narrative, joy and purpose.

There is a twenty-two day period of "Preparation" which is known as the "Triodion." (Liturgically speaking, the Triodion is the period of time from the Sunday of the Publican and the Pharisee through Holy Saturday, when the canon of the Orthros is limited to "three odes" instead of the usual nine, but in contemporary terms, the Triodion is a four Sunday period with the intervening weekdays included). During this period of time, we are supposed to prepare ourselves for Great Lent and the "great fast" which goes with it. Triodion should be a time of reflection and goal setting so that Lent can be a time of spiritual growth and change.

Great Lent begins on a Monday, called Clean Monday, and lasts forty days, including five Sundays. Great Lent is a period of introspection, marked by fasting, additional services, dark colors in church, and confession. Great Lent should be a time when we make positive changes in our spiritual lives. There is a saying that if you can do something for thirty days, it becomes a habit. Making some spiritual changes to your life during Lent, and doing them for forty days, should make for better habits once Lent is over. In the Orthodox Church, we don't focus so much on giving things up or deprivation (only to get them back once Lent is over). Rather we should focus on sharpening our spiritual senses, making small changes and then striving to keep these changes in place once Lent is over.

Holy Week is an eight-day journey that allows us to relive and relearn the events of the Passion and Resurrection of Christ. We relive the narrative in scriptures and in hymns and in liturgical actions, like the Procession of the Crucified Christ, the un-nailing from the Cross, and the journey to the empty tomb.

The Paschal Season is one of joy. During this time we feast and celebrate the successful conclusion of the Lenten journey. We begin all things anew and strive to solidify the habits we began during Lent to become permanent parts of our life. The Paschal season lasts forty days, from Pascha until the feast of the Ascension.

The final three weeks of this journey highlight three feasts—the Holy Fathers, Pentecost and All Saints Day—that define our purpose as a church. We are the church of Pentecost, continually graced by the Holy Spirit. Like the Holy Fathers, we are all called to proclaim the truth of Christ, with the goal of becoming Saints at the end of the journey.

During this period of time, the prayer team will be divided into five units. For the period of the Triodion, twenty-two days beginning tomorrow, we will examine the scriptures of Triodion and Great Lent, primarily the ones that are part of the Sunday readings on each of these nine Sundays, as well as the Saturday of the Souls and the Feast of the Annunciation.

Over the course of Great Lent, we will examine the scriptures that are part of the cycle of Holy Week services in the Orthodox Church. For the period of Holy Week itself, we will highlight *one* scripture reading from each day.

Throughout the Paschal Season, we will examine the post-Resurrection Gospels. For the final couple of weeks after the Ascension, we will talk about Pentecost, life in the early church, and the goal of life in the present church. This unit will end on the Sunday of All Saints Day.

**For those who are reading this message who are not Orthodox Christians, our date of Easter (referred to as Pascha in these writings) often differs from the rest of Christianity. We cannot celebrate the Resurrection until the Jews have celebrated Passover. Please see the section on "The Format of this Book" to find out when Orthodox Lent and Pascha is celebrated each year.

Each day in these reflections, you will find a scripture verse or verses, a reflection, and a prayer or hymn from one of the liturgical services of the season.

The goal of the Prayer Team is to lead you to pray. The goal of the Lenten and Paschal journey each year is to stimulate you to grow. Spiritual growth and prayer go hand in hand. Thank you for reading these reflections. I hope you will take some spiritual benefit from the journey we are about to begin. These reflections are not substitutions for prayer and scripture reading. They are meant to encourage and help you to pray more, and to help you understand the scriptures you are reading. I encourage you to also read the scripture passages that surround the selected verses each day.

Today's hymns are chanted on all nine Sundays of Triodion and Lent, beginning tomorrow. They remind us of God's judgment, but also His great mercy. As we open the gates and begin our journey to the Cross and Resurrection of Christ, we must open the gates to our souls for a period of examination and growth, so that when we proclaim that Christ is Risen from the dead, we do so not only because we've marked another year of time, but because we've made the journey of repentance, the journey back to God our Father.

Glory to the Father and to the Son and to the Holy Spirit.
Open to me the gates of repentance, O Giver of Life, for early in the morning my spirit hastens to Your holy temple bringing the temple of my body all defiled. But as one compassionate, cleanse me, I pray, by Your loving-kindness and mercy.
Both now and forever and to the ages of ages. Amen.
Guide me in the paths of salvation, O Theotokos, for I have befouled my soul with shameful sins and I heedlessly squandered all of my life's resources. By your intercession deliver me from every uncleanness.

Have mercy on me, O God, according to Your great mercy; and according to the abundance of Your compassion, blot out my transgression.
When I ponder in my wretchedness on the many terrible things that I have done, I tremble for that fearful day, the Day of Judgment. But trusting in the mercy of Your compassion, like David I cry out to You, "Have mercy on me, O God, according to Your great mercy.
(From the Orthros on all Sundays of the Triodion and Great Lent, Trans. by Fr. Seraphim Dedes)

Let the journey begin!

PART ONE—THE LENTEN JOURNEY

The Prodigal Son

Thru the hand of Fr. Anthony Salzman, www.imageandlikeness.com

Sunday of the Publican and the Pharisee

Time for a Check Up

Now you have observed my teaching, my conduct, my aim in life, my faith, my patience, my love, my steadfastness.
2 Timothy 3:10
(Epistle on the Sunday of the Publican and the Pharisee)

Depending on what kind of car you drive, every 3,000-5,000 miles you need to take it in for an oil change. I remember an OLD commercial where a car dealership advertised a 19-point inspection for $19. Yes, that had to have been a long time ago! I remember going to the car dealership and the mechanic looking at his checklist of the 19 points and telling me how my car checked out—a little low on brake fluid, tire pressure good, etc.

The period of the Triodion, which begins today, is a time for us to evaluate ourselves on a spiritual scale. Saint Paul, in his Epistle to Timothy, offers us a good "seven-point inspection" of our spiritual lives. So, as an exercise, take a few moments and evaluate yourself on these seven points. Perhaps even a scale of 1 to 10, rate how you are doing:

My teaching—what kind of Christian example are you setting for others? Whether you actively are "teaching" about Christ verbally, we all "teach" by example. What kind of example of Christianity are you modeling for your "students"—your spouse, children, friends, and anyone else you encounter on a regular basis?

My conduct—am I living my life according to the tenets of Christianity and the teachings of Christ?

My aim in life—Do I live with a sense of purpose? Is God the source and center of my life? Is my aim in life to please Him, or to please myself?

My faith—I'm now a year older than I was last year when we celebrated Pascha. Has my faith grown in the past year? Am I excited about my faith? Or stagnant?

My patience—this sin trips up most people on a daily basis. How is your patience on a daily basis? In control? Easily lost?

My love—Every commandment that God ever gave us comes under the umbrella of "love." Fear, anger, lust, sadness, all of these things are the antithesis of love. Joy, chastity, confidence and gratitude are all manifestations of love. Which set of words describes your life best at present: fear, anger, lust, and sadness, or joy, chastity, confidence, and gratitude?

My steadfastness—The journey of life, for most of us thankfully, is long. Along the way, we go through periods of joy and confidence. This is true for life in general and also for faith. There are times when we feel we are getting ahead, other times when we feel like we are falling behind, and other times we are just standing still. IF YOU ARE READING THIS MESSAGE, give yourself at least a FIVE for steadfastness. Steadfastness is being in the game, showing up to play. It doesn't necessarily mean winning!

Going back to the example of the 19-point car inspection, once the inspection is complete, a diagnosis is made. Then the work is done to correct the problem. Finally, the car owner leaves happy that his or her car is in good working condition. Triodion, this period of preparation for Lent, is a period of inspection of our relationship with Christ, with our spiritual life. Lent is the period where we correct the problem, so that on Pascha, we can reclaim our full sense of joy, knowing that our hearts and souls are in good working condition.

Start evaluating, and the evaluation is not good, don't despair. That's why we have this period of time on our calendar each year, to repair and renew. The most important thing in any evaluation is honesty. So, make an honest evaluation of yourself. Look at the end result of the process: a fully repaired you. Then start to tackle the work in between.

> *The Pharisee, who justified himself by boasting about his works, O Lord, You condemned; but You justified the Publican who was modest, and who with sighs prayed for expiation. For You do not accept boastful thoughts, but hearts that are contrite You do not despise. Therefore we, too, in humility fall down before You, who suffered for us. Grant us absolution and great mercy. (Doxastikon from the Orthros of the Sunday of the Publican and Pharisee, Trans by Fr. Seraphim Dedes)*

Make an evaluation today!

> *Note: There is no fasting this week. Because the Pharisee boasted about his fasting, we abstain from fasting during the week following this Gospel reading.*

Monday of the Prodigal Son

He Who Humbles Himself Will Be Exalted

Jesus said this parable: Two men went down to the temple to pray, one a Pharisee, and the other a tax collector. The Pharisee stood and prayed thus with himself, 'God I thank Thee that I am not like other men, extortioners, unjust, adulterers, or even like this tax collector. I fast twice a week, I give tithes of all that I get.' But the tax collector, standing far off, would not even lift up his eyes to heaven, but beat his breast, saying 'God be merciful to me a sinner!' I tell you, this man went to his house justified rather than the other; for every one who exalts himself will be humbled, but he who humbles himself will be exalted."
Luke 18:10-14
(Gospel on the Sunday of the Publican and the Pharisee)

Your motivation for just about anything you do in life can be separated into two categories: it's either all about God, or it's all about you. If it were all about *you*, we would call that "pride." If it were all about *God*, we'd call that "humility." What if it's all about "the other guy," doing something for someone else? Well, that actually fits under the "it's all about God" category, because the Lord tells us that in helping our brethren, we honor Him. This is stated in Matthew 25:31-46, which we will reflect on shortly.

It's not that the Pharisee was a bad person; in fact, he was doing a lot of good things. Fasting and tithing are good things, and he was doing them while refraining from unsavory acts such as extortion and adultery. So, what was his sin? Why would God say that he went back to his home unjustified?

Well, there are at least three things he was doing wrong—Firstly, he was praying "with himself." There is a conflict right there. We "pray" to the Lord. To pray with oneself is to take the role of the Lord, the one who receives our prayers, and give it to yourself. Praying with oneself makes one "his own god." Praying with oneself makes prayer all about us, and not about God.

Secondly, he was boasting—"look at me, I fast, I tithe." Fasting and tithing are good things, but as we will learn shortly, we shouldn't be sounding the trumpet when doing either of these things. If we expect recognition for our fasting and our tithing, then it is hard to argue that we are doing these things for God and not for our own sense of glory.

Thirdly, he was judging the tax collector, as unworthy of God's mercy and redemption, and also as a man who was not capable of repenting.

There was a moment in God's temple, when this man made himself god. It was when he made his good deeds all about himself. In that moment, when he was so confident that he was leaving no room for God to work in his life, God didn't listen to his "prayer."

The tax collector, on the other hand, we do not know what kind of life he had. Suffice it to say, he probably was a thief. He certainly wasn't the person you wanted to greet at your door. Extortion and blackmail were probably a regular part of his life, but there was a moment in God's temple when this man realized that what he was doing with his life was all about him, and none of it was about God. In that moment, when he was so low he couldn't even raise his eyes toward God, he pleaded for God's mercies and God exalted him.

Humility isn't doing everything wrong and coming to God to make it all better. Humility isn't acting pious and expressing self-loathing. Humility doesn't mean you can't have confidence in yourself. It doesn't mean to not be grateful for the blessings in your life.

Humility puts God first in all things. Humility makes it all about God, and not about us. Humility is what St. John the Baptist was talking about when he said, *"He must increase, but I must decrease"* (John 3:30). Humility means "more of God, less about us." Humility means making it about Him, and not about us.

When one strives to be humble, his prayer becomes the prayer of the Publican, because he realizes that he needs God's mercies in order to overcome his shortcomings. The prayer of the Publican, "God have mercy on me a sinner," is the root of the "Jesus Prayer," which says "Lord, Jesus Christ, Son of God, have mercy on me a sinner." In Orthodox theology, we are taught to pray this prayer as often as possible, so that our sense of God's greatness and our need for His mercies are constantly in our minds. Indeed, in the moment we are asking for His mercies, it is impossible to feel pride and make judgments on others. In the moment *after* we offer this prayer, it is possible. In the moment we are offering a prayer for God's mercies, we are right in sync with God. We are making it about Him. This is why we need to ask for God's mercies so often, so that we can live in His mercy, and not in our own sense of self, so that we can make life about Him, and not about us.

> *Recognizing the difference between the Publican and the Pharisee, O my soul, hate the prideful voice of the one, yet emulate the contrite prayer of the other, and cry out, "O God be gracious to me, who have sinned, and have mercy on me." (From the Praises of the Sunday of the Publican and the Pharisee, Trans. by Fr. Serphaim Dedes)*

Seek after God's mercies today, and in so doing, you will find humility.

Tuesday of the Prodigal Son

Your Body Belongs to the Lord

The body is not meant for immorality, but for the Lord, and the Lord for the body . . .
Do you not know that your bodies are members of Christ? . . . Do you not know that your
body is a temple of the Holy Spirit within you, which you have from God? . . .
So glorify God in your body.
1 Corinthians 6:13, 15, 19, 20
(Epistle on the Sunday of the Prodigal Son)

Can you imagine if you went into church one morning with a can of spray paint and started desecrating the walls of the church? Imagine painting over the icons, writing bad language on the doors of the church, taking a chainsaw to the pews, and setting fire to the carpet. Most of us can't conceive of such sacrilege. We love our church building. We appreciate its beauty. If you walked into a vandalized building, you'd wonder, where did all the beauty go?

Our bodies are temples. The Holy Spirit resides in each of us. When God created man, we read in Genesis 2:7, *"He breathed into his nostrils the breath of life; and man became a living being."* In other words, God put His Spirit into each of us, in the form of our souls, and this is how we become human beings. During our lifetime, we are supposed to feed our souls and prepare them for the day when our earthly lives are over, when our souls will separate from our bodies and go back to God for judgment. Our bodies are the "temples" in which our souls live.

We desecrate our bodies when we fill our minds with hateful thoughts, and our mouths with hateful speech. We neglect our bodies when we fill them with bad food and when we are inactive and indifferent to others. We honor our bodies when we maintain good hygiene, good diet, when we exercise, and when we love and serve others. Then our temples are in pristine condition.

In the Epistle of James, we read that, *"every good endowment and every perfect gift is from above, coming down from the Father of Lights"* (James 1:17). Therefore, our bodies are gifts from God and should be honored as such. We are supposed to honor God with our bodies—with what we see, what we hear, what we say and what we do. If we fill our eyes with images of violence and lust, if our ears are filled with hateful thoughts, if our mouths are filled with filthy language and if our hands are used for hurting and taking, then the temple of our bodies will be desecrated, as if spray-painting our church and destroying its contents. Ideally, we want to fill our eyes with images of beauty, our ears with sounds of encouragement, our mouths with words of praise for God and encouragement of our fellow man, and use our hands for helping and giving.

The gap between what is and what should be is called sin. For sin is not only "missing the mark," and doing the wrong thing, sin is failure to do the right thing. Indifference, for example, is a sin. The way for closing that gap is called repentance. This is the theme on the Sunday of the Prodigal Son—closing that gap through repentance. The theme of Lent is the cleaning of our bodies, our temples, so that they shine with the radiance of the most beautiful Cathedral.

The Rev. Dr. Nicon Patrinacos, a Greek Orthodox priest of blessed memory, wrote a beautiful quote that I have always held close to my heart:

Whenever I think of a church Cathedral, I find myself thinking of the Cathedral of one's own soul, in which he, in absolute solitude, and face to face with God, lives the most earnest and most decisive moment of his life. The Cathedral encloses within its splendid architectural lines something more than a physical achievement. In fact, if the walls and the art of this edifice could speak, I am sure that they would voice the presence here and now of the joys and sorrows of our hearts as well as the upward flying of our souls. They would attest to the fact that this building is a living entity, heart-beating and breathing, a treasure that is becoming constantly augmented as we grow in the life of Christ. (From the 1970 Greek Orthodox Archdiocese Yearbook)

While Fr. Nicon was referring to a physical church structure, his referral to the "Cathedral of one's own soul" has always struck a chord with me. As a priest, I spend a great deal of time making sure that the church I serve is clean, that the altar is always prepared and immaculate in its appearance. Most of us spend time cleaning our homes, our cars, our yards, and our clothes. We want them to be immaculate and spotless as well. Patrinacos compares a Cathedral to a living body, heart-beating and breathing as it grows in the life of Christ. Saint Paul encourages us to see our bodies as Cathedrals, with souls that are beautiful, immaculate and spotless. As we are vigilant with our earthly cares, let us remember to take care of our bodies, our temples, as well.

> *The cry of the Prodigal I offer to You, O Lord: I have sinned before Your eyes, O good one; I have squandered the wealth of the gifts You gave me, but receive me as I repent, O Savior, and save me. (From the Praises of the Sunday of the Prodigal Son, Trans. by Fr. Seraphim Dedes)*

Keep your "temple" clean today!

Wednesday of the Prodigal Son

He Came to Himself—The Critical Moment

But when he came to himself, he said "How many of my father's hired servants have bread enough and to spare, but I perish here with hunger! I arise and go to my father, and I will say to him, "Father I have sinned against heaven and before you; I am no longer worthy to be called your son; treat me as one of your hired servants." And he arose and came to his father.
Luke 15:17-20
(Gospel on the Sunday of the Prodigal Son)

One of the most important stories in the New Testament is the Parable of the Prodigal Son. A man had two sons and the younger of the two sons went to his father and asked him for his share of his inheritance. An inheritance is something you only get when your father dies, so in asking for the inheritance, it was as if he was wishing his father were dead. An inheritance is also a gift. It is not purchased, but given from parent to child, in this case from father to son. The father gave the inheritance freely, even though the son had treated the father shamefully.

The son took the inheritance, went to a far country, and in short order, he wasted the inheritance on loose living. When someone has a lot of money, generally they have a lot of "friends." When someone has no money, there are no "friends," because there is no money to have a good time. So, all of his newfound "friends" abandoned the son, who found himself hungry and alone. In order to survive, he got a job tending swine and he ate the food of the swine. It was either that, or perish from starvation.

There was another option. One day, the son "came to himself" and realized that his father's servants lived better than he was living. So, he made the decision to go back to his father and not only ask forgiveness, but ask to be a servant, rather than a son.

What is the difference between a son and a servant? A son is entitled to not only inheritance, but to his father's love. The son, in coming to himself, wanted to ask his father for neither inheritance nor love. He knew he was not deserving of either.

The meaning of this parable is this—the inheritance is our faith, the gift of salvation purchased through the Cross and Resurrection of Christ. It is a gift bestowed to all those who believe. When we sin, we are the Prodigal Son. For in the moment we sin, we are wasting our inheritance, we are squandering our faith. When we sin, we separate ourselves from God. He doesn't separate from us. WE are the ones who leave and go to the "faraway land."

If you know this story well, you know that the father quickly forgave the son. We'll be talking about that in the next reflection. However, that was not the key moment in the story. The key moment was when the son "came to himself" and realized that he needed to go back to his father, to ask his forgiveness and to offer to be his servant. This "coming to" moment is called repentance. Repentance means "a change of direction," and "a recognition that one has missed the mark." Repentance, for each of us, is realizing where we are missing the mark, in relation to where we are, versus where God tells us to be.

Years ago, NASA sent astronauts to the moon. The journey took several days and covered nearly 240,000 miles. At one or two points during the journey, it was necessary for the spacecraft to burn its engine for a few seconds, a maneuver called a "course correction." This made sure that the spacecraft was on target to reach the moon, and not careen into space and certain disaster.

Repentance is our way of "correcting course" in our spiritual lives, to get back on target. This is done in the same way the Prodigal Son made his correction. First you must "come to yourself" and realize you are off the mark. Then you must make the journey back.

> *I revolted senselessly out of Your fatherly glory; I have squandered sinfully all of the riches You gave me. Hence to you, using the Prodigals' words, I cry out, I have sinned before You, merciful loving Father. O receive me in repentance, I pray, and treat me as one of Your hired hands. (Kontakion, Sunday of the Prodigal Son, Trans. by Fr. Seraphim Dedes)*

Think about where you are in relationship to the "target" today!

Thursday of the Prodigal Son

One Happy Father

But while he was yet at a distance, his father saw him and had compassion, and ran and embraced him and kissed him. And the son said to him, "Father I have sinned against heaven and before you; I am no longer worthy to be called your son." But the Father said to his servants, "Bring quickly the best robe, and put it on him; and put a ring on his hand, and shoes on his feet; and bring the fatted calf and kill it, and let us eat and make merry; for this my son was dead, and is alive again; he was lost and is found.
Luke 15:20-24
(Gospel on the Sunday of the Prodigal Son)

Today's reflection focuses on the father in the story of the Prodigal Son. How sad the father must have been to have his younger son, his baby, ask for his inheritance. How sad the father must have been to see his younger son walk away from his home. I imagine the father sitting on his porch, head in his hands, crying for his son. I imagine him looking down the long road wondering if he will ever see his son coming back bounding toward the house.

The father didn't stop the son. He didn't take away his freedom. He didn't send a search party after him. He waited and he hoped that his son would come back to him.

Then one day, the son appeared. He must have been dirty and haggard—he had no money, no place to lay his head, probably hadn't had a shower. Here the boy had left rich and excited, and was returning penniless and shamed. Not only had the son brought shame on himself, he had also shamed his father.

If you pay close attention to this story, you will find a most wonderful detail that is very important and often overlooked. We know that the son was returning home with a plan, to ask his father's forgiveness and to beg to be treated as a servant. We are told that while the son was still a distance away from the house, the father saw him and was filled with compassion. He ran toward his wayward son with embrace and kissed him. His first reaction was one of joy, not anger. He didn't demand to know what had happened. He didn't demand repayment on the inheritance. He embraced him and kissed him.

As I imagine this parable in my mind, I imagine that the son almost had to pry his father off of him and say, "Wait, I have something to say. I have sinned against heaven and before you and I am no longer worthy to be called your son, treat me as a hired servant." It's as if the father wouldn't even hear what his son was saying. He didn't tell his son that he is disappointed, or put the son on probation. He certainly didn't treat him as a servant. He ordered a robe to be brought, a ring to be put on his finger, shoes for his feet and a feast to be thrown in his honor. He was so happy that his son came back. The son's apology was sincere, no doubt, but the father's joy is what ruled the day.

I can't tell you how many times I have thought about this parable when I hear a confession. It's not that the sins people confess are irrelevant, because they most certainly are. As a priest, hearing the sins and the pains of the people, my first reaction when someone comes to confession is always one of joy that one of God's children has come back. I try to remember the father of the Prodigal Son, and to share his joy that his child who was lost has now been found.

This image of the kind and forgiving father is the image we should all have of our Lord. He waits for us to make our way back. He waits to embrace us and welcome us home. Our burden is to make the journey. We don't have to wonder what His reaction will be. It will be one of great joy. Jesus tells us *"there will be more joy in heaven over one sinner who repents than over ninety-nine righteous people who need no repentance"* (Luke 15:7). It took courage for the son to make the journey back, not knowing how it would end for him. For us, we need merely put forth the effort to make the journey back. We know how it will end. Our Heavenly Father will embrace us and forgive us. All we have to do is come back.

The theme of Great Lent is the Prodigal Son, and making our way back to the Father. Why is there such joy on Pascha? Because we celebrate not only Christ's Resurrection, but also we celebrate all those who have made it back to God. As we prepare for Lent in this period of the Triodion, our job today is to think on how we've missed the mark. The journey of Lent is the journey back to God the Father. Pascha is the celebration, when everything begins anew in the Light of the Resurrected Christ for all of God's children who have made the journey back. When we come to the Lord in repentance, when we ask for forgiveness and seek to be His servants, this is when He restores us as His sons and daughters. It takes humility to realize you've missed the mark. It takes repentance to make the journey back. Humility and repentance lead to forgiveness and restoration. These are what lead to true joy.

> *Like the Prodigal Son, I too, have come, O compassionate one; I have spent my whole life in a foreign land; I have squandered the wealth that You have given me, O Father. Receive me as I repent, O God, and have mercy on me. (From the Praises on the Sunday of the Prodigal Son, Trans. by Fr. Seraphim Dedes)*

Identify at least one way in which you are "missing the mark" and start mapping out a way to "come back."

Friday of the Prodigal Son

I Never Left! Not True

[The Older Son] answered his father, "Lo, these many years I have served you, and I never disobeyed your command; yet you never gave me a kid, that I might make merry with my friends. But when this son of yours came, who has devoured your living with harlots, you killed for him the fatted calf!" And he said to him, "Son you are always with me, and all that is mine is yours. It was fitting to make merry and be glad, for this your brother was dead, and is alive; he was lost, and is found."
Luke 15:29-32
(Gospel on the Sunday of the Prodigal Son)

In the Parable of the Prodigal Son, there are three main characters—the younger son, who made a mess of his life, but then returned and repented; the father, who acquiesced to the wishes of his younger son, gave him his share of the inheritance, and who was ready to forgive and restore his son when he came home; and the older son, the one "who never left."

The Parable leads us to surmise that the father was a farmer, as the older son was working out in the field. Presumably, the younger son was sharing the burden of the work prior to his leaving. The older son had plenty of reason to be angry with his brother—his brother had first and foremost, insulted their father. Secondly, he had cut his father's wealth in half by taking his inheritance early. Third, he had left the older brother to do the work of both brothers, so he had increased his labor. As if this wasn't enough, when the younger brother came home, the father not only forgave him, but also threw a party in his honor. When we read the parable, it is the older son who we end up with a bad picture of, not the younger son.

What is the lesson here? First, when the older brother said to his father "I never disobeyed your command." That was not a true statement. No child can ever say that he never disobeyed his father. I was a relatively good child, but I wasn't perfect. I'm sure there were plenty of times I disobeyed my father. If, in the Parable, the Father represents God our Father, then to say we never disobey God is not a true statement for any of us. In fact, it is the height of arrogance.

In some sense, we are all the Prodigal Son. We all "waste" our inheritance when we sin. We all "go away" to a "far country" when we sin because we estrange ourselves from God. Like the Prodigal Son, however, we hopefully have moments where we "come to ourselves" and repent, we come back to God. God our Father forgives us and restores us when we come back to Him.

So, when are we like the older son? There are two instances: first, when we are so arrogant as to think we never do wrong. This puts us in the same place as the Pharisee, in the Parable of the Publican and the Pharisee. It fails to show humility. Second, when we look on those "who come back" with contempt, rather than joy. This happens more than we think. When a person makes a mistake and owns up for it, we sometimes think about retribution and punishment before we think about forgiveness. When we feel that a person has been too easily forgiven and hasn't been thoroughly punished, we tend to become indignant with them. We fail to show mercy.

There is nothing wrong with the loyalty of the older son. The fact that he was obedient to his father (at least most of the time) was a good thing, but no one is obedient all the time. When a lost soul has returned home, we should be rejoicing.

In practical terms, periodically we see someone come back to church after a long absence. What is our reaction? Are we contemptuous, like "where have you been?" Or are we welcoming, without interrogating? How many times in life does someone who has wronged you try to make amends, perhaps even after a long time—it probably doesn't happen often, but it does happen. Are we easy to forgive and easy to entreat, like the Father in the story? Or are we filled with anger and contempt, like the older son?

If God our Father is ready and happy to restore us, we should be happy to restore one another. After all, no one has sinned against me *more* than I have sinned against God. If I expect God to forgive *all* of my sins, then I should be willing to forgive the sins of others. I should rejoice, rather than resent, when someone "comes back" and "makes it right."

> *I have exhausted the wealth of my father's holdings, and have consumed them; I have become destitute, dwelling in the land of wicked citizens. No longer able to bear their company, I return and cry to You, the compassionate Father, "I have sinned against heaven and before You, and I am not worthy to be called Your son. Treat me as one of Your hirelings, O God, and have mercy on me. (From the Praises on the Sunday of the Prodigal Son, Trans. by Fr. Seraphim Dedes)*

See the good in people today!

Saturday of the Prodigal Son

We're All Going to Answer

Jesus said, "When the Son of Man comes in His glory and all the angels with Him, then He will sit on His glorious throne. Before Him will be gathered all the nations, and He will separate them one from another as a shepherd separates the sheep from the goats, and He will place the sheep at His right hand, but the goats at the left."
Matthew 25:31-33
(Gospel on the Sunday of the Last Judgment)

A priest at summer camp gave one of the most memorable sermons I have ever heard, and he entitled the sermon: "Then what?" The story goes like this:

A college senior was stressing out over final exams, so he went to his priest for a little counsel and a prayer. The priest asked him why he was so stressed out. The senior said he was stressed out over his upcoming finals. "It's like the most important thing ever, these finals. They will set the tone forever for me."

The priest asked him, "Once you pass your finals, then what?"

The student asked, "I guess I will go and get a job."

The priest asked, "and then what?"

"Make lots of money."

"Then what?"

"Get married."

"Then what?"

"Have children."

"Then what?"

"Watch the children grow up."

"Then what?"

"Be a grandparent."

"Then what?"

"Retire and travel the world."

"Then what?"

"Well, eventually, I'll probably get sick."
"Then what?"
"Then I'll eventually die."
"*Then* what?"

We are all going to die, and *then*, there will be a judgment before the Lord. Everyone who has ever lived, is going to be gathered before the Lord, and as a defendant before a judge, we will each be called upon to give an account of our lives.

That accounting will be based on one thing: *love*.

Did we love God? Did we love our neighbor?

In Matthew 25:31-46, the Gospel we read on "The Sunday of the Last Judgment" (also called "Meatfare Sunday") the Lord is teaching the disciples about the judgment that will await all the peoples of all the nations. Everyone will be separated into two groups, the way a shepherd separates sheep from goats. This is an image that everyone at the time could understand—Jesus is the shepherd, and we are either in the flock (sheep) or we are out of the flock (goats).

The judgment, we are told, will be based on demonstrating love, to our neighbor. The righteous will be told: "*I was hungry and you gave me food, I was thirsty and you gave me drink, I was a stranger and you welcomed me, I was naked and you clothed me, I was sick and you visited me, I was in prison and you came to me*" (Matt. 25: 35-36). The condemned will be told: "*I was hungry and you gave me no food, I was thirsty and you gave me no drink, I was a stranger and you did not welcome me, I was naked and you did not clothe me, sick and in prison and you did not visit me*" (Matt. 25: 42-43).

Remember the commandment to love GOD and love our neighbor? Jesus tells us that in loving our neighbor, we are showing our love for God. For He said, "*When you did it to one of the least of these My brethren, you did it to Me,*" and to the condemned, "*As you did it NOT to the least of these, you did it not to Me*" (Matt. 25:40, 45). So in loving our neighbor, we show our love for God as well.

When life on earth is over, we will each stand before the Awesome Judgment Seat of Christ, and answer for our lives. We will be judged ready for eternal life, or be sent to eternal punishment. That is the ultimate "Then what?"

> *O what an hour and fearful day shall that be, when the Judge shall sit upon His fearsome throne! Books will be opened, deeds will be checked, and the hidden works of darkness will be made public. Angels speed about, gathering all the nations. Come, hearken, kings and rulers, slaves and freemen, sinners and righteous, rich men and paupers, He is coming who is about to judge the whole world; and who shall bear His countenance, when angels are at hand to accuse your acts, your thoughts, your desires, be they of day or night? O what an hour that shall be! But before the end arrives, O soul, make haste to cry, "O God, convert me, save me as you alone are compassionate." (From the Praises of the Sunday of the Last Judgment, Trans. by Fr. Seraphim Dedes)*

Show love today!

Sunday of the Prodigal Son

It Came Naturally to Them

Then the righteous will answer Him, "Lord, when did we see Thee hungry and feed Thee, or thirsty and give Thee drink? And when did we see Thee a stranger and welcome thee, or naked and clothe thee? And when did we see Thee sick or in prison and visit Thee?" And the King will answer them, "Truly I say to you, as you did it to one of the least of these My brethren, you did it to Me."...
Then they (the condemned) will also answer, "Lord, when did we see Thee hungry or thirsty or a stranger or naked or sick or in prison and did not minister to Thee?" Then He will answer them, "Truly I say to you, as you did it not to one of the least of these, you did it not to Me."
Matthew 25:37-40; 44-45
(Gospel on the Sunday of the Last Judgment)

"You are going to die!"

This is the opening line in a book called *Be a Man* by Fr. Larry Richards, a Roman Catholic priest and writer, and is one of the most unique opening lines of any book I have read. The premise in the opening chapter of this book is to start with the ending of our lives, and where we are going to be, and then work backwards to the present day, making sure that today we are working with that future eventuality in mind.

When the Lord confronted each group of people—the "sheep" and the "goats"—to say that "I was hungry and you gave me food" or "I was hungry and you gave me no food," each group was surprised. The "sheep" asked "When did we see *you* (our Lord) hungry?" As if to say, that in all the years of helping people, they never encountered the Lord. Those who were doing good works were doing them almost "naturally." They weren't ostensibly doing them only for the Lord. Helping others was a normal part of their life. At the end of life, the Lord told them that in loving others, they were showing love to Him as well.

The "goats" were also surprised. When they asked "When did we see *you* hungry and not feed you?" they were saying in essence, that "had we really seen *you* hungry, we certainly would have fed *you*. Had the Lord appeared in the flesh in front of us, certainly we would have known, and cared." For those who weren't helping their neighbors, their indifference was normal for them as well. At the end of life, the Lord told them that in being indifferent to others, they were being indifferent to Him as well.

Every day, probably multiple times a day, we have a chance to show love, or to show indifference to others. There are people who are poor and hungry in every town, people who don't have enough clothes, people who are new in town or new on the job, people who are sick, and those who are imprisoned. Even more frequently, we encounter people who are hungry, not only for food, but for friendship, hungry for compassion, encouragement, empathy. We encounter people who are thirsty for affirmation. There are many people who feel like strangers because they don't have many real friends. There are people who feel naked because they suffer from low self-esteem. There are people who are sick with stress and frustration. There are people who are in prison, serving life sentences of learning disabilities, mental illness or physical handicaps. Do we take time each day to minister to anyone in any of these categories listed above?

In loving others, do we realize that we also love the Lord? When we are indifferent, do we realize we are indifferent to Him as well? Do we make it a goal each day to try to help someone? Is our ministering to other people more "natural" or does it seemed "forced" or "contrived"?

I eventually am going to die and stand before God's throne and I will answer to Him for my love of my neighbor as well as my love of Him. With this eventuality in mind, I should look for opportunities *today* to show love to my neighbor. When we make a point of helping "our neighbor" every day, it becomes a habit, a natural part of our lives. It will set us on the path to being numbered among the "sheep," who were ministering to the Lord, without even knowing that it was the Lord, because their love of their neighbor was a natural part of their lives.

There is no one who is reading this message that does not love the Lord. I am sure of that. Some of us may not know the Lord as well as we'd like, but everyone who is reading this message has some sense of Godliness in them. The challenge then is to take our sense of Godliness and transfer it over to every encounter with every person we meet today, to see God in them, and to love them in the way we love God, the way God loves us.

> *I ponder on that day and hour, when we all, naked and as convicts, will appear before the Judge we cannot bribe. Then a great trumpet will sound and the foundations of the earth will be shaken, and the dead will be raised from the graves and all will become of one stature. And all that which is hidden will be presented overtly before You, and they shall mourn and wail who have never repented, and they shall depart into the outer fire. And with joy and exaltation will the lot of the righteous enter into the heavenly chamber. (From the Praises of the Sunday of the Last Judgment, Trans. by Fr. Seraphim Dedes)*

Help a neighbor today!

Monday of Meat-Fare

Our Piety is Between Us and God

Jesus said "Beware of practicing your piety before men in order to be seen by them; for then you will have no reward from your Father who is in heaven . . . And your Father who sees in secret will reward you."
Matthew 6:1, 6
(Gospel on the Second Saturday of the Souls)

The word "piety" is defined as "the quality of being religious or reverent." Wikipedia has a whole page dedicated to the concept of piety, on which it says, "In spiritual terminology, piety is a virtue that may include religious devotion, spirituality, or a mixture of both. A common element in most conceptions of piety is humility and religiosity." Another definition is "reverence for God or devout fulfillment of religious obligations."

Let's begin with "reverence for God." When a person wakes up in the morning and offers a prayer, or makes the sign of the cross, or kneels at his or her bedside, this is showing reverence for God, it is a pious act. It is also a private act.

When a person goes to worship in church and is intently praying and singing and maintains their focus on the Lord, this is showing reverence for God. Despite the fact that the worship is taking place in a public, in a corporate context, it is still a private act.

When a person helps a neighbor, whether instinctively, or if they are asked, and then focuses on the act of helping, this is showing reverence for God by offering loving support to a neighbor.

When a person helps out expecting a material reward, it does not show reverence for God, because the end goal is payment or recognition, not humble service. When a person calls attention to himself in worship, then there is no humility there either. When a person makes piety a public act, by calling attention to himself in his prayers, or making a big deal out of praying in public, this is exactly what the Lord is warning against.

There is nothing wrong with making a witness for Christ in our lives. There is nothing wrong with talking about Him with others. There is nothing wrong with bowing your head in a restaurant and saying a prayer in a public place. God sees what is in our hearts and knows our every thought.

When an act of piety is done with the express purpose of bringing attention to oneself, this is not pleasing to God. When an act of piety is done privately and with humility, and someone notices and has an experience of God because of it, then this is beneficial to our souls, to the souls of others, and pleases God.

I've shared this with those who read these reflections on several occasions, that as time goes by, I am more and more comfortable leading worship and prayer in a public context. I absolutely love praying with people outside the context of services, something that I used to feel uncomfortable with in the early years of my ministry. I love that part of my "job" that involves helping people. I get the opportunity to minister to others on a daily basis, something for which I am very grateful, but there has to be more to it than that. We have to make sure that we are making time for private devotion and prayer that is seen by no one but the Lord. We have to make sure that we are doing things for others without the expectation of payment, reward, or recognition. We have to temper the almost natural inclination toward self-promotion by shying away from recognition and seeking humility as well as anonymity in our piety and our service to others.

Many of us wear crosses around our necks, and in the Orthodox world, some of us wear prayer ropes or prayer bracelets on our wrists. When we wear a cross or a prayer rope merely in order to display our "religiosity," then we are doing the very thing Christ warns against. Wearing a cross should serve as a reminder for us to be better Christians. Just wearing a prayer bracelet does very little. We have to make the sign of the cross each day in prayer, use the prayer bracelet for its intended purposes of praying, and honor God not only through outward appearance, but inner disposition of the heart. For our faith is not based only on signs and symbols, but on action. Signs and symbols identify us as Christians, but it is our actions that define our Christianity, specifically our actions when no one is looking and when there is no possibility of earthly reward. It is the secret things and the unrewarded acts that are recognized by the Lord, and will eventually be rewarded, not by men, but by Him.

> *As we are shined on by the lightning of the fathers, as if we enter now a most delightful garden, let us fully enjoy the river of Your delight. With wonder we view the excellence of their deeds and virtues, so let us strive to emulate them. Let us pray to the Savior, "By their intercessions, O God, account us worthy to become the partakers of Your kingdom and rule." (Kathisma, from the Orthros of the Second Saturday of the Souls, Trans. by Fr. Seraphim Dedes)*

Don't forget to pray today!

Tuesday of Meat-Fare

What Goes Around Comes Around

Jesus said, "For if you forgive men their trespasses, your heavenly Father also will forgive you; but if you do not forgive men their trespasses, neither will your Father forgive your trespasses."
Matthew 6:14-15
(Gospel on Cheesefare Sunday)

No, we don't believe in karma, but the Lord teaches us that where forgiveness is concerned, there is definitely a "what goes around comes around" element as it relates to the Lord and our practice of the Christian faith. How can we expect God to forgive us, if we cannot forgive one another?

In the verses that immediately precede the verses quoted above, we find the Lord's Prayer, in Matthew 6:9-13. In the Lord's Prayer, when we pray "forgive us our trespasses, as we forgive those who trespass against us," we are not only acknowledging that we need to forgive others because God forgives us, but that we will be forgiven in the *same* way as we forgive others.

If you read this passage in its original Greek, you will see an even higher standard toward others than forgiveness. The Greek word for "forgiveness" is "synoreses." The word "afeseos" means "remission," or blotting out of our sins. "Afeseos" means to "forgive AND forget." In the original Greek, the word, which has been translated "forgive" both in the Lord's Prayer and in these verses, is the word "afeseos." So when we read, "if you forgive men their trespasses, your heavenly Father also will forgive you," what that really means is that "if you forgive AND forget the things others have done wrong to you, if you 'remit' their sins, then your Heavenly Father will also forgive AND forget your sins, He will blot them out from your record of life."

It is an almost "natural" tendency to keep score in relationships. We count the good, and when not enough good is happening, sometimes relationships sour. This is where the phrase "what have you done for me lately?" comes to mind. We have an almost insatiable desire to have good done to us, however, when someone has done good to us, just not lately, we forget easily. We tend to remember the bad. I can't tell you how many times a married couple will come in for counseling and bring their "scorebooks," remembering transgressions that happened many years in the past. If we expect God not to keep score on us—after all, His scorebook would encompass our entire lives—then we cannot keep score on each other. We are to forgive as we go along, working toward strengthening relationships through forgiveness rather than weakening them through grudges.

How does that work on a practical level? By setting parameters so that forgiveness can be possible. I read an article on marriage which encouraged couples to use the words "ouch" and "oops," so that when a person says something offensive to the other, rather than an argument ensuing immediately, the other person can say "ouch," letting the other know that what was said was offensive. The response can be "oops," recognizing that a wrong turn was made, followed by "may I retract what I said and restate?" This can work in other relationships as well. Giving someone the opportunity to restate something that came out wrong will cut down on a lot of misunderstandings.

Affirming relationships is also helpful where forgiveness is concerned. When a person perceives that a relationship will be lost by "coming clean" on something, they will mitigate or lie or misstate the truth. If relationships are built on a foundation of forgiveness, where people are reassured and reaffirmed that the foundation of the relationship is strong, then it is easier to address faults, exchange forgiveness and retain genuine, honest and healthy relationships.

We tend not to use the word "forgive" very often. We say "I'm sorry," but how often do we say "Please forgive me"? Even worse, when we do hear the words "forgive me," do we respond with "whatever," or "no problem," instead of saying, "forgiven" or "I forgive you"?

If we are going to live by this commandment of the Lord to forgive one another, we are going to have to bring the word "forgive" into our conversations and the concept of forgiveness into all of our relationships.

In Psalm 130:3, we read, *"If Thou, O Lord, shouldst mark iniquities, Lord, who could stand?"* Indeed if the Lord added up all of our sins against Him, none of us would stand a chance. So, if we need Him not to be keeping a tally of our sins, we need to extend the same to each other. The Lord is easy to entreat and easy to forgive. We must be so as well.

> *In times of old did Adam sit and cry in sorrow opposite the delights he had in Paradise; his hands upon did his forehead strike, as he said this: O merciful Lord, have mercy on me who have fallen. (Oikos of Cheesefare Sunday, Trans. by Fr. Seraphim Dedes)*

Be patient and forgiving today!

Wednesday of Meat-Fare

And When You Fast

*Jesus said, "And when you fast, do not look dismal, like the hypocrites,
for they disfigure their faces that their fasting may be seen by men. Truly, I say to you,
they have received their reward. But when you fast, anoint your head and wash your face,
that your fasting may not be seen by men but by your Father who is in secret;
and your father who sees in secret will reward you."
Matthew 6:16-18
(Gospel of Cheesefare Sunday)*

When people think of the word "Lent," the word "fasting" is one of the first things that comes to mind. The cornerstone of Lent is not fasting, but repentance and growing in our faith. Fasting is a tool that is used to assist in spiritual growth. Fasting is also mischaracterized as a form of deprivation, rather than a spiritual discipline. Because fasting is so misunderstood, it is many times done incorrectly.

In the Orthodox world, we use the word "passions" to describe tendencies that each person has that lead us to sin. Each of us has a "passion" for anger, lust, power, greed, ego, etc. We do not get through life without wrestling with each of these, sometimes on a daily basis. The most basic "passion" is hunger. While we can go a day without a lustful thought or an angry thought, we can't go more than a few hours without a hungry thought. So, if we can tame our passion for eating, we can hopefully tame our other passions. If we can discipline ourselves to go without certain kinds of food, we can hopefully discipline ourselves so that we can go without certain kinds of behavior that are spiritually destructive. Thus, fasting is not about giving up something only to get it back. Fasting is about getting control of our passions, maintaining control over them, and ultimately giving control of ourselves to God.

It is the Orthodox Tradition to fast from food products that contain blood. So, we fast from meat, fish, dairy products, oil and wine. (Oil and wine, up until the last couple of centuries, were stored in skins of animals. This is why we can eat grapes and olives, but we cannot have wine or olive oil. If the fasting "rules" were ever to be reviewed and updated, the prohibition on oil and wine would have to be examined.) We can eat shellfish because they do not contain blood. Christ shed His blood for us, so we do not consume any "blood" or "animal" products. It is the Tradition of the church to fast for the entirety of Great Lent and Holy Week. The week after the Publican and the Pharisee is fast free, as is the week after Pascha and Pentecost (and Christmas). The week before Great Lent, we are only required to fast from meat, not dairy products. Outside of Lent, it is Tradition to fast every Wednesday (in honor of the betrayal of Christ) and Friday (in honor of His Crucifixion). There is a forty day fast that precedes the Feast of the Nativity (November 15-December 24), a fourteen day fast that precedes the Feast of the Dormition (August 1-14), and the Holy Apostles Fast (which begins the day after All Saints Day and lasts through June 28).

If you've never fasted before, I would not recommend doing a strict fast. Try fasting from meat on Wednesdays and Fridays of Lent (and then throughout the year), then next year try fasting Wednesdays and Fridays plus all of the first week of Lent and all of Holy Week. Then work up from that.

Below is a guide of some levels of fasting:

Level one—Fast from meat on Wednesdays and Fridays and during Holy Week
Level two—Fast from meat and fish on Wednesdays and Fridays and during Holy Week
Level three—Fast from meat the entirety of Lent and Holy Week
Level four—Fast from meat and fish the entirety of Lent and Holy Week
Level five—Level four and eliminate dairy products during Holy Week
Level six—Level four and eliminate dairy products on Wednesday and Fridays and during Holy Week.
Level seven—Level four plus eliminate dairy products during all of Lent and Holy Week
Level eight—Level seven plus eliminate oil and wine during Holy Week
Level nine—The strict fast—no meat, fish, dairy products, wine or oil during the entirety of Great Lent

*Fish is allowed on March 25 (Annunciation), Saturday of Lazarus and Palm Sunday; oil and wine are allowed on Saturdays and Sundays, except for Holy Saturday.

After a few years at one level, challenge yourself to go up a level.

More important, however, than fasting from food, is fasting from the behaviors that are spiritually destructive. We need to fast from things that get us in trouble—perhaps the television, alcohol, inappropriate materials on the computer and in movies, foul language, etc. Fasting also does not mean "looking" deprived, complaining about what you can't eat, or making a show of your fasting. In fact, if you are fasting and you are invited to someone's home for dinner and they serve meat, eat the meat, don't make a big deal out of your fasting. Also, do not pass judgment on others who are not fasting to the degree you are. Saint Paul reminds us in Romans 14:3-4: "*Let not him who eats despise him who abstains, and let not him who abstains pass judgment on him who eats; for God has welcomed him. Who are you to pass judgment on the servant of another? It is before his own Master that he stands or falls."* As Christ tells us, our fasting is seen by our *"Father who is in secret,"* and He will reward us for our efforts.

Again, Lent is not a season of deprivation, nor should we "give up" something only to get it back once Lent is over. Lent is about repentance, and making small and permanent changes to bring us closer to the Lord, changes that will last long after Lent is over. This is the purpose of the Lenten journey. Fasting is an aid to help us in this.

> *The time has come—the start of our spiritual contests, the victory over demons, the full armor of self-control, the angels' dignity, the confidence before God. Thereby did Moses become conversant with the Creator, and heard the invisible voice. Lord, through fasting make us worthy to worship Your Passion and Holy Resurrection, as You love humanity. (Doxastikon of Orthros, Cheesefare Sunday, Trans. by Fr. Seraphim Dedes)*

Give some thought to your fasting plan for Lent today!

Thursday of Meat-Fare

Treasure in Heaven

Jesus said: "Do not lay up for yourselves treasures on earth, where moth and rust consume and where thieves break in and steal, but lay up for yourselves treasures in heaven, where neither moth nor rust consumes and where thieves do not break in and steal. For where your treasure is, there will your heart be also.
Matthew 6:19-21
(Gospel of Cheesefare Sunday)

Most of us think we "cannot live" without our cell phones. We place great value on our little devices that allow us to talk, text, give us directions, check email, surf the Internet, play games and lots of other things. I even did a lesson once with a group of teenagers on "what would you run into a burning house in order to retrieve," and surprisingly, a number of them said they would run in to grab the phone. Actually, there is *nothing* of material value that I would run into a house to retrieve. The most important things in our lives are of non-material value—the people (our families and friends) and our faith.

So many of us spend the majority of our lives chasing material riches. Most of us are not happy with only necessities—we want luxury items as well. Well, the cell phone we so treasure today will be obsolete in six months. Certainly, no one has a phone more than ten years old. Clothes wear out, or we grow out of them. Computers are replaced as well as cars, carpets, couches and chairs. We may live in the same house for our entire life—a rarity, but it still happens—but eventually, when we die, we won't live there either. I've been to many funerals in my work as a priest, and it ultimately comes down to a body in a box. Nobody dies materially rich, because once death comes, all the earthly possessions and our ownership of them ends.

The only thing that survives after death is our soul. Thus we need to be thinking of the state of our souls at all times. As we work toward accumulating earthly treasures, we need to be putting treasure in heaven.

Most of us are familiar with Individual Retirement Accounts (IRAs). This is where we put away money on a yearly basis, so that there is "something there" for us when we retire. Those who put a lot of money into an IRA retire well, and those who put nothing into their IRA find themselves unable to retire, or in trouble when they are older.

Consider for a moment, an Eternal Retirement Account (or an ERA). This is something you put into on a daily basis, storing up treasure in heaven, in the form of gestures that show love for God and for your neighbor. Putting treasure into an "ERA" will have an eternal payout. Failure to put treasure into the ERA will result in an eternal problem.

Jesus tells us that where our treasures are, our hearts are as well. So, if we spend all of our money on ourselves, and we never help the poor, or help the church, it shows that those two latter things are not important on the record of our lives. The same is true for our time. If we spend an hour a day watching television, but we don't have a few minutes to pray; or if we spend 3 hours a week (and usually more) watching sports, but don't have an hour a week to worship, what does this say about how we value our faith?

Truth be told, I've never had anyone I met at the end of their life that wished that they had had one more day to be in their office, or one more day to watch sports. Most people regret not spending more time with family and not doing more to help others, not spending more time in church, or giving more to charity.

There is nothing in the Bible that says we can't own a home or take a nice trip with our families. In fact, in many places we read that God wants us to have sufficiency for ourselves. He does not, however, wish us to have excessive prosperity, at the expense of helping others. If every good thing, starting off with this very day on which we are alive, is a gift from Him, we should make it a priority to give a portion of everything we receive from Him back to Him. He gives us time, so we should give something back to Him in prayer and worship, and service to others. He gives us the means to earn material riches. A portion of these should be given back as well.

Our treasure (and our time) and our hearts work hand in hand. When you put more emphasis on something, it becomes more important to you. When something is important to you, you put more emphasis on it. Whether you lead with your heart and your treasure follows, or you lead with your treasure and your heart follows, make sure that your heart and your treasure are both directed, in some measure, toward the Lord. In order to be ready for "eternal retirement," you need to have put away a good portion of your heart and your treasure into an ERA.

O guide to wisdom, provider of prudence, disciplinarian of fools, and defender of the poor, fortify and discipline my heart, O Master; You, give me a word, O Word of the Father. For behold, I will not hinder my lips from crying to You: O Merciful Lord, have mercy on me who have fallen. (Kontakion, Cheesefare Sunday, Trans. by Fr. Seraphim Dedes)

Put something into your ERA today!

Friday of Meat-Fare

God Crowns Effort

An athlete is not crowned unless he competes according to the rules.
2 Timothy 2:5
(Epistle on the Third Saturday of the Souls)

I have some very good news for you—God is more concerned with effort than with results! You are probably thinking, "How can that be?" Sometimes effort doesn't yield results. Let me give you an example. Let's say I prepare a meaningful sermon for Sunday, and a huge rainstorm hits on Sunday morning so only a few people are in church to hear it. The result is that only a few people hear a meaningful sermon, not the hundreds I had hoped for. On the flip side, it is Palm Sunday, the church is filled, but I give a mediocre, unprepared sermon. The results say "the church was filled," but what about the effort?

Many of us are frustrated in our jobs because we equate success with numbers and dollars, rather than with effort. Sometimes we cannot control numbers or dollars. We can always control effort. Another example—a teacher cannot control whether students learn or not. A teacher can motivate students, can encourage them, but can't force them to learn. A student who just doesn't want to learn is not going to learn. The teacher should focus on "creating an environment that encourages students to learn." This is something a teacher *can* control—he or she can make interesting lessons, send positive messages to students, etc. The teacher can't control the results if half of the students don't want to learn, any more than a priest can control the results if half of the people don't want to listen to a sermon. "Creating an environment" and giving a good effort are things we all can control, and these are the things for which God is concerned.

Let's say that a businessman reaps great financial rewards, but he does it through scrupulous business practices, cheating, lying, extortion, etc. He may look like a successful businessman, and he may earn the paycheck of a successful businessman, but the Lord knows the effort he is making, and how he is making that effort.

It's interesting that in modern times, sports are all about winning. In ancient times, sports were all about competing. It seems as though we are willing to crown champions even if they cheat. In ancient times, cheating was a mark of dishonor and wasn't done. Athletes were crowned for good effort on the field. When a person lost an athletic contest, he went and shook hands with the winner, tipping his hat, so to speak, to the other person. There was no trash talking, no appeals, no bashing others at press conferences.

In our Christian lives, it doesn't matter if we memorize long prayers or only short passages—it matters that we make the effort to pray. It doesn't matter if you feed the hungry or tutor the student who has trouble learning—*help someone*! When you give money to the church, you shouldn't demand to control what is done with it. Your effort in giving is what God rewards.

You don't have to have the perfect marriage, the perfect children, the perfect home or the perfect anything else. God expects an effort. In prioritizing what to do, it doesn't matter if your laundry sits in a pile on the couch for a few days if you have had to take care of sick children, or have had a difficult week at work. God doesn't expect perfection—He *does* expect effort.

Let's say that you have a beautiful, expensive car and everyone compliments you on the car, but you know that you got the car through dishonest means. The compliments might make you happy, but you know deep down that you didn't put out an honest effort to get the car. On the other hand, let's say you drive an old, beat up car, but you work hard and pay for it with honest means and people make fun of your car. At the end of the day, you might not be happy or popular, but you'd know that you'd made an honest effort. I'd rather have honest effort with less success, than success coming with less than honest effort.

Remember, an athlete up until recent years, was not crowned because he won, but because he competed well. The ideal of the Ancient Olympics was to push *yourself* faster, higher, and farther. Similarly, the ideal of the Christian life is for each of us to make an effort to grow in Christ on a consistent basis. The effort is the crowning achievement in the eyes of God.

> *The stadium of virtue is now open; those who wish to compete enter therein, girded for the good contest of Lent, for those who compete according to the rules shall receive their laurels rightfully. Taking up the full armor of the Cross, let us do battle against the Enemy. As an impregnable wall, we have the Faith, prayer as our breastplate, and acts of mercy as our helmet. Instead of sword, there is fasting, which cuts every evil from the heart. He who does this shall attain a true crown from Christ, the King of all, on Judgment Day. (From the Praises of Cheesefare Sunday, Trans. by Fr. Seraphim Dedes)*

Make a good effort today!

First Saturday of the Souls

We Don't Worship the Rules

Jesus entered the synagogue, and a man was there who had a withered hand. And they watched Him, to see whether He would heal him on the Sabbath, so that they might accuse Him. And He said to the man who had the withered hand, "Come here." And He said to them, "Is it lawful on the Sabbath to do good or to do harm, to save life or to kill?" But they were silent. And He looked around at them with anger, grieved at their hardness of heart, and said to the man, "Stretch out your hand." He stretched it out, and his hand was restored.
Mark 3:1-5
(Gospel on the Third Saturday of the Souls)

Without order, there is chaos. Rules are a good way to create and maintain order. This holds true for our society, both outside and inside the church. Imagine a world without traffic laws; it would be totally chaotic and dangerous.

The goal of the traffic laws, for example, is to help people travel safely. Yet, if the speed limit sign says "55 MPH" and traffic is congested, then drivers don't go 55 because it isn't safe. Imagine if someone followed "the letter of the law" and drove 55 mph because they perceived that the "limit" was a "requirement." They would become a source of danger, rather than one of obedience and safety. The overall goal of the traffic laws is to create an environment that allows us to drive safely from one place to another.

If rules are ways to create and maintain good order, this holds true also for the church and for the Christian faith as well. There are lots of "commandments" in the Bible, but we don't "worship" the commandments. We have Traditions in our church, like the Icon of Christ is always to the right of the altar, or that we baptize by immersion (and thousands of other examples), but we don't "worship" the commandments. We worship Christ.

All of the commandments can be summarized in one word, which is "love." God is love. So, in loving others, we show love for the Lord. In worshipping God, we worship "love personified." In the Gospel reading about the man with the withered hand, Jesus was making a point to the leadership of the temple that it is never wrong to love and it is never wrong to help someone. Even though the "rules" of the Jewish faith said that no work could be done on the Sabbath, here was a person who needed to be loved, who needed to be helped. Jesus helped this person on the Sabbath.

There are rules in the church, and for good reason. Without them, we'd have chaos. Again, we don't worship the rules. The canons (the formal name given to the "rules" and practices we follow) indicate that we should abstain from all food on the morning that we are receiving Holy Communion. There are good reasons for this—the chief reason is so that you begin your day by worshipping and receiving Communion, so that the first thing that touches your lips is the Body and Blood of Christ. So, what about the person who is diabetic and can't skip breakfast, or the person who is sick who needs to eat food along with their medication in the morning? Are they therefore banned from Communion because they cannot "follow the rule"? Absolutely not.

In the Orthodox Church, there is the "tradition" of the Spiritual Father, a priest who serves as your "guide" in the spiritual life. He is supposed to be able to discern for each individual when a rule should be relaxed, such as in the case of the person who needs to eat before Liturgy. So, if you are not sure exactly what to do in regards to some of the "rules," ask your spiritual father. If you don't have a spiritual father, sit down with your parish priest; develop a relationship, so that these things can be addressed in conversation and in prayer in a way that is personal and purposeful to you.

I know that as someone who has heard thousands of confessions, thousands of instances when people have confessed to the Lord that they haven't "followed the rules," (God's commandments) that I try to minister to them first and foremost with love. I'm reminded of the Parable of the Rich Man who went away sorrowful, which we read in the Gospels of Matthew (19:16-26) and Luke (18:18-27). When he asked the Lord what he needed to do in order to inherit eternal life, the Lord told him to follow the commandments. The man said that he followed all of the commandments. Then the Lord told him that he still lacked one thing—that he should sell all that he had and give it to the poor and that he would have treasure in heaven. This was not an act of judgment. It was an act of compassion. He was reminding the man that it wasn't purely obedience to rules and laws that was going to save him, but that he needed to show love for others. Jesus was trying to save the man from eternal condemnation by telling him what he still lacked in order to attain salvation.

So, in ministering to the faithful, and in living my own life, I try to let love be the leader, with the "rules" there to "guide" the growth of love. Rules help. Love leads.

> *Once you had taken the Faith of Christ into your heart like a suit of armor, you trampled the hostile forces underfoot, having contended much, and you were crowned with heavenly laurels forever, as one invincible. (Kontakion, Third Saturday of the Souls, Trans. by Fr. Seraphim Dedes)*

Let love be your guide today!

Meatfare Sunday/Sunday of the Last Judgment

Faith Can Move Mountains

And what more shall I say? For time would fail me to tell of Gideon, Barak, Samson, Jephthah, of David and Samuel and the prophets—who through faith conquered kingdoms, enforced justice, received promises, stopped the mouths of lions, quenched raging fire, escaped the edge of the sword, won strength out of weakness, became mighty in war, put foreign armies to flight.
Hebrews 11:32-34
(Epistle on the Sunday of Orthodoxy)

There are many obstacles that can be overcome by rational thought. Materials are used to build buildings. Computers help us solve problems in math, physics and so many other areas. For instance, when I sit down with my son to build with Legos, this involves intellectual skills. From my life experience, I have learned many things about weight, balance and other building skills which come in handy when building with Legos.

Building with toys is not an act of faith, but rather an exercise in knowledge. Many challenges in life, however, are not solved merely by rational thought. They require "a leap of faith." For instance, good grades in high school, good test scores and extra-curricular activities lay the foundation for one to be accepted into college. These things are all achieved through hard work.

When, however, the moment comes for one to go to college, to leave home, go to an unfamiliar city, to a new campus, with new people and totally new dynamics, this requires more than intellect. It requires "faith." This "faith" may be "faith" in yourself, or faith in others, and hopefully faith in God. Intellect is not enough to make the "leap" and go to college. Knowledge is based on what we see—what our mind sees, what our life experience has shown us. Faith is not based on what we see, but trust in what we don't see or haven't yet seen. Faith is when one does not have full knowledge (though it doesn't necessarily mean that they have no knowledge of something) of something and still does it anyway. For instance, to get married requires faith—you may have known the person you are marrying for many years prior to the wedding date, but you get married without knowledge of what it is like to live with your spouse for years, to have children, to survive ups and downs, etc. To get married requires faith in each other, as well as faith in yourself and your ability to adapt to the changes that marriage brings.

So, where is God in the faith equation? Again, we must go to the end of life to find our answer. There is no question that we are going to die, each of us, one day. This is not a matter of faith, but a matter of fact. Faith comes in when we ponder on what will happen next. In the Christian faith, we believe that we will stand before the Lord for judgment and will then be assigned a permanent place in either eternal condemnation (hell) or eternal life (heaven). I've never been to heaven or hell, but I believe that both places exist. I believe because Christ died on the cross and rose from the dead that there is a path to Paradise for those who live their lives in faith.

I have faith that the judgment, the reward and the punishment are real. I believe in God. I believe that God has a plan for my life. I believe that for me that plan includes being a priest, being married, being a father, etc. How these things will work out in my life are a matter of not only my intellect, but also my faith in God and my choice to give Him control over my life. I don't know how long I'll live, how long I'll serve my present parish, and many other things—but I give (or try to give) any anxiety about these things to God, as a matter of faith, that He is going to take care of me and watch over me. I've never "conquered kingdoms," or "stopped the mouths of lions," or "escaped the edge of the sword," as St. Paul writes in his letter to the Hebrews. I believe that I've seen His miracles, felt His mercies, and received strength directly from Him. I believe because I've been part of things that defy rational thought, things that are so beautiful and powerful that they can only come from God.

I've enjoyed God's handiwork in nature—we all have done that. I have felt God's warmth during times of extreme stress, His comfort in times of loneliness, and His reassurance in times of doubt. I've been blessed to do things that I didn't think I should be able to do—preaching, praying, pastoral encounters, directing summer camp. I can't tell you how many times I've felt scared or unsure, and through prayer, have felt a sense of God's presence, with His reassurance that everything will be all right. The only way that these things happen is by putting my faith in God. He leads; I follow. He provides; I accept.

In today's verses, we read about the work of the prophets and Holy people of the Old Testament, who did amazing and unbelievable things through the Power of God. These people worked in concert with God. They put their faith and their very lives in His hands. They allowed Him to lead. They followed. They accepted whatever He provided—whether it was an obstacle, a challenge or even a victory. Many lost their lives while conquering kingdoms, but attained salvation. Many conquered kingdoms, stopped the mouths of lions, escaped the edge of the sword, won strength out of weakness, and became mighty in war precisely *because* they put their faith in the Lord. The lesson of today is that faith is what allows us to do the impossible, because working in concert with God is what makes things that defy rational thought, things in which we can succeed in doing.

This, the mystery of the plan of salvation—this present illumination—did the prophets foretell of old, with divine inspiration, to us who have come to the ages' termination. Receiving knowledge from Him, we know one Lord God, glory giv'n in three hypostases. And in giving Him our sole adoration, being one in Faith and Rite of Immersion, we are vested in Christ, and confessing our salvation, we depict it in word and deed. (Oikos, Orthros of Sunday of Orthodoxy, Trans. by Fr. Seraphim Dedes)

Grow in faith today!

Monday of Cheesefare

Come and See What!

Philip found Nathanael and said to him, "We have found Him of whom Moses in the law and also the prophets wrote, Jesus of Nazareth, the son of Joseph." Nathanael answered him, "Can anything good come out of Nazareth?" Philip said to him, "Come and see."
John 1:45-46
(Gospel on the Sunday of Orthodoxy)

We have all had the experience of being invited somewhere. When we accept an invitation, it is with the expectation that what we will be doing will be a positive experience, like going to a birthday party, or a restaurant.

We have all had the experience of being the "inviter." When we invite someone to do something with us, it is generally with the expectation that the thing we are going to do with them is going to be positive as well.

The Sunday of Orthodoxy, and the Gospel reading of that day, is all about an invitation. The Apostle Philip had an encounter with Jesus, and was so moved by the encounter, that he called his friend Nathanael and told him the good news of this Man whom he had met. However, Nathanael responded to the invitation with skepticism—"Can *anything* good come out of Nazareth?" Philip responded with a confident, commanding, and calming "Come and see."

I sometimes wonder what would happen if I put a large sign outside of our church with the invitation "Come and See" on it. I wonder if people would "come and see." I wonder, more seriously, if they came, what *would* they see? Would they see a parish that is alive with Christ? Or would they notice all the people who come in late? Would they take more note of the beautiful choir, or the damaged roof? What would they think if they saw how much money we give to the poor? Would they think we are a church, or more of a club? I'm thankful to the Lord that my parish is continually improving in all of these areas, but I do realize that we have a long way to go. Are we at a point where we want the "world" to "come and see"? This is an important question for every church community.

What if you wore a shirt that said "come and see" on it, inviting people to Christ via your personal witness for Him? Would people think that *your* life, my life, reflects a Christianity worth "coming and seeing"? Just like the shortcomings of our parish, would our personal shortcomings show more than our faith? Again, this is an important point to ponder, especially during this upcoming season of Great Lent. In fact, the entire purpose of Great Lent is repentance, which is cleaning up our Christian life, and our church communities so that people will want to come and see more of Christ based on our witness of Him.

On the Sunday of Orthodoxy, we boldly proclaim a Synodical Statement from the year 843 that "This is the faith of the Apostles. This is the Faith of the Fathers. This is the Faith of the Orthodox. This is the Faith on which the world is established." (Trans. by Fr. Seraphim Dedes) This is a very bold statement indeed. In many parishes, the "faith" can barely hold up the roof. In the lives of those who are nominal Christians, it is a faith that is nearly irrelevant.

Since we have inherited the faith of the Apostles, we, too, are called to be like the Apostles. We are called to be Philip. We are called to invite others to Christ. Philip was not very educated; he certainly was not educated in the faith. What he had was curiosity, and this bred desire, which led to conviction, and furthermore, to action of recruiting others. Lent is a time for those who are at the "curious" stage to explore the faith deeper. For those who are at the "desire" stage, it is a time to deepen the commitment. For those who are at the "convicted" stage, it is a time to give greater witness. For those out recruiting, it is time to double efforts and recruit even more people to "come and see" the power of God to transform lives.

As a priest, my ministry is one of recruiting others, but that doesn't mean that I shouldn't deepen curiosity, desire, and conviction. Truth be told, we all need continual improvement in all of these areas. "Come and see" should be a motto for all churches and all Christians. Great Lent is a time to reflect on the sincerity and truth of this statement, as it relates to our lives. "Come and see" a person who wears a cross but whose life does not honor that cross, or "come and see" a person who carries his crosses with joy and purpose, radiating God's love to all he meets? "Come and see" a church that can barely hold up its roof, or "come and see" a church that is ready to make a difference in its corner of the universe? Indeed, these are important questions for each of us.

> *Today has been manifested as a day of festivity, as a day full of happiness. The bright light of very true dogmas shines like lightning. And Christ's Church is glowing, for she is once again adorned by the replacement and installation now of holy icons and depictions, and the light that they radiate. And a oneness of mind among the believers has God bestowed. (From the Praises of Orthros on Sunday of Orthodoxy, Trans. by Fr. Seraphim Dedes)*

"Come and see" and encourage others to do the same.

Tuesday of Cheesefare

Being a Good Friend

And when Jesus returned to Capernaum after some days, it was reported that He was at home. And many were gathered together, so that there was no longer room for them, not even about the door; and He was preaching the word to them. And they came, bringing to Him a paralytic carried by four men. And when they could not get near Him because of the crowd, they removed the roof above Him; and when they had made an opening, they let down the pallet on which the paralytic lay.
Mark 2:1-4
(Gospel of the Second Sunday of Lent)

In the Gospel reading on the second Sunday of Lent, we read about Jesus healing a Paralytic. While it is Jesus who performed the miracle and did the healing, there were other people who were important and necessary in order for the miracle to happen; namely, the four friends of the Paralytic. The four friends carried the Paralytic to where Jesus was. Their friend was paralyzed. He couldn't get to Jesus by himself. When they came to the house where Jesus was, they couldn't get into the house because there were so many people in the house. So they got creative. They hoisted their friend up to the roof—*that* must have been quite an accomplishment in itself—then they cut a hole in the roof and lowered their friend down to Jesus, and Jesus healed him.

One of the things we learn from this story is the importance of having friends and the importance of being a good friend. Our friends help our journey to Christ. (Sadly, they can also hurt it.) What are characteristics of a good friend? Good friends are consistent and reliable, they are always our friends, and the friendship does not just depend on the situation. Friends are fun and honest, friends know how to keep a confidence and secret. Friends are forgiving; they have our best interests in mind. They are both good listeners and good advisors. Good friends have good morals and values and encourage us to stay out of trouble.

It is not only important to have good friends, but good Christian friends. Christian friends pray for one another. They encourage us to worship. When our faith is shaken, as happens to all of us at least occasionally, they help to build up our faith again. Christian friends hold us accountable, discourage non-Christian behaviors, and encourage Christian behavior.

All of us need good friends, and all of us need to be good friends to others. It is important that each of us learn how to listen, how to keep a confidence, how to encourage without being overly critical, and learn when to give advice and when we should just listen.

God created us to crave "community." We are social beings by nature. There is a saying that "one Christian is no Christian," and that "no Christian is an island." Part of our work as Christians is to befriend other Christians so that we can encourage them in their Christianity. Even if we are not overtly encouraging others by teaching about Christ, modeling Christian behavior will in itself help to get the message out. Jesus tells us in Matthew 5:16: *"Let your light so shine before men, that they may see your good works and give glory to your Father who is in heaven."* When we are being a good friend, we are letting our lights shine, and through good works, we are showing God's love to others.

In the Gospel of John, chapter 5:1-15, we hear about the healing of another Paralytic. In this instance, the man had been ill for thirty-eight years and had been sitting by the side of a pool that periodically was troubled by an angel who came down and stirred up the water and whoever stepped in first was healed of whatever disease he had. When Jesus saw the man and asked if he wanted to be healed, the man lamented *"I have no one to put me into the pool when the water is troubled"* (John 5:7). When I reflect on this story, I wonder what was worse for this man, his illness or his loneliness. There are people in this world who are paralyzed, not by physical disease, but by extreme loneliness and isolation. There are many people who feel that "I have no one." One of our obligations as Christians is to make sure that there is nobody who has no one. We should all seek to befriend those who do not have many friends. So that everyone has a "someone."

The miracle of the Paralytic would not have been possible without the vigilance and love of four committed friends. The miracle of our salvation, believe it or not, is contingent in part on us having friends who will encourage our faith. Likewise, each of us can play a pivotal role in the salvation of our friends, simply by being a good friend.

> *To those walking in the darkness of their sins You have shone as light, O Christ, during the season of self-control And reveal to us this auspicious day of Your Passion, so that we may cry to You, "Arise, O God, have mercy on us." (Doxastikon from Orthros of the Second Sunday of Lent, Trans. by Fr. Seraphim Dedes)*

Be a good friend today!

Wednesday of Cheesefare

Your Soul is the Most Valuable Thing You Have

Jesus said, "For what does it profit a man, to gain the whole world and forfeit his (soul)?
For what can a man give in return for his (soul)?"
Mark 8:36-37
(Gospel of the Third Sunday of Lent-Sunday of the Holy Cross)

Every time I read the Gospel verse I quote today, I am always disappointed by translation of one word, which fundamentally changes the meaning of the verse. In most translations of the Bible, the verses quoted above read as follows: *Jesus said, "For what does it profit a man, to gain the whole world and forfeit his life? For what can a man give in return for his life?"* When you read the verse in its original Greek, the word which is commonly translated as "life" is the word *psihi*, which is translated correctly as "soul." To give up one's life can be an honorable thing. To die in service of our country, or protecting someone else, is one of the noblest things one can do. To forfeit one's soul, however, condemns one for eternity.

What is a soul? We know how a human being is formed: male and female matter is brought together, and intertwined with them is a spirit—a soul—, which is bestowed by God. This is why, when a husband and wife come together to create a child, they become "co-creators" with God. In the soul, the Divine takes up residence in the human being. When the human being is created, the soul is "deposited" into the body by God. When the body dies and returns to dust, the soul is "extracted" by God, taken back into the presence of God for eternal judgment. Then the soul is sent to live "forever" either in the presence of God (heaven) or away from God (hell).

Our soul contains things like our conscience, our moral barometer. Our "faith" is nurtured in our soul. Our "countenance," the sparkle in our eyes, the spring in our step, comes from our souls. The soul is the God-like part of us.

One way I've used to explain the concept of the soul to people is to imagine that I gave you a shiny new quarter and gave you the task to keep the quarter with you at all times, shiny and new, just as you received it. Let's say that I told you that at some random time in your life, I'm going to come and ask for the quarter back, and if you have the quarter, shiny and new looking, to give back to me, I will give you riches for the rest of your life.

Many people have said in response to my "quarter challenge," that "Father, that's easy, just keep the quarter for my whole life and present it back to you, that's it?" To which I respond, "but you have to be careful, you have to have the quarter with you at all times—what happens to the quarter when you are at the gym, or swimming or sleeping. I could come for the quarter at *any* time." When you think about it that way, to keep the quarter at all times would actually be quite difficult, and so it is with the soul. The soul is not fed merely by going to church occasionally, or even once a week. The soul needs nourishment on a daily basis, especially in prayer. We need to have it ready at all times.

Here is another example—let's say that I made a deal with you that at a random time in the next year, I'm going to show up and ask you to run five miles, and if you can run five miles, I will give you a million dollars. You'd probably agree to this kind of deal. Some people, however, might become complacent, and think, "If he is giving me a *whole year*, what is the likelihood that he will come this week?" If the deal was, "sometime in the next year," it *could* be this week.

I use this example because there are many people who are complacent in life, especially when they are young. Many people reason that they have many years to live, and that they will get more serious about their souls later. In Matthew 24:42-44, we read: *"Watch therefore, for you do not know on what day your Lord is coming. But know this, that if the householder had known in what part of the night the thief was coming, he would have watched and would not have let his house be broken into. Therefore you also must be ready; for the Son of Man is coming at an hour you do not expect."*

The fact is that no one knows the day or the hour when our souls will be required of us. That's why feeding the soul on a daily basis, safeguarding it, protecting it, and cleansing it, has to be part of our daily life. Imagine how wonderful it would be for me to come to collect the quarter, and find you holding the quarter in your hand, polishing it. Likewise, how wonderful it would be for the Lord to come for your soul, and find you in prayer, in worship, or doing an act of kindness.

The soul cannot be replaced. It cannot be ignored. We can gain the whole world, but what will that really matter for eternity! Riches, fame, and fortune—we leave these all behind when we die. The only thing that goes with us is our soul. As we are working for material gain and improvement, let's not forget to work for spiritual gain and improvement. There is nothing you can give in return for your soul. Thus, we shouldn't seek to gain the world at the expense of our soul.

One of the saddest conversations I ever had was many years ago with someone who was ridiculing me for my faith. He said to me "Father, in 100 years, no one is going to remember you. But I'm making money so that my name will be on buildings, to be remembered forever." To which I responded, "The only place I care to be remembered is in God's *Book of Life*. As long as I'm on His list of sheep and not goats, what more is there that I could really want? Having my name on a building and not on God's list of righteous people would make my material fame worth nothing. Not being remembered by anyone, but remembered by God, is the most important thing of all."

> *My soul, O my soul, rise up! Why are you sleeping? The end draws near and soon you shall be troubled. Watch, then that Christ your God may spare you, for He is everywhere present and fills all things. (Kontakion, Canon of St. Andrew, Trans. by Fr. Seraphim Dedes)*

Make your soul shine today!

Thursday of Cheesefare

He Had to Become Like Us in Every Way

Therefore He had to be made like His brethren in every respect, so that He might become a merciful and faithful high priest in the service of God, to make expiation for the sins of the people. For because He Himself has suffered and been tempted, He is able to help those who are tempted.
Hebrews 2:17-18
(Epistle on the Feast of the Annunciation—March 25)

When mankind fell through the sin of Adam and Eve, we severed our oneness, our perfect communion with God. The penalty for that sin was death. Before the Fall, there was no death, no sickness, no strife, and no struggle. Where man was once "like God," in the sense that he could live forever like God, this opportunity for immortality was now gone. At the end of his earthly life, man would be consigned to darkness and death. As Saint Paul writes in Romans 6:23, "*The wages of sin is death.*" This is the penalty that the human beings have to pay because of our choice to sin.

God created the world out of a sense of love. It was (and is) that same love that was the motivation for God to redeem fallen man. How could that come about? God had to become like one us.

We've all had the experience of getting a bill in the mail, and on the bottom of the bill is usually written "remittance," or "please remit with payment." Remittance is what is owed on a bill. Now, let's say that you get a bill from the utility company and it says "please remit $100." Let's say that I offer to pay the bill for you. Does the credit card company care if I pay the bill for you? No, they don't, so long as someone pays the bill. If the wages of sin is death, Christ came to earth, to be like one of us, so that He could remit that bill for us, this is why we say that He died for the "remission" of our sins. He paid the debt for us.

The Feast of the Annunciation, which is celebrated on March 25, falls exactly nine months before the Feast of the Nativity, and thus always falls during Great Lent. (We do not know the exact date that the Nativity occurred, but when the date was fixed as December 25, the church backed up 9 months to set the Feast of the Annunciation.) For one day during Lent, we set aside a strict fast and celebrate a Feast, the day that it was announced to the Virgin Mary that God would take on human flesh and become one of us.

Christ became like us in every way; he got tired, sick, angry, thirsty, and sad. He was tempted, just like we are tempted. He had fears, just like us. When His friend Lazarus died, He wept, just like we do when someone dies. When He contemplated His own death, He was afraid, just like we are.

This is one of the reasons why it is easier to trust in the Lord, because He became one of us. He knows our struggles because He experienced them, and yet, in His human experience, He did not succumb to temptation. He maintained His love for His Father at all times, He remained obedient at all times. He showed us what it is to love, and to empty oneself of all pride. Not only is Christ a faithful "high priest" in the service of God, but He also showed (and continually shows) us what mercy is.

Even though we do not see Him today in the flesh, many people get the "sense" that He walks with them, or that they walk with Him. I don't think of the angels as being like us. I don't think about walking with angels, or flying with angels. Many times when I think of Christ, I do think about "walking" with Him. Because He had the full human experience, I can use human terms to describe my relationship with Him, like "walking with Him," or "talking with Him."

The word "empathy" is often defined as placing ourselves in the shoes of another. Empathy makes us more compassionate toward other people. It is interesting that the etymology of "empathy" comes from two Greek words, "em" and "pathos." "Em" means "in." "Pathos" can be translated "feeling." It can also be translated as "passion," meaning the things we struggle with, and "suffering." We call the sufferings of Christ His "Passion," which comes from the same word. So, the word "empathy" can correctly be translated as "sharing in sufferings." Christ has shared in our sufferings, so He can relate to us. If we share in His sufferings—trials, tribulations, temptations—staying obedient to God as He did, we will "relate" to Him, in *this* life, paving the way for us to live with Him in everlasting life.

> *In His exceeding compassion viewing with mercy our fall, the Co-Eternal Logos of the beginningless Father came down and appeared to the things below, never leaving the things on high. Having assumed Adam's poverty to Himself He has taken on the other's form. (From the Praises of Orthros of the Annunciation, Trans. by Fr. Seraphim Dedes)*

Be Godly today!

Friday of Cheesefare

Behold, I Am the Handmaiden of the Lord

And Mary said, "Behold, I am the handmaiden of the Lord; let it be to me according to your word."
Luke 1:38
(Gospel of the Feast of the Annunciation—March 25)

If you were to divide the history of the world into chapters, the first chapter would be about the Creation of the World. In this chapter, the human race lived in complete harmony with its Creator, in an almost "god-like" state. The second chapter would be about the "Fall" of mankind, and its consequences, when mankind was banished from Paradise and suffered hardship and death. The third chapter would be about the "people of God" living in expectation of a Messiah. This third chapter would begin with the covenant with Abraham, in Genesis 15, where God established a relationship with a people, and those people established a relationship with Him. The covenant with Abraham lasted 42 generations—the names of each of these generations are given in the Gospel of Matthew, Chapter One, and are read the Sunday before the Nativity each year. During these 42 generations, God's people experienced triumph (deliverance from the hands of Pharaoh in Exodus 14) and setback (the fall of Jerusalem and deportation to Babylon in 2 Kings 24). They were given inspiration through the mouths of Prophets like Isaiah and Jeremiah, that one day there would be a Deliverer.

Saint Paul writes in his Epistle to the Galatians (chapter 4) that God sent forth His Son, *"when the time had fully come."* No one knew when this would occur, or how it would occur. We learned from the story of the Paralytic that people work in concert with God in order for God's miracles to happen. The miracles require His power and our faith. The greatest miracle that ever happened was that Jesus Christ died and rose from the dead to save us from our sins. That is a miracle—because it transcends not only the laws of nature, but it transcends even the comprehension of our rational minds. Yes, miracles can also remain enshrouded in "mystery." For instance, it is a miracle that bread and wine are consecrated as the Body and Blood of Christ at each Divine Liturgy, yet we call this "miracle" a "mystery" (sometimes translated as "sacrament"), because even though we believe, we cannot completely comprehend.

The miracle of the Resurrection, which is the centerpiece of our faith, was surrounded by *many* other miracles, many instances where the Lord worked in concert with us to allow extraordinary things to happen. To pave the way to the Crucifixion and Resurrection, Christ worked many miracles, Messianic signs foretold in the Old Testament that revealed Him as the promised Messiah. Before those miracles could occur, Christ had to come into the world, which was caused by another miracle, the Incarnation of God in the flesh. How Christ came into the world is understandable. He had a human birth—we can all understand that. His conception, however, was a miracle.

The Archangel Gabriel came to a village named Nazareth, and visited a young girl named Mary, who, history tells us, was probably fourteen years old at the time of the Archangel's visit. The Archangel brought her extraordinary news: She was going to bear God's Son. The Holy Spirit, not the man to whom she was betrothed, would cause his birth. The angel didn't immediately announce to Mary that her Son would die a horrific death. What would have been apparent right away to Mary was that her reputation would be on the line—how would she explain becoming pregnant to Joseph, or to anyone else? This very young, very alone (remember Mary's parents died when she was very young) woman was being presented with an overwhelming task.

In order for God's miracles to take place, they have involved ordinary people demonstrating extraordinary faith. None was more extraordinary than Mary's "YES" to the announcement by the Archangel. Imagine if she had said "no"? Her answer changed the course of human history. This is why she is said to be *"Greater in honor than the Cherubim and beyond compare more glorious than the Seraphim."* (Megalynarion of Orthros, Trans. by Fr. Seraphim Dedes). Her "YES" was a yes to the greatest task ever given a human being—the responsibility of bearing God's own Son.

Was her "yes" without doubts and fears? Was her "yes" with confidence or trepidation? To completely submit to the will of the Lord has to fill one with all of these things.

The Feast of the Annunciation opened the chapter of salvation in the history of humanity because it sets in motion the Incarnation, the miracles, and THE Miracle, the Resurrection. All of these were made possible as a consequence of the Incarnation, which was made possible by a miracle of God, working in concert with the faith of humanity, in this case, represented by the Virgin Mary. The feast honors the Virgin Mary, for her faith, her humility, and her "YES."

The feast also calls to our minds that we are to do the same—work in concert with God so that we, and others, can experience His miracles. The word "Theotokos" means "God bearer." We use this title for the Virgin Mary, in honor of her bearing God in her womb. This idea of carrying God within us is a call to everyone to be a "theotokos." Christ asks us every day to carry Him in our hearts, our souls, and in our actions. What is our answer? What is your answer *today*? "I am the handmaiden (or servant) of the Lord, let it be to me according to Your will" is the answer we should be offering every day. It is an answer that says; let me work in concert with You, so that Your glory is known through both ordinary and extraordinary things today.

The age-old mystery is revealed today, and the Son of God becomes the Son of man, so that by partaking of what is lower He may impart to me what is superior. Of old, Adam was deceived; and he did not become God, though that was his desire. But now, God becomes man, to make Adam god. Let creation sing for joy, and let nature be exultant. For the archangel is standing with awe before the Virgin and is delivering the salutation, "Rejoice," the reverse of the pain and sorrow. O our God, who in Your tender mercy became me, glory to You! (Doxastikon from Orthros of the Annunciation, Trans. by Fr. Seraphim Dedes)

Work in concert with God today!

Second Saturday of the Souls

I Can *So* Relate to This!

Jesus said "All things are possible to him who believes." Immediately the father of the child cried out and said, "I believe; help my unbelief!"
Mark 9:23-24
(Gospel of the Fourth Sunday of Lent)

I confess that when I was much younger, I used to hear the Gospel on the Fourth Sunday of Lent and think "ho hum, another healing." Now, when I read this passage, I fix my attention on these two verses. Jesus tells a desperate father that all things are possible if he just has enough faith. The father makes one of the most honest and heartfelt confessions in the entirety of the Bible, "I believe," he says. "Help my unbelief!"

There is no question that the man believes that Christ can do something extraordinary for his son. After all, it is the father who has brought the son to Jesus. Jesus did not come to the father's house; the father went to the crowd who had come to see Jesus. There is no question that he believed something.

With so many people thronging about Jesus, this man, like so many others, was not able to get right next to Christ, so he asked the disciples to cast out the boy's evil spirit. His faith must have been shaken when they could not, yet he was undeterred, and eventually made it to speak to Jesus face to face. No doubt exasperated, he explained the whole situation to Jesus. Christ did not ask the father, "Do you believe?" Rather, he made a statement: "If you can! All things are possible to him who believes."

Put yourself in the shoes of the father. We all have something that we cannot fix. In this case, it was a man who loved his son, but couldn't his son's illness. Some of us have children who are sick in some way. Some of us are sick ourselves. Some of us are trapped in circumstances beyond our control, circumstances that cause us stress and sadness. We believe in God, no doubt! There is no one who is reading this message today who doesn't believe in God, at least a little bit. Anyone who is going to take time out of their day to read an inspirational message about Christianity is at least somewhat Christian. The statement, "I believe" applies to you.

There isn't anyone who hasn't had moments of doubt, even on the same day as their moments of faith. All of us scratch our heads at times as we wonder why certain things happen or don't happen in our lives, most especially in the lives of our children and our friends. As a father, I know I'd rather see myself suffer than my son. There are lots of things that happen in our world that leave me wondering, not so much "Is there a God?" but "Where is God in the midst of this?" How many of you have had prayers that have been unanswered? I know I have. Even the same prayer, sometimes offered for years and years, with seemingly no resolution. I do know that God's time and our time move in different ways. In Isaiah we read, *"For my thoughts are not your thoughts, neither are your ways my ways, says the Lord"* (Isa. 55:8). His plans do not necessarily match ours. Like the father in this story, sometimes I cry out to God "Help my unbelief!" Help me to trust that Your will governs all. Help me to have faith that there is a plan. Even my own shortcomings can be part of God's plan.

"I believe! Help my unbelief!" is one of the most powerful statements in the Bible, because it is one of the most honest. The father in this story is really all of us: I believe, but I need God's reassurance in those moments when my faith is tested, when I'm scratching my head wondering.

Jesus concludes the Gospel passage about the healing of the man's son by speaking with His disciples, who ask why they could not cast out the demon. Jesus said, *"this kind cannot be driven out by anything but prayer and fasting"* (Mark 9:29). As we are about to enter Great Lent, and begin the season of heightened prayer and fasting, it is a good reminder to us that our faith is sustained through discipline that comes through prayer and fasting, and friends and community who provide encouragement.

> *Come, let us labor in the mystical vineyard, producing fruits of repentance within it—not laboring for things that are eaten or drunk, but by prayer and fasting attaining the virtues. By such will the Lord of the labor be pleased, and He will grant them the denarius, by which He ransoms souls from the debt of sin, for He alone is greatly merciful. (Doxastikon from Orthros of the Fourth Sunday of Lent, Trans. by Fr. Seraphim Dedes)*

Pray today that God will always strengthen you in your moments of doubt!

Cheesefare Sunday/Forgiveness Sunday

To Serve and Not to Be Served

Jesus said "You know that those who are supposed to rule over the Gentiles Lord it over them, and their great men exercise authority over them. But it shall not be so among you; but whoever would be great among you must be your servant, and whoever would be first among you must be the slave of all. For the Son of Man also came not to be served, but to serve, and to give His life as a ransom for many."
Mark 10:42-45
(Gospel of the Fifth Sunday of Lent)

To truly "serve" someone else is to completely empty oneself of *any* agenda and help. This means to help expecting *nothing* in return—not payment, not a future favor, nothing. It means to help when help is needed. Let's look at an example:

Gus and his family moved to a new city. As they were settling into their new home, their neighbor Chris stopped by and introduced himself. Chris asked Gus, "Is there anything I can do to help you?" Gus said, "Well, my lawnmower didn't survive the trip. If you really wanted to help me, you could mow the lawn so it doesn't get out of control before I'm able to buy a new mower." Chris replied, "Well, I paint houses, can I paint your house?" Gus answered, "No, the house is nice just the color it is." Chris said, "But I paint really well, I'd love to paint your house, I won't charge you much." Gus answered, "No, thank you." One day, Gus came home from work and found his house painted, a color he didn't even like. A bill was on the door. Gus shook his head. Chris had really been no help at all. In fact his "help" was actually hurtful.

While this story about Gus and Chris may seem a little extreme, smaller versions of it take place nearly every day. How many times do we offer to help, in order to be considerate, and when the person we are offering to help says what they need, we're almost sorry we offered because it's not something we really want to do? How many times when we ask for help, does a "Chris" offer to help when really he has another agenda? How many times when we help someone do we wait for a reward or an accolade, or hope for a future "consideration?"

To truly serve someone means to help, as help is needed, without expecting anything in return. If Chris truly wanted to help Gus, he would have mowed his lawn because that's what Gus needed at that particular moment in time. Christ teaches us that we are to serve one another. Just as He came to serve and not to be served, we are to do the same.

It's frustrating, especially in church leadership, that many who step forward to serve have other agendas. Many people will sign up to work at the festival, as an example, and say "I'll do whatever's needed." If they are asked to wipe off dirty tables, they will ask "Is there something *else* I can do?"

It's also hard to truly serve because many times we like to benefit in some way from our "service." I "serve" as a priest, but I also get a paycheck for it. A politician "serves" but also many times has a hard time making a decision that his constituents don't support, for fear of losing their vote. A dad who volunteers as a baseball coach for the team his son is on usually treats his son better than other players, so he "serves," but there is some benefit coming back to him as well.

To truly serve is to empty oneself completely and offer from the heart expecting *nothing* in return. This is the ideal. Everyone falls short of the ideal, for sure. This is the ideal for which we are supposed to strive. This is why it is important to do "volunteer" work. This is why it is important to not just do our jobs, but to go above and beyond what is required at work, so we can "serve." This is why "pro bono" work is important. This is also why it is important to serve our spouses and our children and our friends, even when they are annoying us. To serve only when things are good is really an "exchange" of favors; you be good and I'll be nice. To serve is to give even when the recipient is not deserving. Christ showed us the noblest way to serve; He was willing to die for us. He didn't expect money, or favors, or even loyalty. His disciples eventually all left Him. He served them anyway.

Service starts off with basic courtesy—holding a door open for someone, not playing music too loud, easily forgiving, and being a good listener. We have probably dozens of opportunities to serve every day. Ironically, the more you "serve" the more you receive in the form of God's blessings on your life. For as Jesus says in Matthew 19:30, *"Many that are first will be last, and the last first."* Those who serve with an agenda, who seek to put themselves ahead, will find themselves as "the last" in God's book. Those who put themselves last by serving others are the ones that God will place first, and who will receive His reward.

Serve others as if you are serving the Lord Himself! After all, it's all about Him, not about us. To receive His eternal reward, we've got to make this life about Him. Great Lent, which we begin tomorrow, is about Him and us: what He did for us, how we serve Him, and how we serve Him by serving others. This season is supposed to bring us closer to Him and one another, as we remember His ultimate act of service—His Sacrifice on the Cross!

The Kingdom of God is not food and drink, but righteousness and ascetic practice and holiness; therefore rich men will never enter it, but only those who place their treasures into the hands of the needy. This is what David the Prophet teaches when he says, "Righteous is the man, who is merciful day in and out, who delights in the Lord. He walks in the light; he will not stumble." All of this was written for our edification, that, while fasting, we do acts of kindness; and the Lord will give us, instead of earthly gifts, the things of heaven. (Doxastikon, Orthros of the Fifth Sunday of Lent, Trans. by Fr. Seraphim Dedes)

Serve today!

PART TWO—THE JOURNEY TO THE CROSS

The Extreme Humility

Thru the hand of Fr. Anthony Salzman, www.imageandlikeness.com

Monday of the First Week of Lent

Different Kinds of Healing

Now a certain man was ill, Lazarus of Bethany, the village of Mary and her sister Martha. It was Mary who anointed the Lord with ointment and wiped his feet with her hair, whose brother Lazarus was ill. So the sisters sent to him, saying, "Lord, he whom you love is ill." But when Jesus heard it he said, "This illness is not unto death; it is for the glory of God, so that the Son of God may be glorified by means of it."
John 11:1-4
(Gospel on the Saturday of Lazarus)

As we begin Great Lent today, the focus of these reflections will shift toward the Scriptures of Holy Week. We will spend the Lenten period making a slow journey through the events of the week of Christ's Passion, as told to us in the beautiful scriptures and hymns of Holy Week. The first stop is at Bethany, a village a few miles outside of Jerusalem. Bethany was the home of Mary and Martha, and their brother Lazarus. Jesus was friends with them, and often stayed in their home.

Jesus received word from Mary and Martha that their brother Lazarus was ill. Seemingly out of character, Jesus did not heal Lazarus immediately. Nor did He rush to Bethany to heal him. In fact, He stayed where He was for two days, and only then did He make His way slowly to Bethany. Jesus, knowing everything, allowed Lazarus to die.

Mary and Martha must have had some incredible faith, because they made no request of Jesus to heal their brother. They merely informed Him "The one whom You love is ill." They left it up to Jesus as to what would happen next.

There are three kinds of healing that Jesus did in His ministry, and three kinds of healing that we have access to today. The first kind of healing is "instant healing." One (of many) examples of this is told in Matthew 8:14-15: *"And when Jesus entered Peter's house, He saw his mother-in-law lying sick with a fever; He touched her hand, and the fever left her, and she rose and served Him."*

The second kind of healing is "gradual healing." An example of this was the cleansing of Ten Lepers, told in Luke 17. Jesus encountered ten lepers who asked Him for mercy. *When He saw them He said to them, "Go and show yourselves to the priests." And as they went they were cleansed* (Luke 17:14). In this case, as in others, those seeking healing were given something to do, and having done that, having trusted God to go and show themselves to the priests, they were healed "gradually."

The third kind of healing can be called "ultimate healing." The ultimate healing is "resurrection" from the dead and everlasting life. The only way to get this miracle is to physically die. After death, for the person of faith, comes the ultimate healing, which is salvation. Once one goes to the kingdom of God, there is no more need for healing, for there will never be any more illness. This ultimate healing results in no healing ever being needed again.

Jesus let Lazarus die. That was part of His plan. Because only by letting Lazarus die could Jesus show us what "ultimate healing" is, that He is Lord over the living and the dead, and that life after death is possible—for Lazarus, for Christ, and for us.

Through the miracles of medical science (inspired by God), and sometimes through miracles of God that defy explanation, we experience healing often in this life. Sometimes that healing is instant—a headache can be quickly healed with a pill. A crying child can be healed with a hug almost instantly. Sometimes the healing is gradual—heart disease or cancer is often cured through long protocols of surgery and treatment.

Eventually, for everyone, both instant and gradual healing will fail, and we will die. Death, for the faithful Christian, provides the ultimate healing. It is the only way to receive the ultimate healing. This presents us with at least a couple of challenges. First, it takes faith to place our hope in ultimate healing, because one has to go someplace unseen and permanent (death) in order to receive it. Secondly, as concerns our desire to live and for our loved ones to live, it takes great faith and humility to make the simple plea of Mary and Martha over those who are sick: "Lord, the one whom You love is ill." Imagine that this is the *only* prayer you offer over someone who is sick. This leaves it totally in the hands of God. It asks, as Jesus said, that "God may be glorified by means of it," meaning leaving room for God's glory in the midst of whatever disease or illness is being had and in the outcome, whatever that may be, of that disease. The younger the person is who is very ill, the harder it is to offer *this* prayer. I once ministered to a young woman who was very devout in her faith and who way dying from cancer. She asked me "Father, do you think I will get a miracle?" I answered, "You are either going to get the miracle of restored health or everlasting life, you are either going to get gradual healing or ultimate healing, but either way, you are going to get a 'miracle.' Either way you are going to be 'healed.'" In her case, God gave her ultimate healing.

In our life we will experience instant healing and gradual healing. At some point, we will have to turn our attention and hope to ultimate healing. In order to receive the ultimate healing, however, one has to die, and one has to die trusting God, and giving glory to Him.

Martha and Mary unto the Savior said: If You had been here, O Lord, then Lazarus would not have died. Then Christ, the Resurrection of those who in death have slumbered, resurrected from the dead the man already four days dead. Therefore, O believers all, come let us adore Him who is coming in glory to save our souls. (From the Praises of the Saturday of Lazarus, Trans. by Fr. Seraphim Dedes)

Glorify God in all things—good and bad—today.

Tuesday of the First Week of Lent

Martha Actually Set a Great Example

She said to him, "Yes, Lord; I believe that you are the Christ, the Son of God, he who is coming into the world."
John 11:27
(Gospel on the Saturday of Lazarus)

Most of us are familiar with the story of Mary and Martha, told in Luke 10:38-42. Jesus visited their home. Mary was sitting and listening to Jesus' teaching, while Martha was running around serving. Martha got frustrated and went to Jesus and said "Lord, do you not care that my sister has left me to serve alone? Tell her then to help me." Jesus answered her, "Martha, Martha, you are anxious and troubled about many things; one thing is needful. Mary has chosen the good portion, which shall not be taken away from her."

From this, Martha gets a bad rap, as if she does not have her priorities in order. One might go so far as to question whether Martha was so consumed with material things, whether she had any faith at all. It turns out that nothing could be farther from the truth.

When Jesus came to Bethany, her brother Lazarus had been dead and buried for four days. We read in John 11:20 that when Martha heard that Jesus was coming, it was she, and not Mary, who ran to meet Him. Mary remained in the house. *Martha said to Jesus: "Lord, if You had been here, my brother would not have died"* (John 11:21). This in itself was a statement of faith, that the Lord would have had power to heal her brother. *"And even now I know that whatever you ask from God, God will give you"* (11:22). This is an even greater statement of faith, recognizing that even in this dire circumstance, Jesus could still make a miracle.

We read in 11:19 that *"many of the Jews"* had come to see Mary and Martha and to console them concerning the death of their brother. In 11:31 we read that *when the Jews who were with her (Mary) in the house, consoling her, saw Mary rise quickly and go out, they followed her, supposing that she was going to the tomb to weep there.* Presumably, some of them were with Martha when she went to see Jesus, so the conversation that Martha was having with Jesus was more than likely in the presence of others. When Jesus asked Martha if she believed that He is *"the*

Resurrection and the Life" and that whoever believed in Him even if they died, yet they would live, Martha made the boldest, most public confession that could be: "*I believe that* you *are the Christ, the Son of God.*" Imagine the consequences that this could have had! In the presence of Jews and even Jewish leaders, she confessed Jesus to be the Christ, the Son of God!

Before we give Martha too bad of a rap, we should remember that her pronouncement was a profound example of both faith and courage. As we begin our Lenten journey this week, the first thing we must set about working on is our sense of faith: Do I believe? What do I believe? How strong do I feel about what I believe in? The second thing we must work on is how we witness that faith to others. Do we love others? Do we speak about the faith with others? In a world that seems to be demeaning Christianity at almost every turn, do we stand up for Christ? Do we stand up with Christ?

Indeed it wasn't only Mary that focused on the needful things. Martha, too, had chosen the most needful things: faith, and the courage to live out that faith. May we do the same.

> *Martha cried aloud to Mary: "Come, for the Teacher is here and is calling for you." And she went quickly to the place where her Lord was. And when she saw You, she cried; she knelt; she worshipped. As she covered Your immaculate feet with kisses, she said, "Lord, if You had been here, our brother would not have died." (From the Praises of the Orthros of Saturday of Lazarus, Trans. by Fr. Seraphim Dedes)*

Be courageous today!

Wednesday of the First Week of Lent

Having the Right Values

Finally, brethren, whatever is true, whatever is honorable, whatever is just, whatever is pure, whatever is lovely, whatever is gracious, if there is any excellence, if there is anything worthy of praise, think about these things.
Philippians 4:8
(Epistle of Palm Sunday)

I could write an entire week of reflections on this verse alone! It mentions virtues that are quickly disappearing from our world today. As we reflect on this verse today, think of the meaning of these words, what St. Paul is referring to and how the world has turned these words around.

Truth—Jesus tells us in the Bible, "*The truth shall set you free*" (John 8:32). We live in a world where dishonesty is almost expected, and sadly, in some professions, required. The truth is the highest authority—without truth, none of the virtues that follow are possible. There is no nobility, or justice, or purity, nothing can be lovely, or of good report if it is based in a lie. The ultimate source of truth is the Lord.

Nobility—We are obsessed with control, yet there is no nobility in doing something when you know exactly what the outcome will be. That's why it's a noble thing for a firefighter to rush into a burning building to save someone, or a patient to wage a battle with cancer, or a person to listen to someone who needs comfort, because in any of these situations, a person does not know the outcome, but takes a chance anyway.

Just—Just is what is fair, not in the eyes of society, but in the eyes of God. Just means doing the right thing, even if it is not popular.

Purity—A pure white sheet is a piece of cloth without any stain, wrinkle, or blemish. We were each wrapped in one of these after our baptisms. Purity is under constant attack—it is hard to keep a body pure, to not engage in overindulging in food or alcohol, or for those yet to be married, to stay pure in body and wait for marriage. It is hard to stay pure in mind when we receive messages of violence in movies and distrust of contemporary leaders. It is hard to stay pure in spirit when the faith is constantly under attack, yet to fight the battle for purity is not only noble, it is rewarding.

Lovely—There is beauty in each person because each person is created in God's image and likeness. It is so sad when I hear someone call another person "ugly," because it is so untrue. There are no ugly people. There are people who do ugly things, but every person is innately beautiful because God made them that way.

Good report—It's hard to watch the news most days because the reports are anything but good. In fact, a good friend of mine says to me, during the occasional "woe is me" conversation that all of us have with our friends, "tell me something good." Today in your friendships and in your marriages (for those who are married), focus on saying something good to your friends or your spouse. Even if you can't muster anything good to say about them in particular, say something good to them. We need more good reports in the world.

Truth, nobility, justice, purity, loveliness, and good reports—these are virtuous things upon which we should meditate.

One mantra I use to live my life is, "If it's not good, it's not from God." Only good things come from God, so if it is not a good thing, it isn't from Him. Truth, nobility, justice, purity, loveliness, good reports—these are good things that come from God. Dishonesty, distrust, injustice, ugly behavior, bad news—these are not things of God. So meditate on the things of God today, and make an effort to work at *one* of these virtues: truth, nobility, justice, purity, loveliness, or a good report. Work at *one* of these today, and then pick a different one tomorrow until you've had one day with each of them. Then try two on a day, and so on, until all six become part of your daily life.

One last note, which is that on Palm Sunday, we read the Epistle from Philippians 4:4-9. It is unfortunate, in my opinion that the Epistle doesn't continue all the way to Philippians 4:13: *I can do all things through Christ who strengthens me.* This is because Philippians 4:13 provides us one of the best mantras for the Christian life: all things are possible through Christ. Christ will give us the strength to endure every trial. I encourage you to read Philippians 4:4-13, truly a spiritual treasure.

> *In heaven upon the throne, on earth upon the colt, You were carried, O Christ our God; and the praise of the Angels, and the hymns of the children, You received as they cried to You, ⊠Blessed are You, the One, who is coming to call Adam back again." (Kontakion, Palm Sunday, Trans. by Fr. Seraphim Dedes)*

Focus on truth, nobility, justice, purity, loveliness, and good reports today! Or pick one today and a different one for the next several days!

Thursday of the First Week of Lent

We Must Become Like Children

But when the chief priests and the scribes saw the wonderful things that he did, and the children crying out in the temple, "Hosanna to the Son of David!" they were indignant; and they said to him, "Do you hear what these are saying?" And Jesus said to them, "Yes; have you never read, 'Out of the mouth of babes and sucklings thou hast brought perfect praise'?"
Matthew 21:15-16
(Gospel of Orthros on Palm Sunday)

It is interesting to see the world through the eyes of a child. A young child doesn't know what it is like to be cynical. A young child doesn't know what it means to doubt. Little children don't carry grudges—they move from sad to happy, from crying to laughing, very quickly. If you tell them you are going to do something, they easily believe.

So, when Jesus rode into Jerusalem on Palm Sunday, and people were saying, "The King is coming," the children came out and waved palm branches and sang "Hosanna to the Son of David!" Some of the adults, no doubt, were cynical—after all, where were the chariots and the army—If Jesus was a king after all, shouldn't He be entering Jerusalem as a military conqueror?

The Jewish Temple leadership saw Jesus as a threat. There were no armies to be afraid of, but the mere mention of this man as a "king" certainly unnerved them. Jesus was a Jew, and at the top of the Jewish "food chain" were the temple elite.

The Roman authorities had to be concerned. Their "king" was Caesar. A bunch of people crying out for another king could pose a problem for them and threaten their political stranglehold on the region.

It was the children who led the way. Imagine the cry that the "king" is coming, and the children grabbing whatever was at hand to greet Him. There weren't fancy metal and feathered fans as one would find in a king's court (think of the Pharaoh in the movie *The Ten Commandments*), so the children improvised and grabbed palm branches to waive at the "king." Who was this king? For the children, it didn't matter—they heard that a person of importance was passing through and they didn't want to miss out on the event.

When I was a child, I didn't know much about Holy Week. All I remember was that it was the week that the church was filled to overflow and that we got to stay up late, which was good enough for us. We were really excited! I can't say I really knew much about Jesus either. I was told that He loved me and died for my sins and that was good enough too.

As an adult, there are times I have been more cynical about the faith. I've wondered, "How could all of these things we read in the scripture possibly have happened?" rather than taking it on faith. I've questioned God's love and wondered about His intentions as we watch tragedies happen around us. Sometimes worship is a chore rather than a joy.

I'm reminded though, that it is the faith of a child that puts us in good standing to enter the Kingdom of God. We need to have our eyes wide open in wonder rather than squinting with criticism. We need hearts that are soft and easy to forgive, rather than hardened and calloused. We need to remember the mantra we learned in preschool: hands are for helping and not for hurting. We need to remember that it's good to laugh and okay to be silly.

Jesus says in Matthew 18:3, *"Truly I say to you, unless you turn and become like children, you will never enter the kingdom of heaven."* He encourages us to be childlike. As we make our way through Lent and again to Holy Week, let us try to remember the wonder we had as children. Those children who waved palms on Palm Sunday, they didn't hold anything back. They had unbridled joy, they were totally "into it." When I was a child, I didn't totally understand everything. I didn't need to. I remember my priest lifting up the chalice before partaking of Holy Communion and thinking how powerful it was to see God standing over all of us in that moment. I still think that today when I lift the chalice. When is the last time you felt unbridled joy? Try to capture that in your life and faith. This is when you will be better able to meet Christ as your King and God, when you recapture that joy and innocence of the children on Palm Sunday.

Of course, children don't stay children. They learn more about the things they didn't understand as a child. Our understanding of the faith should be more than what we understood as children. We should, however, seek to learn about our faith, but remember to combine a childlike innocence and joy with an adult sense of focus and purpose, leaving cynicism and demands to the side and embracing with trust and optimism.

> *To confirm the general resurrection before Your Passion, You resurrected Lazarus from the dead, O Christ our God. Therefore imitating the children, carrying the symbols of victory, we cry out to You the Victor over death: "Hosanna in the highest! Blessed are You, the One, who comes in the name of the Lord." (Apolytikion, Saturday of Lazarus and Palm Sunday, Trans. by Fr. Seraphim Dedes)*

Look for reasons to be joyful today!

Friday of the First Week of Lent

Come with Conviction, Not Just for the Signs

The crowd that had been with him when He called Lazarus out of the tomb and raised him from the dead bore witness. The reason why the crowd went to meet him was that they heard he had done this sign.
John 12:17-18

I've often wondered how a large crowd on a Sunday could cheer "Hosanna" for Jesus as He entered into Jerusalem, and five days later, many of the same people jeered "Crucify Him!" Did they feel some sense of "conviction" toward either position? Today's verse perhaps offers some answer.

Lazarus was raised from the dead in Bethany, only two miles from Jerusalem. Because it was Passover Week, many Jews were making their way to the Holy City and were no doubt passing through Bethany, a stop on the route to Jerusalem. News like the raising of a dead man would certainly travel fast, and as it is with most information that passes through many different people, the story probably had changed by the time it had been told several times. Was the news that Jesus was the promised Messiah, or just that He had done an unexplainable miracle? John 11:45-46 tells us, *"Many of the Jews therefore, who had come with Mary and had seen what He (Jesus) did, believed in Him; but some of them went to the Pharisees and told them what Jesus had done."* So, there was a division among the Jews—some believed in Jesus as Messiah, others believed that He was a super-healer, and others went to the Jewish authorities either to discredit Jesus or perhaps even to convince them that He was the Christ.

The next day, (or perhaps it was one or two days later as the raising of Lazarus is not "dated" to the day before Palm Sunday, just customarily celebrated that day) Jesus entered Jerusalem sitting on a donkey's colt. Throngs of people went to see Him. Why? Perhaps it was curiosity—they wanted to see if this man was audacious enough to come into Jerusalem when the Jewish authorities were conspiring to kill Him. Perhaps some believed He was going to be a military deliverer and were waiting for armies to enter with Him and take their city back from Roman oppression. Perhaps some were very devout and with humility they came to honor Jesus.

Five days later, on Good Friday, this same crowd came out and screamed for Jesus to be crucified. What changed their mind in five days? Undoubtedly, there were probably some people in Jerusalem who were disappointed because the "Savior" had been in town for five days, and the Romans still hadn't been overthrown. They probably looked behind the donkey Jesus was riding and wondered, "Where are the armies and the chariots?"

I'm convinced that some people in the crowd probably on both days didn't know what they were doing. When some started chanting "Hosanna," the rest started along with them, and on Good Friday, when the cry for crucifixion became louder, some probably felt pressure to jump in. This is how many Christians are—they don't know enough about the faith in order to be "convicted" about it. When it's popular to be Christian, they line up to be counted, but when it is not popular, they don't stick around, because they lack depth of faith.

In sports, there is a term called "fair weather fans." Which means, when a team is playing well, everyone becomes a fan. When a team is not faring well, many fans jump ship and start to root for other teams. The real fans stay loyal, win or lose.

So, the lesson of today is that we should not be fair weather Christians, coming to Christ only when things are going well and turning on Him or ignoring Him when times are tough. Rather we need to seek a deep and abiding faith in Christ.

Many priests joke that people come to the Holy Week services according to what they will "get." So people come Palm Sunday for a palm, Holy Wednesday for Holy Unction, Good Friday for a flower and on Pascha for an egg. They stay away Holy Thursday night when we read about Christ's Passion, not only because the service is lengthy, but because there is no "free gift." The reason why the "crowds" come is because of the sign, or the gift being given. Why do these crowds not come the rest of Holy Week, or the rest of the church year? Is that because for many people, the faith is as lukewarm as the conviction of the people in the crowd on Palm Sunday? It's easy to scream out "Hosanna" when everyone is doing it, but what about when no one is doing it? What about when life is going really wrong, or when it feels like God is far away, or when you need a miracle and it is just not happening?

The rituals of Holy Week are not signs put there for us to worship. We don't worship rituals. We worship the Lord. Signs and rituals are there only as tools to deepen the faith, to express it and practice it. We don't meet the Lord *because* of "signs," but we may meet Him *in* "signs." That way, we may come to a better understanding of the Lord through worship and the sacraments. It is not sacraments or signs that we worship; we worship the Lord.

The journey to Christ is a long and sometimes arduous one. The best way to grow in Christ is to establish a "consistent" relationship with Him. Over time, you will experience "signs" of His power. These do not happen to me on a daily basis, or even a weekly basis, but I feel God's power and I feel it more acutely the more I pray and the more I give my life over to God. For those who come only on Palm Sunday or who come to God with infrequency, the "signs" aren't going to be enough to hold one's attention. It is consistent effort that makes God real.

The people in those two different crowds probably didn't come to Christ to talk with Him. They came only for the hoopla. As we continue to move through Lent, meditate on your motivation to come to meet Christ—the why, the how often, and the where. Then resolve to meet Him in prayer on a daily basis, no matter the circumstances of the day. This is faith. We don't put faith in signs. We put our faith in the Lord!

> *Christ, You mystically shed tears because of Lazarus Your friend, dead and buried in a tomb, and You raised him from the dead, in Your love for humanity displaying compassion. O Savior, when they learned of Your arrival there, the multitude of babes came out to greet You today; and in their hands they were holding palm leaves, and they were shouting Hosanna to You and saying, "Blessed are You, O Savior, for You have come to save the world." (Kathisma from Orthros of Palm Sunday, Trans. by Fr. Seraphim Dedes)*

Meet Christ in prayer today!

Third Saturday of the Souls

God Expects Us to Produce Fruit

Jesus said, "Therefore I tell you, the kingdom of God will be taken away from you and given to a nation producing the fruits of it."
Matthew 21:43
(Gospel on Palm Sunday Evening**)

"Palm Sunday" was a very festive day in Jerusalem, as Jesus made a very public entrance into the city and was greeted by hundreds, if not thousands, of people. That must have been quite a spectacle. The scene shifted the next day.

After spending the night in Bethany, He was walking with His disciples having quiet conversation with them when they came upon a fig tree that had no fruit on it. Jesus cursed the fig tree, saying that no fruit would ever be produced from it. The fig tree was a symbol of prosperity. For it not only yielded fruit, but also it provided needed shade from the harsh sun. It was among the most beautiful and needed of trees. The cursing of the fig tree was also an indictment of the Jewish temple leadership (there are a lot of such indictments in the coming scripture passages) that they were the guardians of the Jewish faith, the covenant between God and the people of Israel, but they had dishonored God by not practicing their faith correctly.

Jesus continued on to the temple, where He addressed the chief priests and elders, who questioned His authority. He taught them in parables. A parable is a story with a hidden meaning and a life application. Some people heard the parables and understood them, and to others, the lesson of the parable was not so obvious. In Matthew 22:33-41, He told the parable of the wicked tenants:

> "Hear another parable. There was a householder who planted a vineyard, and set a hedge around it, and dug a wine press in it, and built a tower, and let it out to tenants, and went into another country. When the season of fruit drew near, he sent his servants to the tenants, to get his fruit; and the tenants took his servants and beat one, killed another, and stoned another. Again he sent other servants, more

than the first; and they did the same to them. Afterward he sent his son to them, saying, 'They will respect my son.' But when the tenants saw the son, they said to themselves, 'This is the heir; come, let us kill him and have his inheritance.' And they took him and cast him out of the vineyard, and killed him. When therefore the owner of the vineyard comes, what will he do to those tenants?" They said to him, "He will put those wretches to a miserable death, and let out the vineyard to other tenants who will give him the fruits in their seasons."

The householder in the Parable is God. The vineyard is the people of Israel. The hedge, the wine press and the tower—the instruments by which to make the vineyard produce a successful crop—are the Law and the things needed to successfully care for God's people. The tenants are the Jewish leaders, who were supposed to safeguard God's people—to shepherd, guide and love them. The Jewish leaders, of whom Christ would be very critical, instead made the temple a place of business, and the faith became a faith of fear and subjugation, rather than one of freedom and hope.

A tenant is a temporary caretaker. Every human being is a tenant of his life. We are not owners, because every life eventually comes to an end. The Jewish temple leadership were tenants, temporary caretakers of the people of Israel. The "servants" sent by the householder to check in with the tenants were the prophets, who by and large, were treated shamefully by the temple elite. Finally, the householder sent His Son, who is Jesus Christ, to check in with the tenants. The tenants killing the son is a foreshadowing of the temple leadership demanding Christ be put to death.

The owner of the vineyard, God, we are told, will not be too pleased with the tenants, for the way they treated His Son. New tenants will be found to safeguard the vineyard. There will be new leadership for God's people, and that will come in the form of the disciples, simple fisherman, who will lead God's people going forward. It will no longer be the Jewish elite either, as Gentiles will assume leadership roles.

The reading concludes with Jesus telling the chief priests and elders that the Kingdom of God will be taken away from them and given to others who will produce fruit.

The life application for us is this: We are the tenants. We are temporary caretakers of the Christian faith, and of our own talents, which we are supposed to use for the glory of God in safeguarding and spreading the Faith. The vineyard is the Church. The hedge, wine press, and tower are all the things we need (and we have them) to successfully spread the message of Christianity. Each of us has something to offer. The fruits that Christ expects from our vineyard are, simply put, the fruits of the Spirit: *love, joy, peace, patience, kindness, goodness, faithfulness, gentleness, and self-control* (Gal. 5:22-23). The parable serves as a warning to us, as it did back then to the priests and elders, that there is an expectation from God that He will receive fruits from His vineyard. For those tenants who are good tenants, there will be a reward. For those tenants who are not good tenants, there will be a punishment.

Think today of God's vineyard, the church, and the role you play in it. Are you actively doing things to preserve, if not share the faith, in your own life, in the lives of your children? Are you living the Christian Faith in a way that anyone will take notice? Jesus says in Matthew 7:20, that we will be known by our fruits. Is your fruit tree in bloom, or are you fruitless like the fig tree? A very serious question indeed.

> *Fearing a similar sentence to that of the fruitless fig tree, brethren, let us bring forth fruits worthy of repentance to Christ, Who bestows on us the Great Mercy. (Aposticha of Bridegroom Service of Palm Sunday evening, Trans. by Fr. George Papadeas)*

Tend to God's vineyard in some way today.

**The Scripture Readings selected for these reflections are cited based on the day in which they are read. For instance, the Service of the Bridegroom, traditionally offered on Palm Sunday night, is in reality an Orthros/Matins service of Holy Monday, offered by anticipation the night before. Historically, this service would have been offered in the early hours of Holy Monday morning. The current placement of the service took place only in recent centuries. Hence, as we go through these reflections, they will be cited based on when the service is held in modern times.

First Sunday of Lent—Sunday of Orthodoxy

Behold the Bridegroom Comes! What Will He Find You Doing?

What do you think? A man had two sons; and he went to the first and said, 'Son, go and work in the vineyard today.' And he answered, 'I will not'; but afterward he repented and went. And he went to the second and said the same; and he answered, 'I go, sir,' but did not go. Which of the two did the will of his father?" They said, "The first." Jesus said to them, "Truly, I say to you, the tax collectors and the harlots go into the kingdom of God before you. For John came to you in the way of righteousness, and you did not believe him, but the tax collectors and the harlots believed him; and even when you saw it, you did not afterward repent and believe him.
Matthew 21:28-32
(Gospel of Palm Sunday Night)

Just like there was a large amount of activity in Jerusalem on Palm Sunday, we experience the same thing in our churches. The churches are overflowing at the Palm Sunday Divine Liturgy. Just like the city of Jerusalem grew quiet between Palm Sunday and Good Friday, it seems that the mood of the church early in Holy Week is perhaps appropriately the same. In Jerusalem, the Lord was speaking quietly to His disciples about His Passion and about the end times. In the Church, we have the Bridegroom Services on Palm Sunday, Holy Monday and Holy Tuesday evenings, as well as the Pre-Sanctified Liturgy on Holy Monday, Holy Tuesday and Holy Wednesday mornings. These services do not have the "action" of the services later in the week, but rather are more quiet and reflective, matching the teachings of our Savior to His disciples, His last instructions to them before His Passion and Resurrection.

The theme of these services is Christ as the Bridegroom. We, the Church, are the bride. As the husband is traditionally the provider of the family, so Christ, the Bridegroom of the Church, provides salvation to us. As the husband is supposed to be the leader in the family, Christ is the leader of our Church. As a father is a protector and servant, Christ is the same, as He dies for the Bride, the Church.

The dominant feature of these early services is the Icon of Christ the Bridegroom. It does not show a man in formal wear about to go to a wedding feast. It shows Jesus with the instruments of His Passion. He is clothed with a purple robe, His hands are bound, in His one hand is the reed with which He was beaten, and He is wearing the crown of thorns. His gaze, however, is not one of pain or sorrow, but one of love. He invites us to the feast, which is Himself. The "banquet" is salvation in the Kingdom of heaven. The "main course" of the banquet is Holy Communion.

The Gospels of early in Holy Week are not "action-filled," but are didactic in nature, as Christ is either teaching the disciples or the Jewish temple leadership. Some of the teachings are gentle in tone, others more harsh, depending on the audience. Now, two thousand years later, *we* are the audience and Christ addresses us, as disciples and members of His church, and we should hear these messages, be they gentle or harsh, with an ear that hears His compassion and love for us.

Today's verses are from a short parable Jesus told to the chief priests and elders. Two sons are asked by their father to work in the field. One says he will not go, but then afterwards repents and goes. The second says he will go, but then does not. The moral of this story is that those who were not doing the will of God but who repented—the harlots and the tax collectors—will enter into the kingdom of God before the Jewish temple leadership, who spoke about love and compassion but had none, who said they were doing the work of God but really were not.

The lesson for us today is that it is not talk that saves us or condemns us, but action. If we speak well, but our actions do not glorify God, then what good are the words? On the other hand, even if we don't "get it" at first and we do wrong, if we repent and come back and do right, this is what pleases God. We have numerous examples of this—the Prodigal Son, Peter (who denied Christ), Paul (who persecuted the church), and the thief on the cross whom we will encounter on Good Friday, among many others.

While our mouths are what get us into the most trouble, it is the hands that save us. Loving God and loving our neighbor are not about talking, but about doing. I'm reminded of the verse in Luke 11:28, when Jesus says, *"Blessed are those who hear the word of God and keep it!"* It reminds us that it is not enough to only hear, or to talk about it, but to *do* it is what matters. Christ, the Bridegroom, will come for each of us at some point. If He were to come today, what would He find you doing? Merely "hearing" the Word of God, or "doing" it!

> *Behold the Bridegroom comes in the midst of the night; and blessed is the servant, whom He shall find vigilant; and unworthy is he, whom He shall find heedless. Beware, therefore, O my soul, that you will not be overcome by sleep, lest you be given up to death, and be shut out from the Kingdom. Wherefore, rouse yourself, crying out: "Holy, Holy, Holy are You, our God, through the Theotokos, have mercy on us." (Hymn of the Bridegroom, Trans. by Fr. George Papadeas)*

Do something to help someone today!

Monday of the Second Week of Lent

Are We in the End Times?
Is Everyone Going to be Saved?

As He sat on the Mount of Olives, the disciples came to Him privately, saying, "Tell us, when will this be, and what will be the sign of Your coming and of the close of the age?" And Jesus answered them, "Take heed that no one leads you astray. For many will come in My name, saying, 'I am the Christ,' and they will lead many astray. And you will hear of wars and rumors of wars; see that you are not alarmed; for this must take place, but the end is not yet. For nation will rise against nation, and kingdom against kingdom, and there will be famines and earthquakes in various places: all this is but the beginning of the birth-pangs. "Then they will deliver you up to tribulation, and put you to death; and you will be hated by all nations for My Name's sake. And then many will fall away, and betray one another, and hate one another. And many false prophets will arise and lead many astray. And because wickedness is multiplied, most men's love will grow cold. But he who endures to the end will be saved.
Matthew 24:3-13
(Gospel from the Pre-Sanctified Liturgy on Holy Monday Morning)

Are we in the end times? Today's scripture passage certainly does make us wonder. The world is filled with "false Christs." Open the newspaper and you can read daily about wars. Nations rise against one another. There are famines and earthquakes. Christians are hated more and more each day it seems. Betrayal and hatred are a part of everyday life. Wickedness seems to increase. Most profoundly, love has grown cold.

The Gospel readings, both on Holy Monday morning and Holy Monday evening (which will be addressed in a future reflection), are probably the harshest scriptures read in the entire year. In today's reading, Christ tells us very specifically that the end times are coming, but He doesn't indicate when. There are certainly "signs" in our times, but there have been signs at many ages of human history. Probably since the time of Christ, people have wondered "are we in the end times?" Whenever I am asked this question, I always reply, "Why do you want to know? Because if I say 'yes,' then you'll take the faith more seriously, and if I say 'no,' it will give you license to be complacent?" Jesus says in Matthew 25:42-44, *"Watch therefore, for you do not know on what day your Lord is coming. But know this, if the householder had known in what part of the night the thief was coming, he would have watched and would not have let his house be broken into. Therefore you also must be ready; for the Son of Man is coming at an hour you do not expect."* If we knew, for instance, that Jesus was coming in exactly 20 years from now, then we might feel complacent for 15 of those years, knowing that there would be five years left to take it seriously. The fact is, your end, or my end, could come *today*. Whether the world ends any time soon, life for any of us can end at any time. So we must be ready to give our "defense" of our life to the Lord at His awesome judgment seat at any moment in time. We don't know the day or the hour, so we have to be vigilant at all times in waiting for the Lord.

Which brings up a second question that I am frequently asked, which is, "Are we *all* going to be saved?" The easy answer to that question is, "I am not God, so it is not my decision to make." Based on scriptural evidence, the answer to this question appears overwhelmingly to be *no*. In Matthew 24:38-41, we read, *"For as in those days before the flood they were eating and drinking, marrying and giving in marriage, until the day when Noah entered the ark, and they did not know until the flood came and swept them all away, so will be the coming of the Son of Man. Then two men will be in the field; one is taken and one is left. Two women will be grinding at the mill; one is taken and one is left.*

We read in the Parable of the Ten Maidens (Matt. 25:1-13) that five were foolish and five were wise. In the Parable of the Last Judgment, the people are divided into sheep and goats. If I were to venture a "guess," and that's all it could be is a guess, based on how I read these passages—one is taken, one is left; five were foolish, five were wise—it seems as though 50 percent are going to be saved and 50 percent will be condemned. So, why doesn't the Bible just say "fifty percent of you will be saved?" Because then we would be obsessed with being in the top 50 percent, and if we thought ourselves better than 50 percent of the population, we would be content being number 49. We might be tempted to become complacent. We shouldn't compare ourselves to others, for we are not competing for salvation, nor will we stand in competition with others at the Last Judgment. *Can* all people be saved? *Yes*. Does everyone have the potential to be saved? *Yes*. Will everyone be saved? According to the scriptures: *no*. That's because it is a choice to be on the journey to salvation, and many people do not make that choice.

Whether we are in the end times or not is not relevant to my life today. My purpose today should be to glorify God in my life. Nor should we obsess over our "percentage" (whether we perceive that we are in the top 50 percent or not, or whether there is a percent that will make it to salvation). Our job today is to do the best we can with what God has given us, glorifying Him and serving our neighbor. If we are doing that today, and tomorrow, and every day, we will be ready for the day He comes and we will be in good stead at His awesome judgment seat. We need to make it our goal to be ready everyday, whether our days are few, or whether they are many.

As for men's love growing cold, this is a sad but very true statement. Love is a choice. Each of us can do our part to reverse this trend by choosing love today—choose to love God! Show love to your neighbor!

> *You, the Wisdom of all, declared to Your Disciples: "Cast away the impurity of human passions, and obtain a wise understanding, worthy of the Divine Kingdom; in which you shall be glorious, and shine more brightly than the sun. (From the Praises of the Bridegroom Service of Palm Sunday Evening, Trans. by Fr. George Papadeas)*

Make the most out of today!

Tuesday of the Second Week of Lent

All You Need to Remember are These Two Things

But when the Pharisees heard that He had silenced the Sadducees, they came together. And one of them, a lawyer, asked Him a question, to test him. "Teacher, which is the great commandment in the law?" And He said to him, "You shall love the Lord your God with all your heart, and with all your soul, and with all your mind. This is the great and first commandment. And a second is like it, You shall love your neighbor as yourself. On these two commandments depend all the law and the prophets."
Matthew 22:34-40
(From the Gospel read at the Bridegroom Service on Holy Monday Evening)

Can you name all Ten Commandments? Most of us can name at least seven or eight of them. Most of us probably forget one or two. At least when we hear the phrase "The Ten Commandments," we know what is being referred to.

Did you know that in the Old Testament, there are actually 613 "commandments?" There are the ten we are most familiar with, as well as 603 others. These rules are not "suggestions," they are "commandments." They comprise what is called "The Mosaic Law" and they are found in the Old Testament Books of Exodus, Leviticus, Numbers and Deuteronomy. Here are two random "commandments" from the list of 613:

If you lend money to any of my people with you who is poor, you shall not be to him as a creditor, and you shall not exact interest from him (Exod. 22:25).

You shall not muzzle an ox when it treads out the grain (Deut. 25:4).

Having read over the list of the 613 commandments, the list is daunting to merely *read*, let alone memorize, let alone put into practice. In the Old Testament, it was the priests who were charged with keeping and enforcing the law. Of course, we realize back then, that most people did not read. They lived a simpler, agrarian lifestyle. This opened the door for abuses by the temple priests to bind heavy burdens on the people who couldn't follow the Law. Who *could* follow the Law, every last commandment of the 613? No one!

Jesus simplified all of this when He condensed all of the Law, all 613 commandments, into *two* commandments: love God, and love your neighbor. Everything in the Law falls under one of these two commandments. Take just the Ten Commandments:

Having no other gods before us, not worshipping graven images, not taking the Lord's name in vain, and remembering the Sabbath to keep it holy fall under the commandment to love God. Honoring father and mother, not killing, not committing adultery, not stealing, not bearing false witness, and not coveting fall under the commandment to love our neighbors.

Imagine the anger of the temple elite, who came to "trap" Jesus by goading Him into answering the question about which of the laws was the greatest. He took the plentitude of the Law, which had been mastered only by the priests, and made it accessible to all the people.

As Christians today, we don't have to memorize the Mosaic Law. We don't even necessarily need to memorize the Ten Commandments. If we are loving God and loving our neighbor, we are following God's law. If even *two* commandments are too much to remember, you can summarize the entirety of all the commandments in one word: *love*. If we think about it, all sins can have one cause: failure to love. Failure to love is what causes us to sin. That's why Jesus talks about love so much, because love is the basis for God creating the world. Failure to love God is what led to the fall of mankind. John 3:16 tells us, *"For God so loved the world that He gave His only Son, that whoever believes in Him should not perish but have eternal life."* The potential for salvation is rooted in God's love. Finally, our judgment before God and His decision to admit us to His Kingdom will be based on whether we have loved (Him and our neighbor), and on His mercy and love toward us.

Christianity is not a contest to memorize laws. Rather it is supposed to be a life centered on loving God and loving others. We don't worship rules; we worship the Lord. We do that by loving Him and one another.

> *Into the splendor of Your Saints, how can I, the unworthy enter? For should I dare to come into the Bridal chamber, my vesture will reproach me, not being a wedding garment; and bound, I shall be cast out by the Angels. O Lord, cleanse the impurity of my soul, and save me. (From the Praises of the Bridegroom Service of Holy Monday, Trans. by Fr. George Papadeas)*

Show love for God and for your neighbor in all that you do today!

Wednesday of the Second Week of Lent

What Is Your Foundation Made Of?

Unless the Lord builds the house, those who build it labor in vain.
Unless the Lord watches over the city, the watchman stays awake in vain.
Psalm 127:1
(Read at every Pre-Sanctified Liturgy)

Our son loves to build things with Legos. One day, we were building a "skyscraper," taking all of the Legos and building a tall tower. Nicholas was much younger back then, and as he was building, he had left some empty spaces on the lower rows of the building. As the building got taller and taller, it started to lean, about to collapse. He couldn't add another brick without the whole thing toppling over. It was a perfect opportunity to teach him about what a "foundation" is.

There were two problems with his building. One was that for the height of the building, the "footprint" was too small. The base needed to be bigger. The second problem was that the bottom rows of the building needed to be solid blocks. There was a problem with the foundation. I said to Nicholas, "We're going to have to take this building down, redo the foundation and then build it back, and it will stand tall and strong." Of course, there was no reasoning with a six year old (at the time). He didn't want to undo his work. He kept building, and, in short order, the whole building fell down. Why? It didn't have a good foundation. He learned an important lesson that day, and his buildings no longer fall down. I guess, in some sense, it was good that he had that failure, because it is through failing that we learn. Also, in case he is a future engineer or architect, better to make your mistakes with Legos than with real buildings. There are plenty of buildings and bridges that fall down because the designer didn't learn enough about foundations.

One of the Psalms read at the Pre-Sanctified Liturgy throughout Lent speaks to us about foundations. It reminds us that unless the Lord is the foundation of our life, we are building a life that will eventually collapse. Unless the Lord is protecting our lives, our souls, they will eventually be lost, because we cannot protect them by ourselves. Unless the Lord is at the center of our church community, the community can never succeed.

When the foundation of life is damaged, we don't just keep building. We have to go back and repair the damage. When we build without the Lord, eventually our building is going to crumble.

Jesus says in Matthew 7:24-27:

> *Everyone then who hears these words of Mine and does them will be like a wise man who built his house upon the rock; and the rain fell, and the floods came, and the winds blew and beat upon that house, but it did not fall, because it had been founded on the rock. And everyone who hears these words of Mine and does not do them will be like a foolish man who built his house upon the sand; and the rain fell, and the floods came, and the winds blew and beat against that house, and it fell; and great was the fall of it."*

When our life has Jesus Christ as its foundation—its source and center—then our souls will not fall or fail. When Christ is not the foundation, eventually life will crumble. Look at how society has changed, even over the past twenty-five years. Twenty-five years ago, Sundays were still a day for the family. People went to church. You could pray in public. Society has systematically worked to remove Christ from public view. Too many things compete for our attention and churches are losing members. Is there any wonder that our society continues to devolve? We've slowly managed to destroy its foundation: faith and family.

The good news is that if Christ is not your foundation, you can solidify your life by repairing your building and filling the holes that are empty. That might involve a slight tweak or a radical makeover. When the footprint of our life is Christ, only then can the "building" stand tall and strong. Having Christ as our "footprint" gives us the confidence to stand strong in any storm, knowing that our foundation is built on the "rock" of Christ.

> *You have edified me on the rock of faith. You have opened wide my mouth against my enemies; for my spirit has rejoiced in singing: "There is none Holy as our God, and there is none righteous, save You, O Lord." (9th Ode from the Bridegroom Service of Holy Tuesday evening, Trans. by Fr. George Papadeas)*

Build your life with Christ today!

Thursday of the Second Week of Lent

When You Need Comfort, Go Read a Psalm

When the righteous cry for help, the Lord hears, and delivers them out of all their troubles.
The Lord is near to the brokenhearted, and saves the crushed in spirit.
Many are the afflictions of the righteous; but the Lord delivers him out of them all.
He keeps all his bones; not one of them is broken.
The Lord redeems the life of his servants;
none of those who take refuge in Him will be condemned.
Psalm 34:17-20, 22
The Lord is gracious and merciful, slow to anger and abounding in steadfast love.
The Lord is good to all, and His compassion is over all that He has made.
The Lord upholds all who are falling, and raises up all who are bowed down.
The Lord is near to all who call upon Him, to all who call upon Him in truth.
Psalm 145:8-9, 14, 18
(Read at all Pre-Sanctified Liturgies)

The Pre-Sanctified Liturgy is a Traditional part of the Orthodox Christian journey. This service affords us the opportunity to partake of the Eucharist without the full celebration of the Divine Liturgy, as we do not have the joyful celebration of the Liturgy on the weekdays of Lent. It gives us an opportunity to receive Christ through Holy Communion each week in the middle of the week, in order to sustain us through the discipline of the Fast. It gives us the opportunity to hear many Psalms read. There are eighteen Psalms read as part of the Pre-Sanctified Liturgy (an additional three if you include the 9th Hour). These Psalms, in many instances, bring many words of comfort. They sooth the mind, heart, and soul. I'm continually amazed that the Psalms cover feelings and emotions that I have in a way that is more articulate than I could ever be.

The two Psalms that I quoted here are offered at the end of the Liturgy, as we depart the service and reenter the world. How comforting to hear that "The Lord is near to the brokenhearted," and "the Lord upholds all who are falling." Many times this is *exactly* what I need to hear when I'm about to go back to the stresses of life.

The book of Psalms consists of 150 chapters. Each one captures a different emotion. If you've never read the book of Psalms, I recommend that you read it and keep a notepad next to you. After each Psalm, write down the emotion that it evokes, and what kind of circumstance in your life would be captured by each Psalm. Then refer to the Psalms when you are feeling each emotion. Allow me to share some of my favorites:

One of many Psalms I pray, to praise God, is Psalm 18—*I love Thee, O Lord, my strength. The Lord is my rock, and my fortress, and my deliverer, my God, my rock, in Whom I take refuge, my shield, and the horn of my salvation, my stronghold. I call upon the Lord, Who is worthy to be praised, and I am saved from my enemies* (Verses 1-3).

When I need comfort, I pray Psalm 23—*The Lord is my Shepherd, I shall not want . . . even though I walk through the valley of the shadow of death, I fear no evil; for Thou art with me* (Verse 1, 4).

When I have made a mistake, I pray Psalm 51—*Create in me a clean heart, O God; and put a new and right spirit within me* (Verse 10).

When I need reassurance, I pray Psalm 91—*Because he cleaves to me in love, I will deliver him; I will protect him, because he knows My name* (Verse 14).

When I don't know what to do, I pray Psalm 143—*Teach me the way I should go, for to Thee I lift up my soul. Deliver me, O Lord, from my enemies! I have fled to Thee for refuge! Teach me to do Thy will, for Thou art my God!* (Verses 8-10).

These two Psalms from Pre-Sanctified Liturgy reassure me that the Lord is always near, *especially* in the times when life is hardest. Notice how I used the verb "pray" when referring to the Psalms, as opposed to just "reading" them. Many of the Psalms are beautiful prayers. They are used extensively in the hymns and prayers of our services, not only the Psalm Readings. In fact, the only book of the Bible that finds its way into *all* of our services is the book of Psalms.

> *Lord, I have cried to You; hear me. Hear me, O Lord. Lord, I have cried to You; hear me. Give heed to the voice of my supplication when I cry to You. Hear me, O Lord.* (Sung at every Vespers service, including the Pre-Sanctified Liturgies and Vespers Services of Holy Week, Trans. by Fr. Seraphim Dedes)

Pray a Psalm (or a few of them) today!

Friday of the Second Week of Lent

The Story of Job

And the Lord said to Satan, "Have you considered my servant Job, that there is none like him on the earth, a blameless and upright man, who fears God and turns away from evil?" Then Satan answered the Lord, "Does Job fear God for naught? Hast thou not put a hedge about him and his house and all that he has, on every side? Thou hast blessed the work of his hands, and his possessions have increased in the land. But put forth Thy hand now, and touch all that he has, and he will curse Thee to Thy face" . . . While he was yet speaking, there came another, and said, "Your sons and daughters were eating and drinking wine in their eldest brother's house; and behold, a great wind came across the wilderness, and struck the four corners of the house, and it fell upon the young people, and they are dead; and I alone have escaped to tell you." Then Job arose, and rent his robe, and shaved his head, and fell upon the ground, and worshiped. And he said, "Naked I came from my mother's womb, and naked shall I return; the Lord gave, and the Lord has taken away; blessed be the name of the Lord." In all this Job did not sin or charge God with wrong.
Job 1:8-11; 18-22
(Read at the Pre-Sanctified Liturgies of Holy Monday [1:1-12]
and Holy Tuesday [1:13-22])

Many of us have heard the phrase, "The patience of Job." It refers to all of the trials and tribulations that afflicted Job and how he stayed faithful to God. Though, having read the book of Job, I can't exactly say that he always stayed patient. There were times that even Job was lamenting his lot in life.

For those unfamiliar with the book of Job, it consists of 41 chapters. On Holy Monday, Holy Tuesday, and Holy Wednesday at the Pre-Sanctified Liturgy, we read from the first two chapters of the book of Job. At the Vesperal Liturgy on Holy Thursday and the Vespers on Good Friday afternoon, we read from the last chapters.

Job, as we learn, was a "blameless and upright man," who walked in the way of the Lord. The Lord had blessed him with many possessions and a nice family. Satan one day approached

God, challenging God that if God allowed Satan to ruin Job's life, that Job would eventually turn against God. So, God allowed Satan to afflict Job with all kinds of bad things, He only instructed Satan that he couldn't kill Job. So, Satan afflicted Job by taking his possessions, destroying his home, destroying his health and killing Job's children. Job's wife even told him to curse God and end his life, but Job remained faithful to God. In all that happened to him, "Job did not sin or charge God with wrong."

The first two chapters of Job are where God allows Satan to attack Job. From Chapter 3 through Chapter 41 (yes, for 39 chapters!), Job laments his situation. Privately, his heart is broken. Then Job's "friends" come to give him advice. They tell him to blame God, or to blame himself for his sufferings, yet Job, who has lost everything, remains faithful to God, even though he doesn't quite understand why God let all of these bad things happen to him. He believes that God has a plan for him, even though he doesn't understand what that plan is. Who could? With all the death and destruction that came upon Job's life, how could God possibly allow all of that?

At some point in life, we can probably all relate to Job. Life gets hard, our outlook seems bleak, we feel as if we lose more than we win, we might even wonder if we have fallen out of favor with God or if God has abandoned us. We've already learned about the importance of having good friends, and good friends who are Christian, who pick us up when we are down. Unfortunately for Job, his friends added to his misery by challenging him to give up on God.

So, after two chapters of affliction, and thirty-nine chapters of Job's lament, during which he is sometimes frustrated but always faithful, we hear about Job's reward. God significantly rewards Job's faithfulness. Job confesses to God that he is sorry for not being even more faithful. Job's confession is mature and humble. It acknowledges that God has plans for us that may be hard for us to understand, and that perhaps do not match with the plans we have for ourselves. Job says to God:

> *"I know that Thou canst do all things, and that no purpose of Thine can be thwarted. Who is this that hides counsel without knowledge? There I have uttered what I did not understand, things too wonderful for me, which I did not know. Hear, and I will speak; I will question You, and You declare to me. I had heard of Thee by the hearing of the ear, but now my eye sees Thee; therefore I despise myself, and repent in dust and ashes"* (Job 42:1-6).

In the end, we see that God was faithful to Job. God restored Job's fortune, giving him twice as much as he had had before.

Many people's lives resemble Job's life, at least at some point. It's hard even to find a silver lining sometimes when everything is going wrong, but the lesson of Job mimics the Passion of Christ, who stayed faithful to God even as He was being tortured and murdered. The lesson for us is the same—stay faithful at all times to the Lord, and He will reward you. Perhaps, not in *your* time or in *your* way, but He will reward us abundantly in His time, in His way. Our goal should be the faithfulness of Job. Ideally in no situation should we curse the name of the Lord, but rather trust in His plans, as well as His reward to those who are faithful to Him.

> *O Lord and Master of my life, deliver me from the spirit of indolence, meddling, vain ambition, and idle talk.*
> *Grant to me, Your servant, the spirit of prudence, humility, patience and love.*
> *Yea, Lord and King; grant me that I may see my own faults, and to not judge my brother.*
> *For You are blessed to the ages of ages. Amen.*
> *Prayer of St. Ephraim the Syrian*
> *(Prayed throughout Lent and at the Bridegroom Services, Trans by Fr. George Papadeas)*

Be patient in your "trials" today!

Saturday of the Second Week of Lent

Everyone Has Some Talent— He Expects Us to Use Them

Jesus said: "For it will be as when a man going on a journey called his servants and entrusted to them his property; to one he gave five talents, to another two, to another one, to each according to his ability. Then he went away. He who had received the five talents went at once and traded with them; and he made five talents more. So also, he who had the two talents made two talents more. But he who had received the one talent went and dug in the ground and hid his master's money. Now after a long time the master of those servants came and settled accounts with them. And he who had received the five talents came forward, bringing five talents more, saying, 'Master, you delivered to me five talents; here I have made five talents more.' His master said to him, 'Well done, good and faithful servant; you have been faithful over a little, I will set you over much; enter into the joy of your master.' And he also who had the two talents came forward, saying, 'Master, you delivered to me two talents; here I have made two talents more.' His master said to him, 'Well done, good and faithful servant; you have been faithful over a little, I will set you over much; enter into the joy of your master.' He also who had received the one talent came forward, saying, 'Master, I knew you to be a hard man, reaping where you did not sow, and gathering where you did not winnow; so I was afraid, and I went and hid your talent in the ground. Here you have what is yours.' But his master answered him, 'You wicked and slothful servant! You knew that I reap where I have not sowed, and gather where I have not winnowed? Then you ought to have invested my money with the bankers, and at my coming I should have received what was my own with interest. So take the talent from him, and give it to him who has the ten talents. For to everyone who has will more be given, and he will have abundance; but from him who has not, even what he has will be taken away. And cast the worthless servant into the outer darkness; there men will weep and gnash their teeth.'
Matthew 25:14-30
(From the Gospel at Pre-Sanctified Liturgy on Holy Tuesday Morning)

My favorite story in the entirety of the Bible is this one! THIS is the story that I meditated on almost constantly before making the decision to follow God's call to the priesthood. The lessons in this parable are MANY:

Everyone has a talent. Everyone received something from God. Everyone has SOME talent. There is no one who has NO talent. Many times people lament, "I'm not good at anything." That is simply not true. They just haven't discovered what they are good at, because everyone is good at something. God gave EVERYONE the ability to contribute a talent for the betterment of our world AND for the projection of the Gospel. Yes, everyone has a talent, and EVERYONE has an ability to spread the Gospel in some way.

Everyone has a different talent. Not everyone is going to grow up to be a doctor. That's a good thing. Who is more important, the doctor or the farmer? Most parents would probably rather see their children grow up to be doctors than farmers, but without farmers, we'd have no food. With no food, there would be no need for doctors, because none of us would be alive. Let's not discount the value of the truck driver who gets the produce from the field to the market. Or the mechanic who keeps the truck in working order. Or the clerk who puts the food on the shelf. Or the architect who built the store. Yes, we need all the talents to make the world go right!

God rewards equally based on effort. We see from the parable that God rewarded the one who ended up with four talents *equally* to the one who ended up with ten, because both doubled what they were given. The world may equate higher salaries with certain jobs, but in the eyes of God equal effort merits equal reward regardless of what you do and how much salary you earn.

More can be less in the eyes of God. Let's say that the man with the five talents made only one more talent and ended up with six, and the man who had the two talents ended up with four. In our society, we'd say the one with six is better than the one with four because six is more than four. However, in this scenario, in the eyes of God, the one with six would be considered a failure, because he started out with five. The one with four would be the more successful in the eyes of God since he started with only two.

Fear is not an excuse. There are many people who feel called by God to do something, but they are afraid to do it for some reason. This was me, when I was thinking about the priesthood. I knew that this was my calling, yet I was afraid to act on this for fear of losing control of where I'd live, among other things. I was afraid of cold weather, living outside of California (my home state), and of some other things. I remember meditating on this verse and thinking how God punished the man who was afraid because he didn't use what he had been given. I thought what would it be like to go and meet God on the day of my judgment and have to admit to Him "but for a little fear, I should have been a priest." This was the verse that "tipped the scales" for me. Ironically, I did live in cold weather climates for ten years, and have never served as a priest in my home state. Those "fears" came true but my trust in God has helped to overcome those "fears."

To the one who is given more, more is expected. The more talent God gives you, the more responsibility you are expected to assume, the more account you have to give. To the one with the five talents, God expects ten. For the one who has one, God only expects two talents. So, the one who has one talent should not protest that he has only one and why can't we all be the same. We are not all the same and that's a good thing. Focus on doing the best you can with what *you* have, rather than bemoaning what you don't have. This is what God expects from us.

The master is the Lord. The talents are the gifts each of us has, both to love God (witness for Him, spread the faith) and love our neighbor (do our part to improve the world). Each of us has a talent, and each talent is different. When the master returns, that is the Second Coming, we will each have to make an account of what we did with the talents He gave us. Remember, God expects us to use our talents not only to help our fellow man, but in order to spread the Gospel! Which brings me to the final lesson of this parable:

Give God the glory!—Many times we see successful people, be they athletes or executives, call attention to themselves because of their accomplishments. I sometimes think (and this is a judgment on me), "Who do you think gave you the talent to hit a ball or run a business?" God gave us whatever talent we have. Whether you are a doctor, or a teacher, or a homemaker, or a baker, the talent you have has come from a mind that was given to you by God. So, let us use whatever talent we have to glorify Him!

> *Come, you faithful, let us eagerly work for the Master, for He distributes His wealth to His servants; accordingly then, let us increase the talent of grace. Let one, be graced with wisdom through good works; let another, celebrate a service of splendor; let another, faithful to the word communicate this to the uninstructed; and yet another, distribute wealth to the poor; for thus, we shall increase what is entrusted to us, and as faithful stewards of His Grace, we may be worthy of the Master's joy. Of this, deem us worthy, O loving Christ, our God. (From the Aposticha of the Bridegroom Service on Holy Monday Evening, Trans. by Fr. George Papadeas)*

Use your talents to glorify God today!

Second Sunday of Lent—St. Gregory Palamas

Our Traditions Are Scripture-Based

Truly, truly, I say to you, unless a grain of wheat falls into the earth and dies, it remains alone; but if it dies, it bears much fruit.
John 12:24
(From the Gospel of the Bridegroom Service on Holy Tuesday Evening)

What is a "Tradition" and where do our Traditions come from?

For instance, it is a "Tradition" that we fast for forty days before Pascha. Why fasting? Why forty days?

In Exodus 34:27-29, we read:

> *And the Lord said to Moses, "Write these words; in accordance with these words I have made a covenant with you and with Israel." And he was there with the Lord forty days and forty nights; he neither ate bread nor drank water. And he wrote upon the tables the words of the covenant, the Ten Commandments. When Moses came down form Mount Sinai, with the two tables of the testimony in his hand as he came down from the mountain, Moses did not know that the skin of his face shone because he had been talking with God.*

In His encounter with God, Moses prepared by fasting for forty days.
In Matthew 4:1-2, we read:

> *Then Jesus was led up by the Spirit into the wilderness to be tempted by the devil. And He fasted forty days and forty nights.*

Jesus was preparing for His ministry, and He fasted in order to do so. Likewise, we are preparing for an encounter with the Lord, in the sacraments and services of Holy Week, so we also fast, and we fast for forty days. Now, nowhere in the Bible do we read about Lent and Holy

Week. Those terms were created by the church centuries after the Resurrection to mark the time we commemorate the Passion of Christ, as well as the time we prepare for the week. The Tradition of fasting is itself based on scriptures, and universally accepted by the church. That is what Tradition is—a practice rooted in Scripture, which is universally accepted and practiced by the Church.

Today's verse of scripture is read on Holy Tuesday evening at the Bridegroom service. From this verse of scripture comes our Tradition of boiled wheat, or kolyva, which is used at memorial services. In the Orthodox Church, is the Tradition to offer a memorial service when someone passes away. The service is done forty days after someone has passed, because the day one falls asleep in Christ is like their personal Resurrection. Forty days after the Resurrection was the Ascension. This is why the interval is forty days. In order to do this service, the faithful boil wheat, which we call kolyva, and this is what is offered during the service. This Tradition comes from the Gospel of John 12:24.

Entire books have been written on the Traditions of the Church and where they come from in scripture. There is nothing dogmatic in our church that isn't done without purpose, without scriptural "origin," and without agreement by the entire church. While the Bible doesn't specifically say that we are to conduct memorial services on the 40th day after someone has passed away, the elements we use—the 40th day, the kolyva, and the prayers that reference "I am the Resurrection and the Life" (John 11:25)—all of these are found in scripture.

There are people outside of the Orthodox world who claim to be "sola scriptura," meaning that they only do things according to what is written exactly in the scriptures. Some criticize our church for not being "sola scriptura" and having too many things based on Tradition and not scripture. This is incorrect on two fronts: First, our Traditions are rooted in scripture. Second, there is no church that is "sola scriptura." If a church has a gathering every Sunday at ten, and has ten pews on each side of the church, and a pulpit in the center, sings three hymns and then the pastor preaches for 30 minutes, none of these things are written in the Bible either. What makes our church Orthodox is that we have our practices rooted in Scripture and they are universally practiced in something we call "Tradition."

> *The grateful woman was ransomed from her sins through the saving Love of God and a fountain of tears. Washed clean by her confession, she was not ashamed, but cried aloud: "All the works of the Lord, praise the Lord, and exalt Him forever." (8th Ode of the Bridegroom Service on Holy Tuesday Evening, Trans. by Fr. George Papadeas)*

Keep up the Tradition of the "fast" today!

Monday of the Third Week of Lent

We've Got to Get it Right in This Life

Walk while you have the light, lest the darkness overtake you; he who walks in the darkness does not know where he goes. While you have the light, believe in the light, that you may become sons of light."
John 12:35-36
(From the Gospel of the Bridegroom Service on Holy Tuesday Evening)

Most people who know me know that I like to mow the lawn. It is a hobby, exercise I actually like and a kind of "free therapy." When it is the middle of summer, and it is very hot, I try to mow the lawn toward the end of the day. I know how long it takes me to mow the lawn—usually about two and a half hours (yes, I'm very thorough, and usually mow the neighbor's too). I check the paper in the morning to figure out what time sunset is, and then I work backwards from that time and start mowing about two and a half hours before the sun is scheduled to set. Once in a while, I'll come home later than I planned and I'll run to mow the lawn, in order to "beat the dark." Why? You can't mow the lawn in the dark, because you can't see what you are doing. A lawn mowed in the dark would look terrible. Once the sun sets on the day, it is impossible to mow the lawn.

The same can be said for our lives. The purpose of our life is to have a clean soul that we are ready to present to the Lord. Every life has a time of sunset, a day and an hour known only by the Lord. That's the difference between cleaning the lawn of my house and cleaning the lawn of my soul. At home, on a given day, I know exactly how much time I have until the day is over and my chance is gone. In life, we don't know when the sunset will come.

What we do know, is that just like the opportunity to clean the yard ends once the sun sets, the opportunity to clean our souls ends with the sunset of our lives, with our earthly death. After we die, there is no opportunity to acquire faith, to repent, or to do good deeds. When we die, as we have learned from the teaching on the Last Judgment (Matt. 25:31-46), we will stand before the Awesome Judgment Seat of the Lord and answer for what we did in our lives on earth.

We learn in Luke 16:19-31, the Parable of the Rich Man and Lazarus:

"There was a rich man, who was clothed in purple and fine linen and who feasted sumptuously every day. And at his gate lay a poor man named Lazarus, (not the man Christ raised from the dead) full of sores, who desired to be fed with what fell from the rich man's table; moreover the dogs came and licked his sores. The poor man died and was carried by the angels to Abraham's bosom. The rich man also died and was buried; and in Hades, being in torment, he lifted up his eyes, and saw Abraham far off and Lazarus in his bosom. And he called out, 'Father Abraham, have mercy upon me, and send Lazarus to dip the end of his finger in water and cool my tongue; for I am in anguish in this flame.' But Abraham said, 'Son, remember that you in your lifetime received your good things, and Lazarus in like manner evil things; but now he is comforted here, and you are in anguish. And besides all this, between us and you a great chasm has been fixed, in order that those who would pass from here to you may not be able, and none may cross from there to us.' And he said, 'Then I beg you, father, to send him to my father's house, for I have five brothers, so that he may warn them, lest they also come into this place of torment.' But Abraham said, 'They have Moses and the prophets; let them hear them.' And he said, 'No, father Abraham; but if someone goes to them from the dead, they will repent.' He said to him, 'If they do not hear Moses and the prophets, neither will they be convinced if someone should rise from the dead.'"

From the parable, we learn that once someone goes to either heaven or hell, that this placement is permanent. The placement in heaven or hell is based on what one does or doesn't do in life. In the case of the rich man, it wasn't his riches that earned him eternal punishment, but the fact that he was indifferent to a man who would have gladly eaten the crumbs from his table, crumbs he wasn't eating anyway.

Those who are in hell are able to see those in heaven, which is the worst part of the punishment. They are aware of what they are missing out on. There is a chasm between heaven and hell, so that one may not fall out of heaven into hell, nor can one move from hell to heaven.

In hell, the rich man, who had no compassion for poor Lazarus, finally found some Christian compassion, as he began to care about his brothers, and didn't want them also to go to hell and eternal torment. The things he didn't have in his life—compassion and mercy—he now had, but it was too late for him to change his place of eternal residence.

Jesus warns us that we have to walk while we have the light, in this case, not just the light of day, but also the light of life. However, unlike the hour of sunset that we know for today, we do not know the hour of sunset in life. This is why we don't try to "beat the dark" but we live constantly in the *light* of Christ.

The woman who had fallen into many sins, perceiving Your Divinity, O Lord, assumes the role of a myrrh-bearer; and lamenting, she brings the myrrh before Your burial. "Woe to me! She said; "For me, night is an ecstasy of excess, dark and moonless, and full of sinful desire. Receive the sources of my tears, You, Who gathers into clouds the water of the sea. Incline the groanings of my heart, You, Who in Your ineffable condescension bowed down the heavens. I will embrace and kiss Your sacred Feet, and wipe them again with the tresses of the hair of my head. Your Feet, at whose sound Eve hid herself in fear, when she heard Your footsteps while You were walking in Paradise in the twilight. O My Savior and soul-Saver! Who can ever track down the multitude of my sins, and the depths of Your judgment? Do not disregard me Your servant, You Whose mercy is boundless. (Hymn of Kassiani, sung on Holy Tuesday Evening, Trans. by Fr. George Papadeas)

Walk in the Light today!

Tuesday of the Third Week of Lent

The Sin of Judas Was Not the Betrayal

Then one of the twelve, who was called Judas Iscariot, went to the chief priests and said, "What will you give me if I deliver him to you?" And they paid him thirty pieces of silver. And from that moment he sought an opportunity to betray him.
Matthew 26:6-16
(Gospel of Pre-Sanctified Liturgy on Holy Wednesday Morning)

The "Passion" of Christ refers to His sufferings. The first act of the Passion was the betrayal by Judas, one of Jesus' disciples, one of His friends.

The sins of Judas are many. The first sin was greed. We read about the greed of Judas in John 12:3-6:

> *Mary took a pound of costly ointment of pure nard and anointed the feet of Jesus and wiped His feet with her hair; and the house was filled with the fragrance of the ointment. But Judas Iscariot, one of His disciples (he who was to betray Him), said, 'Why was this ointment not sold for three hundred denarii and given to the poor?' This he said, not that he cared for the poor but because he was a thief, and as he had the money box, he used to take what was put into it."*

The devil is a real presence in the world. He seeks to enter into every person who loves Christ, and he tries to exploit our weakest link. In the case of Judas, it was money. The devil couldn't motivate Judas to murder Christ, but used greed to motivate Judas to betray Christ to those who would eventually see to it that He was murdered. In Luke 22:3-6, we read:

> *Then Satan entered into Judas called Iscariot, who was of the number of the twelve, he went away and conferred with the chief priests and officers how he might betray Him to them. And they were glad, and engaged to give him money. So he agreed, and sought an opportunity to betray Him to them in the absence of the multitude.*

The betrayal itself was not an act of violence. Ironically, it was an act of affection. Judas betrayed Jesus with a kiss, a sign of friendship:

> *Now the betrayer had given them a sign, saying "The One I shall kiss is the Man; seize Him." And he came up to Jesus at once and said "Hail, Master!" And he kissed Him. Jesus said to him "Friend, why are you here?" Then they came up and laid hands on Jesus and seized Him* (Matt. 26:48-50).

Up to this point in the story, the actions of Judas are common to *all* of us. We all have weaknesses, and the devil exploits these weaknesses. He enters into each of us through doubt and distraction, which eventually leads to actions that are destructive for us and those around us. He enters into marriages, into friendships, anywhere there is good, you will find him trying to turn good into bad. And most of our sins are not sins of violence, but sins of affection gone wrong. After all, who is it that we sin against the most? Our families and our friends, the ones we are the closest to. While we may never take up a weapon to hurt someone in a physical way, we all use our mouths and our minds as weapons to inflict emotional harm on others. In some way, we all betray friends, confidences, and courtesies and in so doing, we all betray Christ.

The greatest sin of Judas was not greed, giving into the devil or betrayal. The greatest sin of Judas was his failure to repent. It was his failure to believe in the Lord's ability to forgive him and to love him again.

> *When Judas, His betrayer, saw that He was condemned, he repented and brought back the thirty pieces of silver to the chief priests and the elders, saying "I have sinned in betraying innocent blood." They said "What is that to us? See to it yourself." And throwing down the pieces of silver in the temple, he departed and he went and hanged himself* (Matt. 27:3-5).

The door to repentance is open to everyone, no matter what we've done. It was open to the harlots and tax collectors that Jesus forgave and embraced. It was open to Peter, who three times denied Christ. It was open to the thief on the cross. That door was even open to Judas.

The elements of Judas' betrayal are foreshadowed in the fall of mankind. The first sin of Adam and Eve was greed. They wanted the one thing that God told them they were not to have, to partake of the tree of the knowledge of good and evil. They betrayed God in eating from the tree. When confronted, they lied, rather than repenting. Had they repented, would the outcome of the story been different? What if Judas had repented?

There is an old English adage that says *"Still as of old, man by himself is priced. For 30 pieces of silver, Judas sold himself, not Christ."* Jesus paid the price for our sins by dying on the cross. There are two things we must offer in order to collect our reward, salvation: first, faith, and second, repentance each time we fail to live according to the Faith. It wasn't betrayal that doomed Judas and it isn't betrayal that is going to doom us. Repentance means changing direction, from the direction that takes us away from Christ, to the direction that takes us toward Him. Repentance is the key that opens the door to salvation. It could have for Judas. It still can for us.

> *When Your glorious Disciples were enlightened at the washing of the feet before the Supper, then the impious Judas was darkened by the disease of greed, and delivered You, the Righteous Judge, to lawless judges. Behold, O lover of money, the one, who hanged himself for the sake of money. Flee from this insatiable desire, which dared such a thing against the Teacher. O Lord, Who deals righteously with all, glory to You. (Apolytikion of the Bridegroom Service on Holy Wednesday Evening and the Service of the 12 Gospels on Holy Thursday Evening, Trans. by Fr. George Papadeas)*

Repent daily! Repent today!

Wednesday of the Third Week of Lent

The New Covenant

*Now as they were eating, Jesus took bread, and blessed, and broke it,
and gave it to the disciples and said, "Take, eat; this is My body." And He took a cup,
and when He had given thanks He gave it to them, saying, "Drink of it, all of you; for this
is My blood of the new covenant, which is poured out for many for the forgiveness of sins.
I tell you I shall not drink again of this fruit of the vine until that day when
I drink it new with you in my Father's kingdom."
Matthew 26:26-29
(From the Gospel of the Vesperal Liturgy on Holy Thursday)*

A "covenant" is a sacred or solemn agreement. The first covenant was made between God and Abraham. In Genesis 17, "*The Lord appeared to Abram, and said to him, 'I am God Almighty; walk before Me and be blameless. And I will make My covenant between Me and you, and will multiply you exceedingly . . . behold, My covenant is with you, and you shall be father of a multitude of nations . . . I will make you exceedingly fruitful; and I will make nations of you and kings shall come forth from you. And I will establish My covenant between Me and you, and kings shall come forth from you. And I will establish My covenant between Me and you and your descendants after you throughout their generations for an everlasting covenant, to be God to you and to your descendants after you.'*" (v. 1-7)

As a sign of this covenant between God and His people, the Lord required that all males be circumcised (Gen. 17:10-14). This was a sacrifice that required the shedding of blood of each male child. There were other sacrifices, which involved blood as well—rams and bulls and lambs—offered to the Lord as atonement for sin. Even a happy occasion like the birth of a child required an offering of pigeons or doves (Lev. 12).

After the people of Israel were given the Ten Commandments by God through Moses, He commanded them to build an "Ark" in which to keep the Ten Commandments, called the "Ark of the Covenant" (Exod. 25). This "ark" was carried everywhere as a reminder to the people of the covenant between them and the Lord. It was a covenant based on God's love, but practically speaking, it was centered on the Ten Commandments, as well as blood sacrifices to God, a large part of the Law.

At the Last Supper, Jesus instituted a New Covenant. He took bread and wine and offered them to the Disciples, as His Body and Blood. The next day, He shed His blood on the cross for our sins. Whoever, then, partakes of the Body and Blood of Christ, is a participant in the New Covenant.

The New Covenant is without bloodshed. Because Christ shed His Blood for us, there is no need for us to shed any blood for Him or as atonement for sins. Saint Paul writes in Galatians 6:15, *"For neither circumcision counts for anything, nor uncircumcision, but a new creation."* We are no longer circumcised for religious reasons. In Romans 2, we read *"nor is true circumcision something external and physical . . . real circumcision is a matter of the heart, spiritual and not literal"* (v. 28-29). We are no longer circumcised in the flesh, but through baptism (our initiation into the faith) and through the Eucharist (what sustains our faith), we experience a circumcision, or changing, of our hearts.

The Eucharist is a "bloodless" sacrifice, where we present bread and wine to the Lord, and through the Grace of the Holy Spirit, these "gifts" are "consecrated" to become the Body and Blood of Christ. We then partake of them, so that we have the opportunity to touch the Divine God and for the Divine God to touch us.

In Hebrews 9:6-7, we read *"These preparations having thus been made, the priests go continually into the outer tent, performing their ritual duties; but into the second only the high priest goes, and he but once a year, and not without taking blood, which he offers for himself and for the errors of the people.* Continuing on, we read in Hebrews 9:11-12: *"But when Christ appeared as a high priest of the good things that have come, then through the greater and more perfect tent (not made with hands, that is, not of this creation), He entered once for all into the Holy Place, taking not the blood of goats and calves but His own blood, thus securing an eternal redemption."*

The Old Covenant taught us to live in obedience. The New Covenant is to live in love. In the Old Covenant, the people did not have access to the Holy of Holies, only the high priest and he only had access once a year. In the New Covenant, we are welcome to approach Christ in the Eucharist, as many times as we wish.

In the New Covenant, we are to live in Christ, in the way that He lived. We are to be walking "temples" of His love. Through the Eucharist, Christ can live in us. Through continual partaking in the Eucharist, we strengthen our bond with Christ. This is why the Eucharist is offered so frequently.

In Hebrews 9:28, we read that *"Christ, having been offered once to bear the sins of many, will appear a second time, not to deal with sin, but to save those who are eagerly waiting for Him."* The Christian life, then, is not a fearful obedience to rules, but an eager awaiting for Christ to return, and in preparation, we partake of Him continually in the Eucharist. If we believe that heaven is the place where we will partake in divine nature on a permanent basis, meaning that once we go to heaven, we will never suffer the human condition again (sickness, dying, sinning, etc.), then in order to prepare to live with Christ eternally, He gave to us an opportunity to partake of Divine Nature in this life, in the institution of the Eucharist.

The Old Covenant called people to moral living. This was done through obedience to commandments. The New Covenant calls us to eternal life. We honor this covenant through partaking of Christ in the Eucharist.

In our churches, we have a tabernacle on the altar table, as a visual reminder of the New Covenant. It no longer contains the Ten Commandments, but the Body and Blood of Christ, as a reminder that Christ is always present in our churches and in our lives and that we should be eagerly partaking of Him on a continual basis, in preparation for living on a permanent basis in His Heavenly Kingdom.

> *Receive me today, O Son of God, as a partaker of Your Mystical Supper; for I will not speak of the Mystery to Your enemies; nor will I kiss You as did Judas; but as the thief I confess You. "Lord, remember me when You come into Your Kingdom." (From the Vesperal Liturgy on Holy Thursday Morning, Trans. by Fr. George Papadeas)*

Live in Christ today! Invite Him continually to live in you!

Thursday of the Third Week of Lent

Confession: The Manner By Which We Examine Ourselves

Whoever, therefore, eats the bread or drinks the cup of the Lord in an unworthy manner will be guilty of profaning the Body and Blood of the Lord. Let a man examine himself, and so eat of the bread and drink of the cup. For any one who eats and drinks without discerning the body eats and drinks judgment upon himself.
1 Corinthians 11:27-29
(From the Epistle of the Vesperal Liturgy Holy Thursday Morning)

Our participation in Holy Communion is not to be taken lightly. Touching the Divine God through Holy Communion is the most intimate and most holy thing we can do in our lives. In order to receive Communion, we must be "prepared." Saint Paul calls us to "examine" ourselves before receiving Communion.

I'm often asked how frequently people should receive Communion. No one is "worthy" to receive Holy Communion, ever. There is never a day when one should walk into the church and think "I deserve Communion today." That's why we also do not use the verb "take" in regards to Communion. Yes, plenty of people say "I'm going to take Communion," but this is not correct verbiage in regards to partaking. We "take" things out of a sense of entitlement. We "receive" Holy Communion as a gift from God, a gift of which *none* of us is worthy.

Since none of us is worthy to receive, then we must work on our preparation. Many people equate fasting as the sole preparation in order to receive Communion. If that is so, then our understanding of Communion is very in line with the Old Testament way of thinking—that receiving Christ is based on a set of dietary requirements. While fasting is *part* of our preparation, it is not all that we need to do.

In order to receive Communion, first and foremost, one must believe in Christ. It doesn't do any good to receive Christ if one has no faith. What is more important, fasting or faith?

Certainly faith is the most important prerequisite to receiving Communion. Next would be a relationship with Christ through prayer. Fasting without prayer is called "dieting."

One of the other prerequisites for Holy Communion is moral living, living according to the commandments of Christ. Confession is where we examine our lives according to God's Commandments, and not only that, we allow ourselves to be examined by an ordained priest who has been given the blessing to hear confession.

Confession is *not* just a listing of sins, getting a clean slate, and then coming back when the slate is dirty again.

Confession is:

1. A cry for help. It is the cry of the Prodigal Son: *"I have sinned against heaven and before you; I am no longer worthy to be called Your son"* (Luke 15:18-19). The sins of each person that lead them to cry out to God may be different, but the cry is the same—I need help! This is why, as a priest who hears confessions, the sins you bring to confession are not as important as the mere fact that you came to confession. Because it is not the sins specifically that the priest is listening to, but the cry for help, offered with humility, that lets the priest know that one has come with a contrite heart.
2. A recommitment to God. Confession affords one the opportunity to not only purge oneself of sins, but in so doing, one recommits his or her life to God.
3. An opportunity to be rid of guilt. Everyone carries around a certain amount of guilt over past failings. Many people have told me over the years that they "confess" their sins privately, but still feel guilt over them. Through confession and repentance, we are given permission to leave our guilt and depart in peace without further anxiety of the sins we have confessed.
4. An opportunity for some guidance. No one should do it alone when it comes to faith, or the journey to salvation. Developing a relationship with a Spiritual Father (of your choosing) affords you the opportunity to enjoin someone else in your challenges and for them to offer advice as well as prayer for you. There is also something powerful about speaking from the heart in front of someone else. It is validating. It also helps to keep one accountable.
5. An opportunity to receive absolution, a complete wiping out of sin. Jesus gave a command to the disciples, that *"if you forgive the sins of any, they are forgiven"* (John 20:23). By extension, the Apostles ordained bishops who have ordained priests until this very day, who have been given the permission to "loose" sins, so that they are completely wiped off of our record.
6. Confession gives us the opportunity to answer in this life. If our life is a book, and if at the Last Judgment, *"the books shall be opened up, and public knowledge will things hidden be"* (Kontakion, Sunday of Last Judgment, Trans. by Fr. Seraphim Dedes), then confession gives us the opportunity to clean up our books in this life. Whatever things

are offered in confession come out of our book of life, not to be spoken of again, in this life or at the Last Judgment. What a beautiful opportunity to shed our sins as we go, growing closer to God, so that we can look forward to His Judgment, rather than dreading it.

How often should one go to confession? There are lots of different answers to this question. Different priests and different jurisdictions have different answers and different practices. Some will say that one should go to confession each time one receives Communion. That might not be practical for either the penitent or the priest. I personally believe (and this is just my belief, I do not speak for the church), that a person should ideally go to confession once or twice a year, not only to confess sins (which takes only minutes) but to open a dialogue with their priest about the state of one's spiritual life in order to bring one into a closer orientation with God.

We go to a doctor for examination, not only for what we know is wrong, but for things we cannot see, like our cholesterol. Just like we go to the doctor, we should go for confession in times of acute spiritual sickness, and at least once a year for a "spiritual check-up."

Holy Communion, touching the Divine God, is a serious, heavy, holy thing. It should not be treated casually, but with reverence. Part of our reverence is preparation. Part of our preparation is examination, and an important part of examination is confession.

> *Loving Master, Lord Jesus Christ, my God, let not these Holy Gifts be to my condemnation because of my unworthiness, but for the cleansing and sanctification of soul and body and the pledge of the future life and kingdom. It is good for me to cling to God and to place in Him the hope of my salvation. (Prayer of Preparation for Holy Communion, from the Divine Liturgy of St. John Chrysostom, Trans. by Holy Cross Seminary Press)*

Examine yourself today, and if you haven't been in a while, make an appointment for confession with your priest or spiritual father.

Friday of the Third Week of Lent

By THIS All Men Will Know That You Are My Disciples

A new commandment I give to you, that you love one another; even as I have loved you, that you also love one another. By this all men will know that you are My disciples, if you have love for one another."
John 13:34-35
(From the First Gospel on Holy Thursday Evening)

Everyone lives busy lives. We even call our lives "crazy busy" at times. Christ knows that our lives are busy. If you envision scenes from the Bible, we have a picture of "crazy busy" times back then as well—think busy Bethlehem at the Nativity, or the chaos in Jerusalem on Palm Sunday. Christ boiled down all of the commandments and expectations of His followers into *one* word: *love*. *"A new commandment I give to you, that you love one another; even as I have loved you, that you also love one another. By* this *all men will know that you are My disciples, if you have love for one another"* (John 13:34-35). Love. *This* is how people will know that we are His disciples. It doesn't matter what skills we have—we all have different ones. It's not about how big our family is, or how many children we have, or where did they (or we) go to college, or what kind of car we drive. *Love* is the barometer by which others will know that we are Christ's disciples. *Love* is the barometer by which Christ will judge our lives.

Sin is not only doing wrong. Sin is failure to do right. Sin, on the most basic level, is failure to love. The root cause of all sin is failure to love.

Saint Paul writes in his First Epistle to the Corinthians, that *"Love is patient, and kind; love is not jealous or boastful; it is not arrogant or rude. Love does not insist on its own way; it is not irritable or resentful; it does not rejoice at wrong, but rejoices in the right"* (1 Cor. 13: 4-6). In the First Epistle of St. John we read *"There is no fear in love, but perfect love casts out fear"* (1 John 4:17). So where there is jealousy and boasting, arrogance or rudeness, irritability or resentfulness, where there is negativity and fear, there cannot be love, because love is none of these things. Where there is love, there is an absence of fear, and there is patience, kindness, humility, and optimism.

Jesus told His Disciples in John 15:13, that *"greater love has no man than this, that a man lay down his life for his friends."* The greatest love is selfless. It forsakes everything up to giving up one's own life for someone else. After all, what could be a greater gift than for someone to die in the place of another? Jesus did not just preach this; He did it. He laid down His life for us, to not only save us from our sins, but to demonstrate for us what real love is.

Love is not just a nice word we put down on paper, nor is it merely an expression between people who say, "I love you." Love is an action. Love is something taken from me and given to you, or taken from you and given to me. There is no love for oneself; one cannot take from himself and then give to himself. One can have self-respect and self-confidence, but love is taking from oneself and projecting onto someone else.

Which then leads to the question of how we meet gestures of love made toward us. Do we meet them with reciprocal expressions of love, with indifference or with hate? Most certainly we meet them with love. So, if God loved us so much that He sent His Only-Begotten Son to die for our sins; and if Jesus Christ loved us so much that He endured the Passion and Crucifixion for us; and if God loves us so much that He has granted us so many blessings, starting off with the very day we are living in, should we not respond to His love by loving Him, and by loving one another? Going back to the examination of ourselves in confession, it begins and ends with love. This is the barometer on which our final Judgment will be based on, and this is the barometer to use in this life as we make an examination of our conscience and confession.

A popular Christian song says, *"And they'll know we are Christians by our love, by our love."* Indeed, Christ told us that people will know that we are His disciples by our love for one another. This does not mean only our families, but even to those we do not know, we should show love and concern. Finally, there are many people who show love and concern for others and forget to love their families. We are to love everyone. This is how we manifest our love for God. Again, from the words of the First Epistle of St. John, *"We love, because He first loved us"* (1 John 4:19).

> *As brothers in Christ, let us acquire brotherly love. Let us not lack compassion for our neighbors, that we may not be condemned like the unmerciful servant on account of money, or repent like Judas to no avail. (From the Fourth Antiphon of the Service of the 12 Gospels on Holy Thursday Evening, Trans. by Fr. George Papadeas)*

Manifest God's love in your life today!

Saturday of the Third Week of Lent

Let Not Your Hearts Be Troubled

Jesus said to His disciples, "Let not your hearts be troubled; believe in God, believe also in Me. In My Father's house are many rooms; if it were not so, would I have told you that I go to prepare a place for you? And when I go and prepare a place for you, I will come again and will take you to Myself, that where I am you may be also."
John 14:1-3
(From the First Gospel on Holy Thursday Evening)

On a Thursday evening, Jesus gathered His Disciples in an upper room of a home in Jerusalem. There He had a dinner with them, affectionately known as "The Last Supper." At the dinner table, He foretold that one of His disciples, Judas, would betray Him. After dinner, He instituted the Holy Eucharist. After that, He offered a lengthy sermon, a "farewell discourse," to His Disciples. This discourse is recounted in the Gospel of John, chapters 13-17, and is read as the first of twelve Gospel readings on Holy Thursday evening in the Orthodox Church. It is the longest Liturgical Gospel Reading of the year, but it is filled with teachings that are the backbone of how to live a Christian life. The discourse begins with a commandment for the disciples to love one another, which we spoke of in the last reflection.

It continues with Jesus telling the Disciples, *"Let not your hearts be troubled."* What a thing to say! The Disciples surely have figured out by this point that something bad is about to happen. Several times, Jesus has told them that He is going to Jerusalem, where He tells them that He will be killed. The betrayer has already been identified and has left their company to do his job. The mood of what Jesus is saying identifies this as a farewell speech. How could their hearts be anything but troubled!

He continues on that the reason they should not be troubled is that, *"In My Father's house are many rooms"* and *"I go to prepare a place for you"* and *"I will come again and will take you to Myself, that where I am you may be also."* The "house" is heaven. The "many rooms" are places set aside for all the Disciples, and by extension, to all of us who are disciples, who believe in Jesus and who demonstrate that by loving Him and loving one another. The reason why we should not be troubled is that eventually we will be welcomed to the "Father's house," and one of the "many rooms" will be reserved for us. In all of life's troubles and tribulations, this is the hope that we cling to. When all of life is going wrong, this is the hope that sustains us. When we seem to be failing at everything, this is the one success that stays on the table for all of us, all the time. We've all seen people that seemed drained of all hope—because of a job loss, or a marriage failure, or because of a serious illness, or any number of other things—and the message for everyone, especially those who are losing hope, is that God desires for all of us to be where He is, that where He is, we may be also.

Continuing on in John 14, Jesus tells His followers that He will give them a means of sustenance, to help them especially in their hard times. In John 14:16-17, Jesus says, *"And I will pray the Father, and He will give you another Counselor, to be with you forever, even the Spirit of Truth."* The "Counselor" is the Holy Spirit, and the Gift of the Spirit is "Grace" that heals what is spiritually infirm and completes what is spiritually lacking in each person. In verse 18, He says *"I will not leave you desolate; I will come to you."* In verse 26, He says, *"The Counselor, the Holy Spirit, whom the Father will send in My name, He will teach you all things, and bring to your remembrance all that I have said to you."* It is the Holy Spirit that is our "Comforter," bringing guidance, "counsel," strength and spiritual healing to each of us.

On a practical level, how do I let my heart not be troubled? The simple answer is, "Do your best to honor God today." If you are giving your best, what more is there to give? What more can God expect? Our sins and failings come about because we do NOT always give our best. If we work with honesty and integrity, without falling prey to the distractions that take our minds off of what we are supposed to be doing, then we've given our best. On the day we cannot work because we are sick, if we endure with patience, instead of with bitterness, then we've done our best. If our results are not what we'd hoped for, but we've given our best effort, then we need to be content with that. For all of life's circumstances, we are sustained by two things—the "grace" of the Holy Spirit, accessible to each of us in prayer, and by the overarching hope of the "rooms" in heaven, reserved for each of us who believes, and demonstrates that belief through love.

In John 14:27, Jesus reiterates, *"Let not your hearts be troubled, neither let them be afraid."* If you are giving your best and staying faithful, there is no need for hearts that are troubled and filled with fear. Give your best today. Honor God with your best effort today. Whatever the results are, do not be troubled or afraid. God has told us what the promised reward is—a "room" in heaven. He has given us an important tool—the Grace of the Holy Spirit—to guide us and sustain us through this life to that reward.

> *You did say: "See, My friends, that you not be troubled; for now, the hour is near for Me to be given up and slain by the hands of lawless men. All you shall be scattered, forsaking Me; but those, who I shall gather will preach a Loving God." (From the 5th Ode of the Service of the 12 Gospels on Holy Thursday Evening, Trans. by Fr. George Papadeas)*

Have confidence in God today, and let that give you confidence for yourself as well!

Third Sunday of Lent—Veneration of the Holy Cross

The Vine and Branches: Abiding in God's Love

Jesus said to His Disciples, "I am the true vine, and My Father is the vinedresser. Every branch of Mine that bears no fruit, He takes away, and every branch that does bear fruit He prunes, that it may bear more fruit. You are already made clean by the word which I have spoken to you. Abide in Me, and I in you. As the branch cannot bear fruit by itself, unless it abides in the vine, neither can you, unless you abide in Me. I am the Vine, you are the branches. He who abides in Me, and I in him, he it is that bears much fruit, for apart from Me you can do nothing. If a man does not abide in Me, he is cast forth as a branch and withers; and the branches are gathered, thrown into the fire and burned. If you abide in Me, and My words abide in you, ask whatever you will, and it shall be done for you. By this My Father is glorified, that you bear much fruit, and so prove to be My disciples.
As the Father has loved Me, so have I loved you; abide in My love.
If you keep My commandments, you will abide in My love,
just as I have kept My Father's commandments and abide in His love.
John 15:1-10
(From the First Gospel on Holy Thursday Evening)

Have you ever considered what it would be like to not have a place to call home? That is an unfortunate reality for many people. I have never been homeless, and I pray that I will never experience what that would be like. I have wondered, however, what it would be like not to have a home—how would I be protected from the cold of winter, or the heat of summer, the rain and the wind? How would I find food, and how would I cook it? How would basic things like laundry and personal hygiene be taken care of? If I didn't have a place to live, it would be hard to hold a job, because my house is my home base. It is where I rest, where I eat, where I prepare to go to work and where I wind down after work. It is the building that protects me from the elements, which provides warmth on a cold day, and coolness on a hot one.

In these verses from John 15, we read the word "abide" many times. The word "abide," each time it appears in the original Greek text, is derived from the Greek word "meno" or some derivative form of it. "Meno" means "to live." Reread these verses and change the word "abide" to "live," and see what that does to the meaning.

The image that the Lord paints for us is of a vine, where the main stem is the Lord, and we are the branches coming off of the stem. Cut a stem off of a vine and it will die rather quickly. Cut a stem off of a vine and it quickly becomes useless. It loses its beauty and its vitality. Apart from the vine, the branch is nothing. With the vine, each branch lives, and has its own beauty.

When we do not live in God, and we don't invite Him to live in us, we are like the branch that has separated from the vine. Many times at funeral services, someone will say, after seeing their loved one, "they don't look anything like they looked in life." Why is that? Because the God-part of them, the soul, is gone, and with the soul goes not only our life, but also our beauty. A person who is "alive" in the sense that they live and breathe, but whose soul is not aflame with God, does not radiate the beauty which God intended for us to radiate. We bear spiritual fruit and grow in spiritual beauty when we remain with the vine, with the Lord.

When I'm trimming trees in my yard, and I see a dead branch, I prune it from the tree, because the dead branch is useless. It takes away beauty from the tree and if diseased, could even harm other branches. Jesus speaks of the Father as the "vinedresser," the one who prunes off the bad branches so that the vine can be healthy and beautiful. If God is the vine, then we are the branches. Stay on the vine and be healthy. Separate from the vine and it will cause one to wither and die.

What if you are separated from the vine? The answer comes from a special plant that you will see in church today, the third Sunday of Lent. The plant is "Vasiliko," or "basil" in English, and it will be placed near the Holy Cross on a tray that will be carried in a procession around the church today. Vasiliko is the exceptional plant that can come back to life, even after it is cut off from its main "vine." Place a piece of cut basil flower in water, and it will eventually regrow its roots and "come to life" again. When St. Helen went to find the precious Cross of Christ around the year 325 AD, she found basil growing on the hill of Golgotha, where the cross has been buried after the crucifixion. Underneath the basil, the cross of Christ was unearthed. Vasiliko means "of the King," and in this case, refers to the King of Glory, who "died" and then "came back to life." Vasiliko does the same.

When we feel spiritually dead, remember the Vasiliko. Get in some water and regrow your roots. How is that possible? For the nonbeliever, it is through the water of baptism. For the Christian, it is through the water ("tears") of repentance. If you are on the vine, stay on the vine that you may bear much fruit. If you feel like you are separated from the vine, tears of repentance will "graft" you right back onto it.

Now, reread the passage above and exchange the word "abide" with the word "prosper," which means to "live well." If we "abide" in God, and He abides in us, that means that we "live in Him," and that He figures into our daily living. If we "live" in Him, and allow Him to live in us, eventually we will "prosper" in our faith. If we seek to "abide" in God's love on a daily basis, we will be in good stead to "abide" in His love on a permanent basis in His Heavenly Kingdom.

Our God, the God who saves, You teach us justly to thank You for the good things which You have done and still do for us. You are our God who has accepted these Gifts. Cleanse us from every defilement of flesh and spirit, and teach us how to live in holiness by Your fear, so that receiving the portion of Your holy Gifts with a clear conscience we may be united with the holy Body and Blood of Your Christ. Having received them worthily, may we have Christ dwelling in our hearts, and may we become the temple of Your Holy Spirit. Yes, our God, let none of us be guilty before these, Your awesome and heavenly Mysteries, nor be infirm in body and soul by partaking of them unworthily. But enable us, even up to our last breath, to receive a portion of Your holy Gifts worthily, as provision for eternal life and as an acceptable defense at the awesome judgment seat of Your Christ. So that we also, together with all the saints who through the ages have pleased You, may become partakers of Your eternal good things, which You, Lord, have prepared for those who love You. (From the Divine Liturgy of St. Basil, Trans. by Holy Cross Seminary Press.)

Abide in God today! Let Him live in you today!

Monday of the Fourth Week of Lent

Your Faith Will Make You Some Enemies

Jesus said to His Disciples, "If the world hates you, know that it has hated Me before it hated you. If you were of the world, the world would love its own; but because you are not of the world, but I chose you out of the world, therefore the world hates you. Remember the word that I said to you, 'A servant is not greater than his master.' If they persecuted Me, they will persecute you; if they kept My word, they will keep yours also. But all this they will do to you on My account, because they do not know him who sent Me.
John 15:18-21
(From the First Gospel on Holy Thursday Evening)

Love one another! Let not your hearts be troubled! I go to prepare a place for you! Abide in My love!

This all sounds great. Then why is it so hard? Why does doing the right thing seem to get us more enemies than friends sometimes? As His "discourse" continues, Jesus mixes in for His Disciples, not only the temporal and eternal rewards of being a follower, but the reality that following isn't always going to be easy.

Indeed those early centuries of Christianity were anything but easy. Every one of the Disciples except for John was martyred for their faith. They were cruelly tortured and murdered. In the first three centuries after Christ walked the earth, before Christianity became the legal religion of the Roman Empire through the Edict of Milan, Christians were persecuted. Any public declaration of one's faith in Christ risked a heinous execution. Christianity was practiced in secret. Church communities gathered in the catacombs, in the sewers of the city. The only time Christianity was out in the public was when a Christian was caught and killed, oftentimes in arenas in front of thousands of people. This was a demonstration by the Roman Empire designed to strike fear in anyone who was a follower and to make those considering becoming Christians think twice about it. The net effect of this? The Church grew at an astounding rate of 40% per decade! (See Rodney Stark, *The Rise of Christianity,* Princeton, NJ: Princeton University Press, 1996)

Why? Because people saw Christians who were so convicted about their faith that they were willing to die for it. Because Christianity preached a theology of love—they engaged their neighbors, they cared for the sick and the poor. ("Four Reasons Why Early Christianity Grew So Quickly" by Seraphim Danckaert, 2014)

In modern times, there are groups of people who "hate" Christians. There are two reasons to hate Christians: one is that those who espouse violence, greed and fear, feel threatened by those who preach love, peace, and generosity. This is because love, peace, and generosity inevitably wins over violence, greed, and fear. Violence, greed, and fear are not the foundation of strong families, good marriages, or meaningful friendships. They are not the backbone of any legitimate success. It has been said that, "might makes right." The one who has the might creates the rights. However, only love can make what is truly right in the eyes of God. Because we all have some passion for power, ego, and greed, we sometimes develop feelings of anger and hatred toward others. The second reason that people "hate" Christians is because there are many hypocritical Christians, people who espouse the love of Christ but fail to live it.

If you are a genuine Christian, at some point someone will dislike you because of it. Think about if you made an effort to refrain from gossip and were successful in doing so. Some of your relationships would undoubtedly end, because many of our friendships put gossip as their central activity. Take out cattiness, and some relationships would have nothing left in them.

Sadly, we live in a world where Christianity is seen as a threat. Christ tells us very specifically how we are to live in Him, and work our way toward His Kingdom. He outlines certain behaviors that are pleasing to Him and certain behaviors that are not. We are free to choose to follow or not follow. There is no fear in love, remember, so there is no coercion in Christianity.

"Political correctness" teaches that anyone can believe anything and still be right. Every person has an equal voice and every idea should receive equal weight. That means that hatred gets equal play with love. Immorality and moral living are both okay. There are no "sheep" and "goats" if everyone is equal and the same. Political correctness is "nice," in that it doesn't hold anyone accountable for anything, but political correctness is not a Biblical concept. It is not a God-ordained idea. Political correctness is society's idea, not God's.

If anything, God is not politically correct. He tells us to love, not hate. He tells us to live according to certain moral stands and avoid immorality. He tells us that heaven is for those who have prepared—the wise maidens, not the foolish ones; for the ones who used their talents, not the ones who didn't; for the sheep and not the goats (See Matthew 25). When the truth of God runs into the "lie" of political correctness, there is a conflict, and out of conflicts are where "hatred" is born, the same kind of hatred that Christ tells us that the world had for Him, and will have for us as well.

We should not meet hatred with hatred. Nor should we meet "political correctness" with hatred. Neither should we meet it with acceptance and complacency. Jesus says in John 8:32, *"Know the truth, and the truth will make you free."* To accept everything is to accept nothing. To be forced to accept everything is to be denied freedom. To choose Christ is a free choice. Ironically, in a "free country," we see Christianity on the decline. It no longer grows by 40% per decade. In fact some studies suggest that there has been a decline of church attendance by 40% in the last decade. Mediocrity and complacency actually have dealt a greater blow to Christianity than hatred and violence. Reclaiming our Christianity begins with each person's decision to seek after the *truth* of God, not just our own perception of it. Jesus tells us that the truth will set us free, but it is also likely to make us some enemies along the way.

> *Remember, Lord, this country and all those in public service whom You have allowed to govern on earth. Grant them profound and lasting peace. Speak to their hearts good things concerning Your Church and all Your people that through the faithful conduct of their duties we may live peaceful and serene lives in all piety and holiness. Sustain the good in their goodness; make the wicked good through Your goodness... Reunite those separated; bring back those in error and unite them to Your holy, catholic, and apostolic Church... Remember, Lord, those who entreat Your loving kindness; those who love us and those who hate us; those who have asked us to pray for them, unworthy though we may be. Remember, Lord our God, all Your people, and pour out Your rich mercy upon them, granting them their petitions for salvation... Prevent schism in the Church; pacify the raging of the heathen. Quickly stop the uprisings of heresies by the power of Your Holy Spirit. Receive us all into Your kingdom. Declare us to be sons and daughters of the light and of the day. Grant us Your peace and love, Lord our God, for You have given all things to us. (From the Liturgy of St. Basil, Trans. by Holy Cross Seminary Press)*

Stay true to Christ today!

Tuesday of the Fourth Week of Lent

Christ's Hope for Us

Jesus said to His Disciples, "I do not pray for these only, but also for those who believe in Me through their word, that they may all be one; even as thou, Father, art in Me, and I in Thee, that they also may be in Us, so that the world may believe that Thou hast sent Me. The glory which Thou hast given Me I have given to them, that they may be one even as We are one, I in them and Thou in Me, that they may become perfectly one, so that the world may know that Thou hast sent Me and hast loved them even as thou hast loved Me. Father, I desire that they also, whom thou hast given Me, may be with Me where I am, to behold My glory which Thou hast given Me in Thy love for Me before the foundation of the world. O righteous Father, the world has not known Thee, but I have known Thee; and these know that Thou hast sent Me. I made known to them Thy name, and I will make it known, that the love with which Thou hast loved Me may be in them, and I in them."
John 17:20-26
(From the First Gospel on Holy Thursday Evening)

No one knows how long it took Christ to give this discourse. It was probably over a period of a couple of hours. It was a summation of three years of ministry. All the things He had done and taught were about to come to pass, with His impending death now only hours away. The discourse began with hope and with instruction, then turned to the reality of the Christian life, that it is not an easy life.

Jesus followed these words of sober reality with words that again spoke of comfort. He again spoke of the Holy Spirit, in John 16:13, saying, *"When the Spirit of truth comes, He will guide you into all truth."* Not only does the Spirit guide us to know the Truth, but sustains our hope and confidence in that truth. This is one of the many reasons why we celebrate the Liturgy so often, so that the Holy Spirit may come down upon us and upon the Gifts we are presenting to God (See the Prayer of Consecration at the Divine Liturgy).

Jesus warns His followers, then and now, that we will be sorrowful at times because we are Christians and because the world will hate us. He makes the comparison of a woman giving birth, who suffers great pain, which is quickly forgotten when a child enters the world. He says this is the kind of pain we will feel in this life, but also the kind of joy we can expect as we prepare for eternal life. He says that when we find that joy, our *"hearts will rejoice, and no one will take your joy from you (us)"* (John 16:20-22).

In John 16:33, Jesus said to His Disciples *"I have said this to you, that in Me you may have peace. In the world you have tribulation; but be of good cheer, I have overcome the world."* Likewise, those whose lives are filled with peace and love will overcome the tribulations of the world as well.

Christ ended His farewell discourse with a prayer for His Disciples. The prayer was offered to God the Father, on behalf of His Disciples, as well as everyone who will ever become a disciple, which means that this is a prayer for us living in the world today. Christ's prayer is not only His prayer for us, but should become our prayer for ourselves. It offers up His hopes for us.

Verse 21—*that they also be in Us*—that we live in unity with God.

That the world may believe—that we spread the Word of God and that our witness is accepted by the world.

Verse 22—*That they may be one even as We are one*—that we seek unifying relationships with one another, and that we manifest God-like love in our relationships.

Verse 24—*that they may be where I am*—meaning to be with Christ in heaven, at the right hand of God the Father.

To behold My glory—to gaze upon Christ with our own eyes and to not only see His glory, but to share in it.

Which Thou hast given Me in Thy love for Me before the foundation of the world—For us to share the glory of God with God, in the same way that God was before the Creation of the world, meaning for us to exist in a state of perfect love with God and with one another, free from the sin of the fallen world, and to share this state of existence on a permanent basis.

Nowhere in this prayer does Christ ask for things to be easy for us. He asks the Father, *Holy Father, keep them (us) in Thy name.* (17:11) In verse 26, He asks that, *"the love with which Thou hast loved Me may be in them, and I in them."*

Christ's hope for all of us is to one day be with Him, in the way He was with God before the creation of the world. He wants us to live in a world the way the world was before the Fall, when it was perfect. The means to that end are to live a life here on earth with faith, demonstrated by love, aided by the Holy Spirit, which sustains us and guides our church until the day that we are graced with salvation, a permanent oneness with God. To be one with God needs to be a daily prayer and a daily pursuit in every Christian life. To ask God to show us His glory in some way, large or small, should be a prayer and a hope for each day as well.

> *Grant peace to the world, O Merciful Lord; You, Who for Your servants' sake, condescended to take on flesh from the Virgin. Therefore with one voice we praise You, as a loving Lord. (From the 10th Antiphon of the Service of the 12 Gospels on Holy Thursday Evening, Trans. by Fr. George Papadeas)*

Do something for your salvation today!

Wednesday of the Fourth Week of Lent

Will You Stay When it Counts?

And when they had sung a hymn, they went out to the Mount of Olives.
Then Jesus said to them, "You will all fall away because of Me this night; for it is written,
'I will strike the Shepherd, and the sheep of the flock will be scattered.' But after I am raised
up, I will go before you to Galilee." Peter declared to him, "Though they all fall away
because of you, I will never fall away." Jesus said to him, "Truly, I say to you, this very night,
before the cock crows, you will deny Me three times." Peter said to him,
"Even if I must die with you, I will not deny you." And so said all the Disciples.
Matthew 26:30-35
(From the Gospel of the Vesperal Liturgy on Holy Thursday Morning)

Most people who are committed Christians would probably say that they would stay loyal to Christ, no matter what. We certainly wouldn't deny Christ! Right?

We see more and more Christians in the world today under attack, killed for just being a Christian. We lull ourselves into thinking that this is happening halfway around the world and could never happen here in our country. I wonder though, if things keep going the way they are, will there be a day when we are asked to choose between Christ and dying. Which would you choose?

No one is asking you to die for Christ today, but on many days, we are tempted to deny Christ. Back when I was a child, there were no sports on Sunday mornings. Sunday was reserved for families, to attend church, to have lunch, to do whatever families do together. Now it is almost impossible to play competitive sports and not have them interfere with Sunday morning worship. Young people who work are oftentimes scheduled to work on Sunday mornings as well. In many corners, people are told, or at least it is inferred, that one must "deny Christ" on Sunday mornings or he can't play on the team, or "deny Christ" and risk losing a job. Many of us are still finding ourselves in the role of Peter—a loyal disciple, who under the threat of something negative happening to him, turned and ran away, denying Christ at the moment of truth.

In today's society filled with anti-Christian sentiments, where the "Shepherd" is continually stricken, what is happening to the sheep? It seems that many sheep are scattering. I have wondered what might have happened had the Disciples not fled, had they galvanized the followers of Jesus to fight for Him, would the story have turned out any different. Did the Disciples just "let" Jesus die, without putting up a fight?

Obviously, we know that God's will governs over all. God let His Son die for our sins. Jesus told those who arrested Him that He could have *"appealed to My Father and He will at once send Me more than twelve legions of angels. But how then should the Scriptures be fulfilled, that it must be so?"* (Matt. 26:53-54). So, allowing Jesus to die was part of God's plan. Is it His plan that Christianity continues to be pushed to the margins of society as is happening in many pockets of the world? Or is it His plan that all should come to know the Truth, and that we are thwarting His plan and His purposes?

Saint Paul answers this question in his First Epistle to Timothy:

> *First of all, then, I urge that supplications, prayers, intercessions and thanksgivings be made for all men, for kings and all who are in high positions, that we may lead a quiet and peaceable life, godly and respectful in every way. This is good, and it is acceptable in the sight of God our Savior, who desires that all men should be saved and come to the knowledge of the Truth* (1 Tim. 2:1-4).

We know that God's desire is for all people to be saved. Therefore denying Christ, and denying people the opportunity to know Christ goes against God's plan. Merely not denying Christ is not enough. We have to live in Christ, and we have to acknowledge Christ, to bear witness to Him, to let others know that we know Him. This does not mean we need to stand on street corners handing out flyers, but it does mean living a Christ-centered life where others recognize Christ at work in you in some way large or small.

It is the Orthodox Tradition to offer incense in a vessel called a "Thimiato" or "censer." The censer has 4 chains, one for each of the Evangelists, and 12 bells, one for each of the 12 Disciples. The bells make considerable noise when the censer is swung, reminding us that good Disciples spread the Word of God by talking to others about Jesus. During Great Lent, the censer is often used without bells, reminding us that at the moment of truth, the Disciples all forsook Christ and left, and is a reminder to us not to do the same.

At some point, it's not enough to "just go along" with Christ. At some point, we've got to stand up and be counted.

While permitting the lawless men to seize You, O Lord, You thus declared: "Though you strike down the Shepherd, and scatter the twelve sheep, My Disciples, yet I could have summoned more than twelve legions of Angels by My side; but I forbear, so that the unknown and secret things, which I revealed to you through My prophets, may be fulfilled." O Lord, Glory to You. (From the 7th Antiphon of the Service of the 12 Gospels on Holy Thursday Evening, Trans. by Fr. George Papadeas)

Stand up for Christ in some way today!

Thursday of the Fourth Week of Lent

The Importance of "Watching"

Then Jesus went with them to a place called Gethsemane, and he said to His Disciples, "Sit here, while I go yonder and pray." And taking with Him Peter and the two sons of Zebedee, He began to be sorrowful and troubled. Then He said to them, "My soul is very sorrowful, even to death; remain here, and watch with Me."
Matthew 26:36-38
(From the Gospel of the Vesperal Liturgy on Holy Thursday Morning)

The first "act" of Christ's Passion was His betrayal by Judas. This was revealed in the context of the Last Supper. Then Jesus began a lengthy discourse to His Disciples. In the midst of this, He revealed that Peter would deny Him, another "act" of the Passion. Jesus eventually left the upper room, and *"went forth with His Disciples across the Kidron Valley, where there was a garden, which He and His Disciples entered"* (John 18:1), the Garden of Gethsemane. This place was very familiar to Jesus, *"for Jesus often met there with His Disciples"* (John 18:2). It also set the scene for His arrest, for *"Judas, who betrayed Him, also knew the place"* (John 18:2).

Jesus, knowing all things, knew that as He entered the garden a free man, that He would be exiting the garden shortly as a prisoner. He knew that it was only a short time before an excruciating day of pain and torture would commence. He knew that He would endure a humiliating and painful death.

He had just spent a "peaceful" evening having supper and speaking with His Disciples, His friends. Now His mood began to change. He asked Peter (whom He still loved, even though He had predicted Peter's denial), and James and John, the sons of Zebedee, to "watch" with Him while He prayed. Why? He did not want to be alone. He didn't ask these Disciples to pray *for* Him. He didn't ask them to pray *with* Him. He didn't ask them to share in His sufferings *with* Him. He asked them only to watch with Him while He was praying, so that He wouldn't feel alone.

Loneliness is a very powerful feeling. It makes one feel debilitated at best, and hopeless at worse. There are many people who have lots of friends, who live in the public eye, and at times they are lonely. There are many jobs where the person at the top is lonely, in the sense that he or she stands alone to make decisions. For example, in a household where there is only one mother caring for a small child or small children, she is virtually their entire world. She is responsible for their entire well-being and this is a lonely job. Teachers stand alone, trying to impart knowledge, in front of a class of thirty-five students. Doctors, surgeons, dentists, architects, business executives, salespeople, all of these people can feel lonely as well.

From personal experience, I can say the priesthood is like this at times. For instance, at a funeral, I may stand in front of a church filled with people, many of whom I consider friends, but I am the only one up in front, and sometimes that is a lonely feeling.

The point of this is that at some point, we are all going to feel like Jesus—alone, sorrowful. We won't need to necessarily have someone take away our burden, but to have someone "watching" is a comfort in itself. The sorrow of Christ in the garden was not only because of His impending suffering, but because at that moment He experienced the human emotion of loneliness and it made Him sorrowful.

It is important that when you are lonely, you find people who can "watch" with you. Perhaps they can lend a sympathetic ear or a few words of encouragement. Many times that, in and of itself, is enough to bring comfort. It is critically important that when a friend asks you to "watch" with them, that you come with an attentive ear and a sympathetic heart. So that they know that while they may feel stressed out and lonely about their situation, they won't feel "alone" because someone will be "watching" with them.

Remember that Christ didn't ask the Disciples on that night to suffer with Him, or to do anything other than to "watch." In times when "help" is needed, then one must actively "help." There are times when compassion is needed, and it is in these times when it is important to "watch."

> *"Shake off sleep now from your eyelids, O My Disciples," said Christ. "With prayer watch, lest you be overwhelmed by temptation; especially you, Simon, for the trial is greatest to the strong. O Peter, know me, Whom all creation blesses, glorifying to all Ages." (8th Ode from the Service of the 12 Gospels on Holy Thursday Evening, Trans. by Fr. George Papadeas)*

"Watch" with someone today!

Friday of the Fourth Week of Lent

Leaning on God When You Are in Agony

And going a little farther He fell on His face and prayed, "My Father, if it be possible, let this cup pass from Me; nevertheless, not as I will, but as Thou wilt." And there appeared to Him an angel from heaven, strengthening Him.
Matthew 26:39; Luke 22:43
(From the Gospel of the Vesperal Liturgy on Holy Thursday Morning)

Jesus went to a place that was very familiar to Him—The Garden of Gethsemane. He went with people whom He was comfortable with—His Disciples. He did something that was very familiar to Him—He prayed. This is where the comfort ended. For in the prayers of this night, He confronted His own impending suffering and death. He was about to do something that had never happened to anyone. He was about to suffer as no man had ever suffered.

Jesus' response to His situation was a very human response. At the tomb of Lazarus, He shed human tears, as He mourned His friend who had died. In the Garden of Gethsemane, He shed the tears of fear and sorrow, as He meditated on His own impending death.

His prayer cried out to God for deliverance and relief. In confronting what was going to happen to Him, Jesus had the human emotion of wishing for the cup of suffering to pass from Him. His overwhelming thought, even in the midst of personal suffering, however, was a desire to remain obedient to God, to place His trust in God. Immediately upon asking if the cup of suffering could be lifted, He placed it in the hands of God, leaving it up to God's will and not His.

Many times in life, we feel like Christ. This is why Christ understands us. He understands our pains because He lived them. Many times in life, we wish for a "cup of suffering" to pass from us, or to leave us. We beg and plead for God to take away pain and sorrow. Many times the prayer ends there—we offer our plea, and we hope that He will offer deliverance.

However, the most spiritually mature person will offer to God, in addition to a specific request, a humble surrender and submission to the will of God. In Isaiah 55:8-9, we read, *"For My thoughts are not your thoughts, neither are your ways My ways, says the Lord. For as the heavens are higher than the earth, so are My ways higher than your ways and My thoughts than your thoughts."* Our requests may not be in line with God's will for our lives. So, we should always leave room for His will to be done.

If you are the parent of a young child, you know that if that child had his or her way, he or she would probably want to eat pizza or French fries for every meal. On occasion, we, as parents, grant this request, but if we always granted that request, we would be irresponsible guardians. Children are free to make any requests they want, but at the end of the day, ideally, they acquiesce to the will of parents, who provide for them, guard them, and have their best interests in mind.

The same thing applies to God. Sometimes our will is in line with His. We desire something and He desires it for us. There are other times when His will and our will are not in line, and this is where we have to trust and be obedient to His will, as our Father, our Provider, and our Guardian.

In Luke 22:44, we read that Jesus, *"being in agony, He prayed more earnestly; and His sweat became like great drops of blood falling down upon the ground."* This depth of sorrow and stress is hard to comprehend. We are told that in this moment, *"an angel appeared from heaven, strengthening Him"* (Luke 22:43).

One of the greatest comforts is knowing that God does not abandon us, especially in our moments of suffering. Sometimes it takes great faith and trust to realize that He is right there with us, even when it feels like we are alone, or that He is far away. We pray in the Divine Liturgy *"For an angel of peace, a faithful guide, a guardian of our souls and bodies"* to be with us at all times, to comfort us in our times of sorrow.

I've seen several depictions of Christ praying in the Garden of Gethsemane. He is kneeling over a large rock, pouring out His sorrows. I've seen some depictions where an angel is hovering above Him, in a posture of prayer, as if praying over Him. I've seen depictions where the angel is putting his arm around Him, embracing Him. I bring these depictions to my mind in my moments of sorrow, that God sends His angels around me to comfort and protect me. Many times, I have felt their "presence" and warmth.

At times in every life, we've all felt "agony." It is not necessarily the agony of impending pain and suffering, but the agony of a "cup" that we wish would pass from us. When you are in agony, ask the Lord for His will to be done, and ask for comfort and strength from His angels to help you in whatever challenge is at hand.

> *The One, Who at all times, and at every hour, both in Heaven and on earth, is worshipped, and glorified, O Christ, our God, long-suffering, plenteous in mercy and full of compassion, Who loves the righteous and is merciful to sinners, calling all to salvation, through the promise of blessings to come, accept our supplications in this present hour, and direct our lives according Your commandments. Sanctify our souls; purify our bodies; set aright our minds; cleanse our thoughts; and deliver us from all affliction, evil and distress. Surround us with Your Holy Angels, that*

guided and guarded by their interposition, we may attain the unity of faith the knowledge of Your ineffable glory. For You are blessed unto the Ages of Ages. Amen. (Prayer of the Hours, offered at the Royal Hours on Good Friday Morning, Trans. by Fr. George Papadeas)

May God send His angels over you today!

Saturday of the Fourth Week of Lent

Syncing Up the Flesh With the Spirit

And He came to the Disciples and found them sleeping; and He said to Peter, "So, could you not watch with Me one hour? Watch and pray that you may not enter into temptation; the spirit indeed is willing, but the flesh is weak."
Matthew 26:40-41
(From the Gospel of the Vesperal Liturgy on Holy Thursday Morning)

Jesus asked three of His Disciples to "watch" with Him while He prayed. His prayer was one of great agony. Not only did He feel the weight of the enormous, almost unthinkable, task at hand, but also the sorrow of loneliness, knowing that He would bear the Passion alone. An angel came to comfort Him. When He returned to His Disciples, however, He found them sleeping. This wasn't betrayal. It wasn't denial. Still, it had to hurt.

As for the Disciples, why did they fall asleep? Were they just too tired and the task of "watching" was too great for them? Did they not care about Jesus and His obvious struggle? He had just spent hours telling them about His Passion, saying "goodbye" to them. I would venture to say that when Jesus asked the three Disciples to watch while He went yonder to pray, that the "intention" of the Disciples was to do exactly that, to watch. I don't think Jesus left their company and immediately they started saying "He'll be gone awhile, why not catch a few zzz's?" I'm positive that they started out with the best of intentions in their spirits, but their bodies just didn't keep up, and they fell asleep. The spiritual opportunity lost out to a material concern.

If we think about this verse, it is very appropriate to the struggle to be a Christian. There are many spiritual opportunities. These opportunities are not hidden. We know what they are. We know what the right thing is to do, yet many times material concerns override our desire to do the right thing. How many times have people opted to sleep late rather than go to church? How many times have we forgotten to pray? Or we've said that we'll pray, but we put it off, and before we know it the day has gone by and no prayer has been said? How many times do we have the opportunity to stand up for our Christianity, but we don't out of some kind of fear?

How many times do we say "I've got to treat my body better with better diet and more exercise," only to fail on both counts?

"The spirit is willing but the flesh is weak" is a reality that challenges each of us. I'm reminded of an Old Indian story by the title "Two Wolves." It reads as follows:

> *One evening, an elderly Cherokee brave told his grandson about a battle that goes on inside people. He said "My son, the battle is between two 'wolves' inside us all. One is evil. It is anger, envy, jealousy, sorrow, regret, greed, arrogance, self-pity, guilt, resentment, inferiority, lies, false pride, superiority and ego. The other is good. It is joy, peace, love, hope, serenity, humility, kindness, benevolence, empathy, generosity, truth, compassion and faith." The grandson thought about it for a minute and then asked his grandfather, "Which wolf wins?" The old Cherokee simply replied, "The one that you feed."*

Like the "two wolves," there is a battle in each of us between the flesh and the spirit. There is, however, a third "player" at work in each of us and that is the mind. The human being is composed of body (flesh), spirit and mind. So, one has to decide what will lead in life—will it be the body leading with the mind and spirit following? Will it be the mind leading, or will it be the spirit leading? The truth is, whatever leads, the other parts follow. So, if we lead with our flesh—filling our bodies with bad food, and filling our minds with bad thoughts, then our spirits will not be strong and in moments of temptation, the spirit will be weak. If we lead with our spirits, seeking after God and allowing Him to lead, then the mind and the body will follow in ways that are edifying to us and helpful to others. Ideally, we let the spirit lead, and everything else follows.

How, on a practical level, is that accomplished? Here is one practical idea: Eliminate the word "try" from your life. Many people say, "I'll *try* to pray" or "I'll *try* to exercise" or "I'll *try* to eat better" or "I'll *try* to make better choices." Perhaps the Disciples said to one another, "We'll *try* to stay awake." I'm reminded of the scene in the Star Wars movie *The Empire Strikes Back* when the old sage Yoda challenges Luke Skywalker to lift his X-wing fighter out of a swamp using his mind. Luke says to Yoda "Master, moving stones around is one thing. This is totally different!" Irritated, Yoda responds "No! No different! Only different in your mind. You must unlearn what you have learned." Luke replies, "All right, I'll give it a try." Then Yoda says one of the most memorable lines of the movie: "Do, or do not. There is no try."

The way to bring the flesh in line with the spirit is to not try, and just do. Don't try to pray. Pray. Don't try to get to church. Go to church. Don't try to follow the commandments. Follow them. Make a choice to do, and not to try. When the voice of the one "wolf" comes into your head, the voice of doubt and discouragement and distraction, know that that voice is the voice of the devil. Silence him through prayer and focus, and don't forget the important ingredient of friends. There were three Disciples who fell asleep. At the beginning of the watch, they could have agreed to keep each other awake and focused. Instead, as they began to nod off, perhaps they all agreed, "What was the big deal anyway?"

Focus. Get your friends to help you focus. Stop trying and start doing. *"The spirit is willing but the flesh is weak"* sounds like an excuse but it isn't. It shows us the reality of our human condition and that we need to get the flesh in line with the spirit by doing.

> *Create in me a clean heart, O God, and put a new and right Spirit within me. Cast me not away from Thy presence, and take not Thy Holy Spirit from me. Restore to me the joy of Thy salvation, and uphold me with a willing Spirit. (Psalm 50/51, read at all Orthros services in the Orthodox Church, including all the evening services of Holy Week)*

Let your spirit lead today!

Fourth Sunday of Lent—St. John of the Ladder

My Kingdom Is Not of This World

Jesus answered, "My kingship is not of this world; if My kingship were of this world, My servants would fight, that I might not be handed over to the Jews; but My kingship is not from the world."
John 18:36
(From the Fourth Gospel on Holy Thursday Evening)

What comes to mind when you think of the word "kingdom"? Have you ever thought what it would be like to be a "king?" Perhaps you've never thought about "kings" and "kingdoms" as we see in medieval movies, with castles and armies, but it is probably safe to say that most of us have the idea of having something "under our authority." That's what drives us to seek material gain. We are "in love" with the idea of amassing property and power. No, we're not going to own a feudal state, but a nice home and a nice car are good goals. We're not going to command an army, but being the boss over a few employees probably feels good. It's probably safe to say that most of us give a lot of attention to material advancement—buying clothes falls under this category and I don't know anyone who doesn't like to get new clothes at least once in a while. All of these material things cost money, and so a good amount of time is spent earning the money to get the "stuff" that we want.

It's very easy for life to go by quickly and for someone who is at the end of life to wonder, "What will become of my stuff?" On a person's deathbed, when asked what they regret the most, no one says "I wish I had put in more hours at the office," or "I wish I had more money." Most people would say they wish they had more time to live and that they had spent more time with their families. Look at life, for most of us who are in the rat race, our lives are "kingdom-centered," in the sense that they revolve around our jobs and our materials things.

Jesus identified Himself as a "king." He redefined the terms "king" and "kingdom." As a "king," Jesus was not a tyrant. Rather, He was a servant. He didn't stand up and demand respect and bark out orders. Rather, He stooped down to wash the feet of His Disciples. He didn't ride into Jerusalem on a chariot, but on a donkey.

After Jesus was arrested, He was taken to the Jewish authorities, who handed Him over to Pontius Pilate for the purposes of condemning Him to death. The Jews were not allowed to execute criminals; only the Romans could do that. While the Jewish authorities had no real charge against Jesus, they were both jealous and insecure that He was going to wrestle their power away from them. So, they delivered Him to Pontius Pilate on the accusation that He had made Himself "King of the Jews" and therefore posed a threat to both the Jews and the Romans, whose king was Caesar.

So, when Pilate questioned Jesus as to whether He was a king, Jesus answered Him that His Kingship was not of this world. His "kingdom" would not be established through conquest and power, but through service to others and love. Jesus calls on us to radically change our thinking. His "Kingship" is centered on being a servant. His "Kingdom" is centered on benevolence.

So, in our desire to be "kings," (owners and controllers of things), we have to shift our thinking to being "servants." The greater the authority one has, the greater of a servant He should be. Jesus said, *"Many that are first will be last, and the last first"* (Matt. 19:30).

Going back to the Fall of mankind, the initial sin of Adam and Eve was the sin of ingratitude. God had given the human beings Paradise, the entire world, to be at their disposal. He told them, *"You may freely eat of every tree of the garden; but of the tree of the knowledge of good and evil you shall not eat, for in the day that you eat of it, you shall die"* (Gen. 2:16-17). Adam and Eve, instead of saying "thank you" for the vast "kingdom" that God had given them, said, in essence "we want the tree also." They ate of it and fell.

The Kingdom of God, to which we are working to go in our spiritual life, is going to be as it was before the Fall, when everything was in abundance and the human beings lived in a state of "perfection." The roadmap to the Kingdom of God is based on people "divesting" themselves of things, not on material acquisition. It is based on "giving" of love, attention and help to others, rather than just on getting. This is not a call to "communism" but rather a call to "stewardship" and "faith." "Stewardship" is using what you have to take care of someone or something, in this case, using some of your time and talent and resources to care for others, either through the church or through other means. It means being charitable to both neighbor and stranger. The Bible fixes the percentage at ten percent of these things. "Faith" is the idea of living "for God," "with God," and "in God," so that one's work and indeed one's life is all about *Him*!

So, while my "job" might bring material wealth to me, it should also bring glory to Him. While my material wealth may accumulate to bring me temporary joy, I should share a percentage of it with others through the church, or in other ways, so that my material things honor Him as well. In these ways, our lives become centered more on His Kingdom than on our kingdoms. Because no matter how big our earthly kingdom might be, the goal of life is to end up in the Kingdom of God and not be shut out of it.

Because of a tree, Adam was estranged from Paradise; because of the wood of the Cross, the thief abode in Paradise; for the former, in tasting, disobeyed the commandment of the Creator; but the latter, who was crucified with You, confessed, admitting to You, the concealed God. O Savior, remember also us, in Your Kingdom. (From the Beatitudes of the Service of the 12 Gospels on Holy Thursday Evening, Trans. by Fr. George Papadeas)

Focus on His Kingdom today, in addition to yours!

Monday of the Fifth Week of Lent

What is Truth?

Jesus answered, "You say that I am a king. For this I was born, and for this I have come into the world, to bear witness to the truth. Every one who is of the truth hears My voice."
Pilate said to Him, "What is truth?"
John 18:37-38
(From the Fourth Gospel on Holy Thursday Evening)

Pontius Pilate questioned Jesus as to whether He was a king? Jesus answered Him that His purpose in coming into the world was to bear witness to the truth, that everyone who is of the truth hears His voice. Then Pilate asked one of the greatest questions a human being has ever asked: "What is truth?"

Let's go back to Genesis 3, the Fall of mankind. If the first sin was ingratitude, the precursor to the first sin was a lie. We read:

Now the serpent was more subtle than any other wild creature that the Lord God had made. He said to the woman, "Did God say, "You shall not eat of any tree of the garden?" And the woman said to the serpent, "We may eat of the fruit of the trees of the garden; but God said, 'You shall not eat of the fruit of the tree which is in the midst of the garden, neither shall you touch it, lest you die.'" But the serpent said to the woman, "You will not die. For God knows that when you eat of it your eyes will be opened, and you will be like God, knowing good and evil (Gen. 3:1-5).

So, Eve "thought about it," *and when she saw that the tree was good for food, and that it was a delight to the eyes, and that the tree was to be desired to make one wise, she took of its fruit and ate; and she also gave some to her husband, and he ate* (Gen. 3:6).

Immediately, they knew that they had been lied to: *Then the eyes of both were opened, and they knew that they were naked; and they sewed fig leaves together and made themselves aprons* (3:7). When they were confronted with God about their nakedness, rather than just telling the truth, they told a lie. Since that time, the human race has battled between telling the truth and telling lies.

I heard a great definition for lying recently: Lying is rewriting history. If one has a sense of truth, he accepts history as it is, consequences and all. Think about when you lie—it's because the lie is more appealing than the truth. Think about that first lie—the devil rewrote history and mankind fell for the lie.

A couple is asked by some friends to go on a twenty-mile bike ride. The husband thinks to himself, "I don't know how to ride a bike." Then he mulls over what to do. He can tell his friends the truth, that he doesn't know how to ride a bike, and risk disappointing them or having them ridicule him for not knowing how to do something most people learned to do as a young child. He can say that he is busy, but this will also be disappointing to them. He can go for the big lie: "I am actually a bike racing champion, but I hurt my knee and am no longer allowed to ride a bike," which will engender respect, sympathy and admiration. Or he can tell his wife, "Perhaps you'd be willing to teach me to ride a bike, and not make fun of me while I'm learning." Most people in this scenario go for the big lie. It preserves our ego, so we think.

Another lie we often find ourselves in, is when we ask, "How are you?" We ask the bank teller, "How are you?" That's a lie. What if the bank teller tells us that she is going through a divorce? Are we willing to speak with her for half an hour, or do we want to just make our transaction and leave? When you say to someone, "How are you?" ask yourself if you are really willing to stop your day and minister to them if they are in trouble.

When I give out antithoron (the blessed bread) and greet people at the end of the Divine Liturgy, I offer a truthful statement and say, "Nice to see you." That is truth. To ask "How are you?" when I know there are another hundred people in line to greet is not a true statement. If the answer is anything less than positive, there is no time to slow down and talk.

So when we live in a society that doesn't promote being truthful, it is easy to fall into the trap of lies and less than truths. Jesus says in John 14:6, *"I am the way and the truth and the life; no one comes to the Father, but by me."* This is truth. In John 8:31-32, Jesus says, *"If you continue in my word, you are truly my disciples, and you will know the truth and the truth shall make you free."*

Speaking the truth with love is another skill we can all improve. There is a way to speak the truth while also preserving someone's dignity when we have to lodge a complaint. Perceptions also distort the truth, but being careless with the truth leads to a misperception. For instance, when we're constantly checking our phones, it leads to the negative perception that we are not interested in the conversation when we very well might be. Being patient and humble is part of creating a more truthful society. Think of the humility of an adult who has to ride a bike with training wheels and the patience of the person who has to teach him, but this beats the big lie that has to be told to cover a deficiency. We all have deficiencies. If we can all have the humility to admit them and the patience to work through them or help others work through them, think about how much more truthful our world would become.

The Fall was caused by a distortion of the Truth, a lie. The path to our salvation is open through the Truth of the Gospel of Jesus Christ. Attaining salvation will only be possible based on our adherence to the Truth. This starts with us being truthful with one another, speaking the truth in love, and putting aside perceptions of truth. Rther than rewriting history with lies, live it in truth the first time around.

> *The law-transgressors verily did buy the Ordainer of the law from a Disciple. And they brought Him before Pilate as a law-breaker, shouting "Crucify the One, who gave them manna in the wilderness!" But we, emulating the righteous thief, cry out in faith: "Remember also us, O Savior, in Your Kingdom. (From the Beatitudes of the Service of the 12 Gospels, Trans. by Fr. George Papadeas)*

Be truthful in all things today!

Tuesday of the Fifth Week of Lent

Stop Passing the Buck!

So when Pilate saw that he was gaining nothing, but rather that a riot was beginning, he took water and washed his hands before the crowd, saying, "I am innocent of this man's blood; see to it yourselves."
Matthew 27:24
(From the Fifth Gospel of Holy Thursday Evening)

Pontius Pilate, depending on one's perspective, is almost a "tragic" figure in the Passion of Christ. Because he wanted to do the right thing, he knew what the right thing was and he still couldn't do it.

Pilate was the "prefect" of the Roman Province of Judea from 26-36 AD, during the reign of the Emperor Tiberius. Judea was not a glamorous assignment by any means. Far removed from Rome, Pilate lived among Jews and Gentiles who resented Roman rule. The Romans, even though they had power, were outnumbered. Had the people gotten themselves organized, perhaps they could have overthrown their Roman overlords. So, Pilate's grip on power was tenuous at best. He had to make alliances with the Jewish Temple leadership in an effort to "keep the peace" so he could keep his position.

Even though Pilate was known to have a ferocious temper, he also had a conscience and struggled with what to do when presented with the "case" of Jesus of Nazareth. In all four Gospel accounts, Pilate believes that Jesus is innocent. In the Gospel of Mark, Pilate openly questions the crowd in the Praetorium, *"What evil has He done?"* (Mark 15:14). In the Gospel of Luke, Pilate proclaims that Jesus is innocent not once, but three times, *"A third time he said to them 'Why, what evil has He done? I have found in him no crime deserving death; I will therefore chastise Him and release Him'"* (Luke 23:22). In the Gospel of John, Pilate says, *"See I am bringing Him out to you, that you may know that I find no crime in Him"* (John 19:4). In the Gospel of Matthew, it was not only Pilate who had reservations, but also his wife Claudia, who went to Pilate and said *"Have nothing to do with that righteous man, for I have suffered much over Him today in a dream"* (Matt. 27:19).

With this amount of staggering sentiment recounted in ALL the Gospels about Pilate's reservations about condemning Jesus, how could such a powerful man have gone against his own beliefs? Peer pressure, popularity and security are three compelling reasons, reasons that we all still fall prey to at times. First, it was the chief priests claiming that Jesus forbid his followers to pay tribute to Caesar (Luke 23:2). Then it was the crowed crying out *"If you release this man, you are not Caesar's friend; everyone who makes himself a king sets himself against Caesar"* (John 19:12). Pilate even tried to pacify the crowd by offering to release Jesus, or a murderer named Barabbas, hoping, and even believing, that the riotous crowd would most certainly not want a murderer released into their midst. Ultimately, Pilate "washed his hands" of the whole thing, as if to absolve himself of Jesus' demise. Except that, had Pilate stood up and not allowed the crucifixion to proceed, it most certainly could not have. The betrayal, the chief priests, and the riotous crowd are all complicit in the death of Jesus. Pontius Pilate is complicit as well. Ultimately, his wife Claudia Procles was made a saint for her defense of Christ.

Pilate "washed his hands" and "passed the buck" because he feared the crowd. Perhaps he feared reprisals from the emperor. We don't know if in the moment before he washed his hands, he "saw his life pass before him" and wondered what kind of life he would have if he were to be accused of betraying Caesar. So, he allowed the crucifixion to happen. Ironically, not even ten years after the crucifixion, Pilate fell out of favor with the emperor Caligula, was exiled to Gaul (France) and killed himself there.

Pontius Pilate offers two lessons to us: First, his question "What is truth?" is an existential question we should all seek answer to. Our life should be a pursuit of the "truth" of Christ. Somewhere in his mind, Pilate wanted to know the truth. Somewhere in his mind, he believed the words of his wife, that Jesus was a "righteous man." Even as he washed his hands, he knew that he was doing wrong.

The more important lesson we learn from Pontius Pilate is that it is not only important to seek after and know truth, but to stand up for truth. This is where Pilate fell short. He fell short because of peer pressure, popularity, and his desire for job security. Our unwillingness to stand up for the truth today is still affected by these things. In our lives, we have to have morals, truths, and principles that we stand up for. If you had a well-paying job and you were asked to do something illegal to keep it, would you keep your morals or your money? If you were asked to slander someone else or lose popularity, would you tell a lie to keep your friends or tell the truth and risk losing them? These are hard questions. While the answers are easy, the life application of them is hard.

The easy answer is that we do not take money or friends with us to our grave. Money can't buy us a favorable judgment at the awesome judgment seat of Christ. And our friends won't be there to stand with us. We will take the "truth" of our lives with us. The lies will be made known, the mistakes will be revealed. Live in the truth, even if it costs you popularity or security. The *"truth will make you (us) free"* (John 8:32) and those who follow after Jesus as *"the way, the truth and the life,"* (John 14:6) will follow that truth into eternal life.

Come, O Christ-bearing people; let us see what Judas the traitor has plotted with the lawless priests against our Savior. Today, they condemned to death the Immortal Word. They delivered Him to Pilate, and crucified Him on the Place of the Skull; and as our Savior suffering these things, He cried out saying: "Father forgive them this sin, that the Gentiles may know of my Resurrection from the dead." (From the 6th Hour on Good Friday, Trans. by Fr. George Papadeas)

Stop passing the buck and stand up for truth!

Wednesday of the Fifth Week of Lent

Even Christ Had Help Carrying His Cross

As they went out, they came upon a man of Cyrene, Simon by name; this man they compelled to carry His cross.
Matthew 27:32
(From the Sixth Gospel of Holy Thursday Evening)

Many years ago, as we prepared to open up the Diakonia Center (the place we use for summer camp) in South Carolina, I was working with a group of people setting up the ropes course that we use. The camp was opening in just a few days and there was pressure to get all of our tasks done, so we labored outside even though it was a stormy afternoon. One of our tasks was to place large wooden beams around some of the elements of the course. I was carrying one long beam on my shoulders, and I kept sinking in the muddy soil, kept losing my balance, and kept wondering if I would ever finish this task. I started to pray to God to give me strength. I'll never forget two things that happened at this moment: First, I suddenly was filled with joy. I'm very much into experiential learning, and I realized that this experience was helping me understand what it must have felt like for Christ to carry His cross—staggering, struggling to walk another step. Secondly, one of my co-workers came up to me and offered to help carry the beam. I would later help him carry his. We realized that the only way we were going to accomplish our task was to work together.

In Mark 8:34, Jesus tells His followers, *"If any man would come after Me, let him deny himself, take up his cross and follow Me."* Jesus not only preached that. He lived it. After hours of beatings and torture, a heavy cross was placed on His shoulders for the march to Golgotha, where He would be crucified. Christ suffered, in a very human way. Movies about the Passion all show Christ dehydrated, bruised, battered, staggering under the weight of the cross. The Gospel accounts of the Passion tell us that a passer-by, Simon of Cyrene, was forced to help Jesus carry His cross. Jesus "took up His cross" for the salvation of humanity. Even He needed help to carry it.

Each of us carries some "cross" in our lives. That cross might be a medical condition, a difficult child, a challenging marriage, a difficult job, financial difficulties, or any number of other things. The devil adds to the weight of each cross by creating doubt and distraction. Many times we feel "crushed" by the weight of our crosses, as if we have been beaten down and battered by our challenges. This is where each of us needs three things. First, we need resolve to keep going, to put one foot in front of the other. Second, we all need a "Simon of Cyrene" to help us carry our crosses. We all need friends and supporters who can come in and help when we've had enough or when we seem to not be able to take another step.

Third, and perhaps most important, we need to understand that our struggles in life are temporary. I once gave a sermon where I laid a fifty-foot rope down the middle aisle of the church. On the rope I put one paper clip on its side. Imagine that that one paper clip, which takes up a miniscule space on the rope, represents your life. The rope represents eternity. The paper clip against the rope registers hardly a blip. It's the same with our lives when registered against eternity. If you have the best life, but you have no faith, then when the joy of your life ends, you will have an eternity of misery. If, however, on the other hand, you have a terrible life, unspeakable suffering, the heaviest cross that could be, if you survive your life filled with faith and with hope, then you will have an eternity of happiness.

We each have a cross. There is no one who does not carry one of some kind. Our crosses are heavy for each of us. We all need friends to help us carry our crosses, but we have to keep our crosses in perspective of the span of eternal life. Every struggle is temporary. Hard as it may be, we are supposed to glorify God, even in our struggles. This is where friends are so important. On the day when I cannot carry my cross alone, it is the friend who helps. Even on the day when I can carry it, I still need encouragement. Finally, if we need and hope for help in carrying our crosses, we should eagerly embrace the role of Simon of Cyrene, and rush to help others in carrying theirs as well.

It is important to remember the comparison between our temporary suffering and God's eternal glory. We need to maintain focus and motivation to carry our crosses of temporary suffering, so that one day we can leave them at the door of heaven, and experience His eternal glory.

You ransomed us from the curse of the Law by Your precious Blood; You have shed forth immortality upon mankind by being nailed to the Cross and pierced with a spear. O Savior of us all, glory to You. (From the 15th Antiphon of the Service of the 12 Gospels on Holy Thursday evening, Trans. by Fr. George Papadeas)

Carry your cross with hope today! Help someone else carry theirs!

Thursday of the Fifth Week of Lent

The Greatest Example of Forgiveness!

And when they came to the place which is called The Skull, there they crucified Him, and the criminals, one on the right and one on the left. And Jesus said, "Father, forgive them; for they know not what they do."
Luke 23:33-34
(From the Eighth Gospel of Holy Thursday Evening)

In Matthew 18:23-35, Jesus tells us a parable about an unforgiving servant. A man owed his king more money than he could ever pay. When he begged the king for mercy, the king forgave the entire debt. This same man, who had been forgiven for so much, then found a servant who owed him a small amount of money. When that servant asked for mercy, he refused, and put him in prison. When the king heard about this, he put the first servant in prison. The lesson of this parable, said Jesus, is that this is what *"my Heavenly Father will do to every one of you if you do not forgive your brother from your heart"* (18:35).

There are MANY teachings on forgiveness offered by our Lord. In the Lord's Prayer, we are taught to ask God to *"forgive us our debts, as we also have forgiven our debtors"* (Matt. 6:12), meaning that we are to forgive in the same way we expect to be forgiven. He tells us in Matthew 6:14, *"For if you forgive men their trespasses, your Heavenly Father also will forgive you; but if you do not forgive men their trespasses, neither will your Father forgive your trespasses."* In Matthew 18:21, we read *"Peter came up and said to Him, 'Lord, how often shall my brother sin against me, and I forgive him? As many as seven times?' Jesus said to him, 'I do not say to you seven times, but seventy times seven.'"* That's a lot of forgiveness!

As He was being crucified on the cross, in the midst of pain, suffering, and humiliation, Jesus asked His Father to forgive those who were killing Him! What greater example of forgiveness can there be!

"Forgiveness" and "mercy" are concepts that are closely related. When I hear the word "mercy," I think of someone who is about to be executed, who asks to be spared, and is shown pity. "Mercy" means giving someone better than what he deserves. In the Divine Services of our church, the phrase we hear most often is "Lord, have mercy," which means "Lord, give me the thing I don't deserve, the thing I don't have any right to, pity me and allow me to have it anyway."

Every time we commit a sin, we are either sinning against God alone, or against both God and our fellow man. If I sin once against ten people, it is also ten sins against God. While I might be able to count the number of sins I have committed against someone, there is no way I can keep track of the number I have committed against the Lord.

Mercy and forgiveness go hand in hand. If I expect mercy and forgiveness of my sins, the total number that I commit against God, which are innumerable, then I must be able to forgive my fellow man when he sins against me. After all, how can I expect great forgiveness from God if I can't offer small forgiveness to someone else? I will indeed receive God's mercies and forgiveness according to how I offer mercy and forgiveness to others.

How many times must we forgive our neighbor? As many times as we hope God will forgive us. To what depth of sin must we forgive? Well, Christ forgave those who were murdering Him. We certainly should be able to forgive sins that are less horrific than that.

Forgiveness does not mean one has to be friends with everyone who has wronged them. For instance, if someone were to hit my car and damage it, I can forgive them. I am not required to befriend them, but let's use the more frequent example of forgiveness between friends, spouses, and families. We all sin, and we all sin every day. Thus, we are all in need of forgiveness on a daily basis, from the Lord and from one another. If we do not learn how to forgive as we go along, we will build walls and grudges and our relationships will quickly break down on a fundamental level. If we learn how to forgive one another, we will be able to create long and lasting relationships. We will be able to learn how to build real relationships, because every relationship has problems. Sweeping problems under the rug doesn't make for a healthy relationship, and neither does being unable to forgive problems. Having mechanisms to confront problems and being able to effectively forgive and ask for forgiveness sets each relationship not only on a more stable path, but sets each relationship under the umbrella of Christ, and follows His example of forgiveness. The Crucifixion and Christ's forgiveness from the Cross opened the door of reconciliation between God and humanity. It also gave us the greatest example of how to forgive and reconcile with one another.

> *"Israel, My first-born son, committed two evil deeds. He forsook Me, the source of the Living water, and hewed out for himself a broken well; and he crucified Me on the Wood, and asked for the release of Barabbas. The Heavens were aghast at this, and the sun hid its rays. But you, O Israel, were not ashamed, and delivered Me to death. Forgive them, O Holy Father, for they know not what they have done." (From the Praises of the Service of the 12 Gospels on Holy Thursday Evening, Trans. by Fr. George Papadeas)*

Ask for forgiveness! Offer forgiveness! May God forgive all of us!

Friday of the Fifth Week of Lent

Salvation is Possible Until the Very Last Moment, But Don't Wait

One of the criminals who were hanged, railed at Him, saying, "Are you not the Christ? Save yourself and us!" But the other rebuked him, saying, "Do you not fear God, since you are under the same sentence of condemnation? And we indeed justly; for we are receiving the due reward of our deeds; but this Man has done nothing wrong." And he said, "Jesus, remember me when You come into Your kingdom." And He said to him, "Truly, I say to you, today you will be with Me in Paradise."
Luke 23:39-43
(From the Eighth Gospel of Holy Thursday Evening)

Jesus was crucified between two thieves. This was to fulfill the Prophecy of Isaiah, *and He was numbered with the transgressors; yet He bore the sin of man, and made intercession for the transgressors"* (Isa. 53:12). One of the criminals looked at the Lord and thought of his own selfish needs. He asked Christ to save him, if He were really the Christ.

The other thief didn't ask for reprieve. He owned up for his sin to Jesus, saying that he was justly under a sentence of condemnation. In his dying moments, he believed in the power of Jesus to save not his life, but to save his soul. He said to Jesus *"Remember me when You come into Your kingdom"* (Luke 23:42). Jesus answered the thief, *"Truly I say to you, today you will be with me in Paradise."*

A priest once joked with me "the thief was such a good thief, that he stole Paradise in the last moment of his life." Joking aside, I don't believe that one can "steal" Paradise. He believed in the Divinity of Jesus Christ in that final moment. How do we know this? He asked to be remembered in His Kingdom. The other thief believed there was nothing after this life. This is why he pleaded for his life to be extended. The repentant thief had a recognition in a life in God's Kingdom—faith. He asked not to be placed there, but merely to be "remembered"—humility.

The keys to salvation are faith and humility. Because faith is the belief we place in our Lord, and humility is the foundation of a desire to serve others. The repentant thief had a luxury that we do not have—he knew when his dying breath was going to be. We do not. Hence, we must make not only the "confession" of the thief, but also the application to our life today, before the unknown day of our last breath. For even in his dying breath, it wasn't too late to repent and believe. After one has died, however, it is too late.

There are two other things that jump out from today's scripture verses. First, the statement of the repentant thief to the unrepentant one: "Do you not fear God?" I often ponder on this question as we witness acts of unspeakable horror in our world today—from terrorism, wanton violence, white collar criminals who embezzle and steal, etc. I wonder, "do they not fear God?" Because anyone with a fear of God is going to think twice before doing some of the things that we do. When I examine my own life, I sometimes shudder with horror at things I have done and said, and then try to remember that we all, myself included, need to have a healthy fear (and love and respect and awe) of God, to keep our temptations and desires in check. Anyone who has gossiped or lied about someone is a thief—because lying and gossiping steals self-esteem and self-worth of others. Let us not be like the unrepentant thief who had no concept of God, and whose exposure to the very Son of God only feet away from him produced no repentance in him.

The second thing that also jumps out is the message of Christ to the repentant thief, "TODAY, you will be with Me in Paradise." Jesus said "TODAY," not at the second coming, or in a long time from now, but the very day you die, you will experience the Kingdom of God. There are lots of conjectures about what happens when we die. The story of the Last Judgment (Matt. 25:31-46) speaks of all the nations being gathered before Christ TOGETHER for the final judgment. His words to the repentant thief point to a judgment that is immediate, which points to two possible interpretations. In 2 Peter 3:8, we read *"But do not ignore this one fact, beloved, that with the Lord one day is as a thousand years, and a thousand years as one day."* If God's time and man's time move at different speeds, then in God's time, the Judgment could be "today," even though in man's time the Judgment may be thousands of years away. A second interpretation is the belief that one receives a "partial" judgment upon his earthly death—either a foretaste of Paradise or a foretaste of condemnation—and receives the full measure of reward or punishment at the Last Judgment. These are two explanations of the use of the word "TODAY" in Jesus' speaking to the thief.

Finally, in many depictions of the crucifixion, the Cross of Christ has bars above or below Him that angle up to the right. This symbolizes that the repentant thief, the one to the right of Christ (the same side as the "sheep" on the right hand, Matthew 25:33), went "up" to Paradise. The angling of the bar down to the left symbolizes the unrepentant thief who was numbered among the "goats" and went "down" to Hades (Matt. 25:33).

> *The thief upon the cross spoke in a low tone, but found great faith. In an instant he was saved, and being the first to open the Gates of Paradise, he entered. O Lord, Who accepted his repentance, glory to You. (From the 14th Antiphon of the Service of the 12 Gospels on Holy Thursday Evening, Trans. by Fr. George Papadeas)*

Make your journey to salvation an important part of every day, starting with today!

Fifth Saturday of Lent

The Establishment of the Church

When Jesus saw His Mother, and the Disciple whom He loved standing near, He said to His mother, "Woman, behold, your son!" Then He said to the Disciple, "Behold, your mother!" And from that hour the disciple took her to his own home.
John 19:26-27
(From the Gospel of the Ninth Hour on Good Friday Morning)

What a profound moment that took place between the Lord, His Mother and His beloved Disciple John! Jesus had endured betrayal by one disciple, denial by another, and abandonment by all the rest. He had endured rejection from His own people, and the scourging by the Roman soldiers. He had been hung on a cross by nails driven into his hands and feet. He had been mocked and humiliated. Now, as His earthly body was quickly shutting down and heading toward human death, Jesus had a brief exchange between His Mother and His Disciple John, from which we take away several lessons.

First, one of the Ten Commandments instructs us to honor our parents. Even in the greatest pain and suffering a human being has ever endured, Jesus found a deep love for His Mother and earthly concern about her well-being. He wanted to make sure that she was taken care of before He passed away. The term "Woman," in Greek "Yine," with which he addressed His Mother was an address of great respect and admiration.

Jesus entrusted His Mother to His beloved Disciple because His earthly father and protector, Joseph, was already deceased. Orthodox and Catholic traditions differ on the life of Joseph. In the Orthodox Church, Tradition holds that Joseph was an older man, who had been widowed and had children from his previous marriage (see Matthew 13:55-56, for mention of Jesus' brothers and sisters, likely half-brothers and half-sisters). By the time the Crucifixion occurred, Joseph was deceased. This would have left Jesus, as the only son, with the obligation and expectation to care for His Mother. With His death imminent, He did the kind act of entrusting His Mother's care to His beloved Disciple, John. We also hold that Mary remained "Ever-Virgin," that she had no other offspring. Had there been other offspring, Jesus would have entrusted her to them. The belief in her eternal virginity is supported by this act of Christ.

However, the way He did it accomplished much more than establish a caregiver for Mary. It set in motion the creation of the Church. When He said to His mother, "Behold your son!" He was asking the Virgin Mary not only to see John as a son, but to see all of His Disciples and followers, from then until now, as her children. When He told John to "Behold your Mother!" He was instructing John, and by extension all of us, to see the Virgin Mary, as our mother. In taking the Virgin Mary into his own home, we are receiving an example that we are to take the model of the Virgin Mary into our own homes, as the best representation of what it means to be a servant of God, imitating the Virgin Mary in her obedience and servitude toward God.

Every Christian has three mothers. One is our birth mother. The second mother is the Virgin Mary, Mother of all Christians. Her example nurtures us. Her prayers strengthen us. Her intercessions help us. Her love comforts us. Our third mother is the Church, established in this act of Christ entrusting His Mother to His Disciple John. We have the Church, which like a mother, guides us, teaches us, sometimes chastises us, and provides for us.

It is important for us to know that we are not alone. Christ, when He was forsaken by nearly everyone, was never abandoned by His Mother and His beloved Disciple. When we have our tough times, it is important to remember that we are not alone either. We always have the Virgin Mary to intercede for us. We always have a Church to go to.

We are supposed to have one another to lean on for support as well. For if the Virgin Mary is the "Mother" of us all, then we are all "brothers and sisters." For those of us who have siblings, just about all of us fought with them when we were children. As adults, hopefully we see our siblings as our closest friends. As we mature spiritually, we should develop friendships that center on spirituality, to help one another and encourage one another to grow in Christ.

We are supposed to call one another "brother" and "sister." We are supposed to see the church as our "family." We are supposed to regard the Virgin Mary as our "Mother," rendering her the honor due to our birth mothers, allowing her example to nurture and teach us, so that through her, we may be led to spiritual maturity.

Saint Paul speaks of the church as family when he writes, in Ephesians 4:11-13: *"And His (Christ's) gifts were that some should be apostles, some prophets, some evangelists, some pastors and teachers, to equip the saints for the work of ministry, for building up the body of Christ, until we all attain the unity of the faith and the knowledge of the Son of God, to mature manhood (personhood), to the measure of the stature of the fullness of Christ."* The Father of our Family is Christ Himself. The Mother is the Virgin Mary. The children are all of us!

> *Seeing You hanging on the Cross, O Christ, your Mother cried aloud: "What strange mystery do I see, my Son? How, do You, the Giver of Life, with Your flesh transfixed, die upon the Wood?" (From the 15th Antiphon of the Service of the 12 Gospels on Holy Thursday Evening, Trans. by Fr. George Papadeas)*

Honor your "Mothers" today—Your birth mother; the Virgin Mary; and the Church, by honoring one another!

Fifth Sunday of Lent—St. Mary of Egypt

What Will Your Last Words Be?

It was now about the sixth hour, and there was darkness over the whole land until the ninth hour, while the sun's light failed; and the curtain of the temple was torn in two. Then Jesus, crying with a loud voice, said, "Father, into Thy hands I commit my spirit!"
Luke 23:44-46
(From the Gospel of the Sixth Hour on Good Friday Morning)

The "Hours" according to Tradition, mark the time of day according to the hours of sunlight. In Biblical times, there were no watches. So, the "first hour" was when the sun arose, the "third hour" was mid-morning. The "sixth hour" was midday. The "ninth hour" was mid-afternoon. The "twelfth hour" was the sunset. The "hour" was not a sixty-minute period of time. In winter the "hours" could be much shorter. In summer they could be much longer. In modern times, if one counts the "hours" as equal periods of time, that would make the first hour about 6:00 A.M., with the third hour being 9:00 A.M., the sixth hour between noon, the ninth hour being 3:00 P.M., with the twelfth hour, or sunset, being 6:00 P.M.

At the sixth hour, in the middle of the day, the sun's light failed, and so did the light of the moon. There was darkness over the whole land. When I think of this scene, I think of the juxtaposition of the Nativity. At the Incarnation, in the middle of the night, the sky was brightened by a multitude of angels. All creation—the powerful (magi), the simple (shepherds), the animals, stars, angels and the earth itself (the cave)—came to worship the Creator, Incarnate in its midst. At the Crucifixion, it was as if all of Creation was mourning the death of its Creator. The great light, the sun, hid its face, unable to bear the sight of its Creator being put to death by His Creation.

The temple, seen by the people as God's home on earth, was breaking apart in an earthquake. The curtain, which prohibited the people from seeing the Holy of Holies, was ripped in two. Jesus said, "*I thirst*" (John 19:28). This showed us His human condition of fatigue and dehydration. It also reminds us of our own state of fatigue and how our thirst is quenched only when we thirst for Christ.

The last words of Christ showed His total trust in God, to His last breath. He said, *"Father, into Thy hands I commit my spirit."* Then we read in John 19:30, *"He bowed His head, and gave up His spirit."* In most movies, when someone dies, first the last breath is taken, and then there is a "dramatic" falling of the head. In the case of the crucifixion and death of Christ, He first bowed His head, and then yielded up His spirit, an act of both trust in God, and His Lordship, that He is Lord even in His own death.

Many people are familiar with a team-building activity called the "trust fall." In this activity, a person mounts a platform several feet off of the ground. Below him or her are assembled many people who will "catch" him or her. The person stands with his or her back to everyone else, crosses arms over the chest, closes his or her eyes, stands totally straight, and falls backwards, trusting in the others to catch him or her. This activity requires total trust. Because to uncross arms, or to look backwards, or to fall without being totally stiff, could cause injury to either the person falling or the people catching. I have done this exercise many times, and as soon as one gets over the initial fear of falling and not being caught, as soon as one learns to have faith in the people catching, this experience is actually very liberating, because it allows one to just "let go" and trust.

The ultimate "trust fall" occurs when we die. When we close our eyes for one last time, take one final breath, and "fall asleep" in death. I would think that the ultimate way to pass from this life is with the hope of eternal life, and with the words of Christ, *"Father, into Thy hands I commit my spirit,"* with the faith of Christ, to bow one's head, and let go, knowing that God will "catch" us.

If one doesn't believe in God, I would think his last words would be something like "no, no, no!" words of fear that indeed everything is coming to an end, that an unknown or empty future is about to begin. Spend a moment today thinking about what your last words on this earth would be. I'm sure in them there would be words of love expressed to our families and friends, but what would be the last words that we expressed to our God? I would think that they would be the words of the repentant thief—*"Lord, remember me in Your Kingdom"*—or the words of Christ Himself—*"Father, into Thy hands I commit my spirit."*

> *He who clothed Himself with light as with a garment, stood naked at the judgment; and received blows on His cheeks from the hand which He had fashioned. When the lawless people nailed the Lord of glory to the Cross, then the veil of the temple was rent, and the sun went dark, unable to endure the spectacle of God blasphemed, before Whom all the universe trembles. Him let us worship. (From the 10th Antiphon of Service of the 12 Gospels on Holy Thursday evening, Trans by Fr. George Papadeas)*

Think about your "last words" today!

Monday of the Sixth Week of Lent

The Passover in the Old and New Testaments

Since it was the day of Preparation, in order to prevent the bodies from remaining on the cross on the Sabbath (for that Sabbath was a high day), the Jews asked Pilate that their legs might be broken, and that they might be taken away. So the soldiers came and broke the legs of the first, and of the other who had been crucified with Him; but when they came to Jesus and saw that He was already dead, they did not break His legs. But one of the soldiers pierced His side with a spear, and at once there came out blood and water. He who saw it has borne witness—his testimony is true, and he knows that he tells the truth—that you also may believe. For these things took place that the scripture might be fulfilled, "Not a bone of Him shall be broken." And again another scripture says, "They shall look on Him whom they have pierced."
John 19:31-37
(From the Gospel of the Vespers on Good Friday Afternoon)

We know that the Bible is divided into two parts: the Old and New Testaments. The Old Testament contains the history of God's people—Creation, the Fall, the Law, and the Prophecies of the Prophets foretelling of the coming Messiah who would save the people from their sins, from their fallen state and banishment from Paradise. The New Testament contains the earthly and salvific ministry of Jesus Christ, the establishment of the early church, and pastoral letters to the early churches.

The "prophecies" of the Old Testament are fulfilled in the person of Jesus Christ. The Crucifixion is "foretold" as far back as the Old Testament book of Exodus, with the establishment of the Passover. Most of us know that the children of Israel were enslaved in Egypt. Pharaoh was their taskmaster. God told Moses to go to Pharaoh and tell him to let the people go. Pharaoh refused. So, God, through Moses, afflicted Egypt with a series of plagues. After each plague, Pharaoh would agree to let the people go, but then his heart would harden and he would refuse.

The tenth plague was the death of the first-born son in all the Egyptian homes. The angel of death would "pass over" all the houses and kill the first-born son in each house. The people of Israel would have their children spared by placing the blood of a lamb over their doorways, and in this way, the angel would "pass over" their homes and spare their children. The blood of the lamb would be the sign that they were God's people and would lead to the "saving" or "salvation" of their children. This "passing over" is the origin of the Jewish feast of the Passover.

In Exodus 12, we read about some of the details of this Passover:

The lamb had to be without blemish. Verse 5

The people shall eat the flesh of the lamb. Verse 8

God said, "The blood shall be a sign for you, upon the houses where you are; and when I see the blood, I will pass over you, and no plague shall fall upon you to destroy you, when I smite the land of Egypt." Verse 13

The Passover would be a memorial day, kept forever as a feast to the Lord. Verse 14

Lambs were to be selected and killed. Verse 21

Not one bone of the Passover lamb could be broken. Verse 46

All of these preparations for the Jewish Passover prefigure the Crucifixion of Christ. In the act of the Crucifixion and Resurrection, we receive a "new" Passover. Let's look at a comparison of the original Passover feast with the Crucifixion:

Jesus is the "Lamb of God." In John 1:29, John reveals Jesus by saying *"Behold, the Lamb of God, who takes away the sin of the world!"*

Jesus remains without blemish, without sin.

We are to partake of His flesh and blood: *"He who eats My flesh and drinks My Blood abides in Me and I in Him"* (John 6:56).

The blood of Christ, both His shedding of it for us, and us partaking of it, is what allows us to "pass over" from death to eternal life. It is the only way by which we can do this, the only thing that will spare us from death. We still keep Pascha (the "new" Passover) as a feast to the Lord.

Jesus was crucified at the same hour as the Passover Lambs in Jerusalem on Good Friday.

Not one of His bones was broken.

Christ is called "The New Passover," because by His blood we are saved from death.

Passover is what allowed the Egyptians to be delivered from Pharaoh. The New Passover, Pascha, the Resurrection of Christ, is what allows us to be delivered from death and to attain eternal life.

> *Christ, our God, Who is our Passover, is sacrificed for us; therefore let us not keep the Feast as the Judeans, but let us cleanse ourselves from every defilement, and sincerely beseech Him: "Arise, O Lord, and in Your mercy, save us." (From the 15th Antiphon of the Service of the 12 Gospels on Holy Thursday Evening, Trans. by Fr. George Papadeas)*

Prepare for your personal "Passover" today and every day.

Tuesday of the Sixth Week of Lent

The Executioner of Christ, Who Became a Saint

When the centurion and those who were with him, keeping watch over Jesus, saw the earthquake and what took place, they were filled with awe, and said, "Truly this was the Son of God!"
Matthew 27:54
(From the Gospel of Vespers on Good Friday Afternoon)

It is truly amazing how the Lord calls all kinds of people in all kinds of circumstances to serve Him. Some people who have committed the greatest sins and mistakes have become saints. It is said that every saint has a past and every sinner has a future. It is not a person's past mistakes that costs one the ability to live a saintly life. Repentance, change, is what allows any person to be a Godly person, and even allows one who has committed a grievous sin to become a saint! Consider the life of St. Longinus:

Longinus was a Roman centurion, a military officer with one hundred soldiers under his command. When Jesus was crucified, it was a band of soldiers under Longinus who conducted the execution. Because the Crucifixion occurred on Friday afternoon, the Jewish leaders were concerned that it be concluded before the Sabbath, for no work, not even an execution was allowed on the Sabbath. So, the soldiers broke the legs of the two thieves, because unable to raise themselves to breathe, they would quickly expire. They did not break the legs of Jesus, because He was already dead and there was no need to.

As we read in the previous reflection, after Jesus expired on the Cross, *"one of the soldiers pierced His side with a spear and at once there came out blood and water"* (John 19:34). This soldier, according to Church Tradition, was Longinus, the Centurion. In fact, some historians are not sure if Longinus was the actual birth name of the Centurion, or rather a name now given to him since he was the one who held the spear, which is "longhi" in Greek.

Longinus had a disease in his eyes and was healed of his affliction when the blood and water poured forth from the side of Christ and touched his eyes. Looking upon all that had happened shook Longinus to the depths of his soul, and he confessed his faith that "Truly this was the

Son of God." Longinus and his band of soldiers also stood guard at the tomb and were present at the Resurrection. The Jewish authorities attempted to bribe the soldiers, but Longinus and two others refused to be paid for their silence. They declared their belief in Christ and in the Resurrection. They left the military service, were baptized and they went out to preach the good news of Christ in Cappadocia.

Upon hearing of mass conversions in Cappadocia, the Jewish authorities persuaded Pontius Pilate to send soldiers to Cappadocia to kill Longinus and his companions. They beheaded the three of them, taking the head of Longinus back to Pontius Pilate. Pilate ordered the head be thrown into a garbage heap outside of the city. A blind woman whose son was ill and died was "led" by a dream about Saint Longinus to find his head, which, when she touched it, caused her sight to come back. She buried the head of St. Longinus together with her son. Saint Longinus is commemorated on October 16 in the Orthodox Church and on March 15 in the Roman Catholic Church. (Some of the above information was gathered from the website of the Orthodox Church in America, or OCA, under the lives of the saints section.)

There are at least three lessons to take away from the story of St. Longinus. First, even a sinful person can become a saint. Here was the man who presided over the Crucifixion of Christ, who is now remembered as a Saint, not as an executioner. Second, Longinus had a moment of conversion, when his whole life changed. Each genuine Christian will have one (if not more) conversion moment(s), when something will happen that will erase all doubt that Jesus Christ is the Son of God, our Savior. Third, Longinus seized on the moment and allowed it to change his life. He went from soldier of Rome to soldier of Christ, from leader of armies to leader of the Christian army; from killer of Christ, to leader of Christ's church. We have to seize on our moments of conversion to move us to change, and to become not only loyal soldiers, but also devout and enthusiastic leaders.

> *Your Cross, O Lord, is life and resurrection to Your people; and trusting in it, we praise You, our crucified Lord. Have mercy on us. (From the 15th Antiphon of the Service of the 12 Gospels on Holy Thursday evening, Trans. by Fr. George Papadeas)*

Allow our Savior to change your life today!

Wednesday of the Sixth Week of Lent

Will We Be Seekers? Attendees? Masters?

Joseph of Arimathea, a respected member of the council, who was also himself looking for the kingdom of God, took courage and went to Pilate, and asked for the Body of Jesus. And Pilate wondered if He were already dead; and summoning the centurion, he asked him whether He was already dead. And when he learned from the centurion that He was dead, he granted the Body to Joseph. And he bought a linen shroud, and taking Him down, wrapped Him in the linen shroud, and laid Him in a tomb which had been hewn out of the rock; and he rolled a stone against the door of the tomb. Mary Magdalene and Mary the mother of Joses saw where He was laid.
Mark 15:43-47
(From the Tenth Gospel on Holy Thursday Evening)

Joseph of Arimathea is, in my opinion, one of the honorable figures in the Passion narrative. He was, as we read in the Gospels, "a respected member of the Council," who at the same time "was also himself looking for the kingdom of God." He did not pretend to be a "know it all" as some of his contemporaries were doing. Instead he was seeking something greater than himself. Pontius Pilate had a moment where he contemplated "what is truth," but then couldn't allow himself to see truth for fear of what it might cost him. Joseph, on the other hand, not only contemplated "truth," but also he "took courage" and did something—He "went to Pilate and asked for the Body of Jesus." This was a courageous act that could easily have led Joseph to suffer a similar demise as the Lord did. After all, Joseph was going to the very man who had handed down a death sentence. Pilate had no reason to be loyal to Joseph. Though perhaps, having washed his hands of the whole thing, Pilate was anxious to have the whole episode behind him and the faster someone could bury the Body of Jesus, the quicker the whole thing might go away.

We are told in John 19:39 that Joseph was accompanied by Nicodemus, who had approached Jesus secretly (John 3) to ask Him questions. Nicodemus had also defended Jesus, reminding his peers in the Sanhedrin that the law required a trial before a person could be judged (John 7:50-51). Nicodemus was a Pharisee, so this was a courageous act for him as well.

As I reflect on the story of Joseph and Nicodemus, two men of authority in the Jewish temple who were also courageous "seekers," it leads me to three classifications of people who witnessed the Crucifixion: masters, attendees and seekers. The "masters" were the Jewish and Roman authorities who were directly responsible for the death of Christ. They carried out the event with violence and arrogance, masters of tragedy, masters filled with hatred and ego. They weren't interested in hearing about Christ, they had already made up their mind what was truth.

The "attendees" were all those who stood silently by. If they believed, they lacked the courage to express it. If they felt an injustice was being done, they didn't step forward to stop it. It is probably unfair to say that they were complicit with the "masters" in carrying out the execution of the Lord, but we also know that while hatred is a sin, indifference can be as well.

The "seekers" are those who had not necessarily "grasped" the entire truth of Christ, but they were eager to learn more. The "seekers" included Joseph and Nicodemus, as well as the myrrh-bearing women who ministered to Jesus in death.

Many Christians fit into one of these three categories. In contemporary context, there are the "masters" of the faith, who in some cases, work against the faith. There are entire books written on the subject of "Antagonists in the Church." There are some Christians who are not necessarily antagonistic, but who have no desire to learn more about Christ—they know what they know and are content with that. Even as they get older, and become concerned for their mortality, they are closed off to growing in their faith. The irony is that there are no "masters" of the faith—we *all* have a ways to go. Only saints who have lived in Christ and died in Him can truly be considered masters of the faith.

There are some Christians who are "attendees." They "attend" services, either seldom or even regularly, but they really don't grasp what is going on. They attend in body, but the mind and the spirit do not attend with them. They also seem content to not stretch their comfort zones when it comes to growing in the faith.

Which brings us to the category of "seekers." To be a "seeker" one has to be an "attendee," he has to be present in body. To be a "seeker" one has to realize that he is not a "master," that he still has room to grow in his faith. In order to be a "seeker," one must be present not only in body, but in mind and in spirit, with a mind that is humble enough to admit it doesn't know everything, and a spirit that is open to pushing the bounds of one's comfort zone in order to more deeply experience the faith. Indeed, it takes "courage" to be a seeker.

Joseph and Nicodemus inspire and motivate me because, while they didn't start off in the right place (masters), they certainly ended up in the right place (seekers). This inspires me that there can be hope for anyone who comes to God as a seeker. The scriptures confirm this in their use of the word "seek." Notice how Jesus' teachings below do not use the word "attendee" or "master," but rather emphasize the importance and the reward of being a "seeker."

"Seek first His kingdom and His righteousness, and all these things will be given to you as well" (Matt. 6:33).

"Ask and it will be given to you; seek and you will find; knock and the door will be opened to you. For everyone who asks receives; the one who seeks finds; and to the one who knocks, the door will be opened" (Luke 11:9-10).

As you attend services this Holy Week, and as you approach your Christian life in the months and years to come, do not consider yourself a "master," or be content with being an "attendee," but come to Christ continually as a "seeker" because it is the seeker who finds Christ!

> *You Who clothed Yourself with light as a garment, Joseph with Nicodemus, brought down from the Cross, and seeing You dead, naked and unburied, felt deeply a sympathetic lament, and in grieving said: "Woe to me, sweetest Jesus! Whom, but a short while ago, when the sun beheld You hanging on the Cross, enshrouded itself in darkness, and the earth quaked in fear, and the veil of the Temple was rent asunder. But lo, I now, see, that You willingly underwent death for my sake. How then shall I array You for burial, my God? Or how shall I wrap You in a shroud? And with what hands can I touch Your sacred Body? Or what dirges shall I chant for Your funeral, O Merciful One? I magnify Your Passion; I praise in hymn Your Burial, with Your Resurrection, crying aloud: Lord, glory to You." (Doxastikon of the Vespers on Good Friday Afternoon, Trans. by Fr. George Papadeas)*

Be a seeker today!

Thursday of the Sixth Week of Lent

The Fulfilling of a Journey

*He was despised and rejected by men; a man of sorrows, and acquainted with grief;
and as one from whom men hide their faces He was despised, and we esteemed Him not.
Surely he has borne our griefs and carried our sorrows; yet we esteemed Him stricken,
smitten by God, and afflicted. But He was wounded for our transgressions, He was bruised
for our iniquities; upon Him was the chastisement that made us whole,
and with His stripes we are healed. All we like sheep have gone astray; we have turned
every one to his own way; and the Lord has laid on Him the iniquity of us all.
He was oppressed, and He was afflicted, yet He opened not his mouth;
like a lamb that is led to the slaughter, and like a sheep that before its shearers is dumb,
so He opened not His mouth. By oppression and judgment He was taken away;
and as for His generation, who considered that He was cut off out of the land of the living,
stricken for the transgression of My people? And they made His grave with the wicked and
with a rich man in His death, although He had done no violence,
and there was no deceit in His mouth.
Isaiah 53:3-9
(From a Prophecy Reading at the Vespers on Good Friday Afternoon)*

The Passion of Christ is told in all four of the Gospels in the New Testament. In each Gospel account, the story unfolds in consecutive chapters in a way that is easy to follow. The entire story of the Passion of Christ is also told in the prophecies of the Old Testament. However, unlike the New Testament, it is not told in consecutive chapters. If you read an "annotated" Bible, you will see references to Old Testament scriptures throughout the accounts of Christ's Passion. One of the places His Crucifixion is foretold is in the Prophecy of Isaiah, which is quoted above and read on Good Friday afternoon.

The Prophecies in the Old Testament told God's people what was coming for two reasons: First, so that they would recognize what was happening when Christ came, that HE was going to be the fulfillment of ALL of these things. When all of these prophecies came to fulfillment in ONE person, certainly He would be unmistakably recognized as the Christ. Second, so that until Christ came, the people would have hope that indeed the Messiah was coming, and in the long years of waiting, they would not lose hope for salvation.

Christ has come, and did all the things that it was foretold that He was going to do. The people in Old Testament times were told to wait for the Messiah. In New Testament times, we have been taught by Christ to wait for His return, and for the inheritance of His Heavenly Kingdom. Christ gave us teachings on what is going to happen and how we are to live as we await this future eventuality. So, as in the Old Testament times, we, too, live in an age of expectation. Unlike Old Testament times, we also live in the age of Christ. We have our Messiah. We have His glory in the here and now. We have His promise for greater glory to come. The Church is here to teach us about Christ and to sustain us in our hope in this life as we journey to everlasting life. Life's journey will have its fulfillment in eternal life.

This week marks the end of the Lenten journey, which will have its fulfillment in Holy Week. The whole point of Triodion and Lent, this journey which now nears completion of its ninth week, was to lead us to this point. We have been given all the signs—humility, repentance, charity, fasting, prayer, and confession. Hopefully, we have embraced these signs. Even if we haven't, there is still time, the Holy Week journey has not yet begun. We are now on the fast road to the fulfillment of these signs in the Holy Week journey—healing, recommitment, and renewal.

In these reflections, we've met people who saw signs and missed them—Judas, the Pharisees, the crowds. We've met people who saw the signs and couldn't act on them—Peter, Pilate. We saw people who missed all the signs and still found redemption—the repentant thief, the centurion, Joseph of Arimathea, Nicodemus.

We—you and I—we have seen the signs. If you've read these reflections throughout Lent, we've studied them. There are two steps left. The first remaining step I will share today. The second and final step I will share tomorrow. The first of the remaining steps is the Holy Week journey that is about to be upon us. Will we stand with Christ, will we put ourselves there with Him? At the tomb of Lazarus, in the streets of Jerusalem on Palm Sunday, in the quiet teaching moments of Holy Monday and Holy Tuesday, in the upper room for the washing of our bodies and souls, at the table of the Eucharist, watching in the garden, standing at the cross, weeping at the tomb, and finally seeing the tomb empty on Pascha.

The prophecies of the Old Testament were fulfilled in Christ. The teachings of Christ will be fulfilled in eternal life, after we first pass before the awesome Judgment Seat. The journey of Lent is about to be fulfilled in Holy Week. If you've seen the "signs," prepare yourself to see them fulfilled. Even if you've missed all the signs, it's not too late. Plan out your time these next two days so that beginning Saturday you can put the Holy Week journey as your primary focus—having repented, fasted, and prepared, let us move toward healing, renewal, and recommitment.

The Lamb, which Isaiah proclaimed, comes willingly to the slaughter, and gives His back to scourging, and His cheeks to blows. HE turns not away His face from the shame of spittings, and He is condemned to a dishonorable death. The sinless

One, willingly submits to all, that unto all He may bestow the resurrection from the dead. (From the Vesperal Liturgy on Holy Thursday Morning, Trans. by Fr. George Papadeas)

Make your Holy Week plan today if you haven't already!

Friday of the Sixth Week of Lent

Who is Going to Step Forward?

For Thy name's sake do not give us up utterly, and do not break Thy covenant, and do not withdraw Thy mercy from us, for the sake of Abraham Thy beloved and for the sake of Isaac Thy servant and Israel Thy holy one, to whom Thou didst promise to make their descendants as many as the stars of heaven and as the sand on the shore of the sea. For we, O Lord, have become fewer than any nation, and are brought low this day in all the world because of our sins. And at this time there is no prince, or prophet, or leader, no burnt offering, or sacrifice, or oblation, or incense, no place to make an offering before Thee or to find mercy. Yet with a contrite heart and a humble spirit may we be accepted, as though it were with burnt offerings of rams and bulls, and with tens of thousands of fat lambs; such may our sacrifice be in Thy sight this day, and may we wholly follow Thee, for there will be no shame for those who trust in Thee. And now with all our heart we follow Thee, we fear Thee and seek Thy face. Do not put us to shame, but deal with us in Thy forbearance and in Thy abundant mercy. Deliver us in accordance with thy marvelous works, and give glory to Thy name, O Lord! Let all who do harm to Thy servants be put to shame; let them be disgraced and deprived of all power and dominion, and let their strength be broken. Let them know that Thou art the Lord, the only God, glorious over the whole world."
(This text appears in two places in Scripture. It appears in the Septuagint translation of the Book of Daniel, Chapter 3:35-45; and in the Revised Standard Version as an Apocryphal Book called "Song of the Three Young Men," which consists of one chapter, of which these are verses 11-22)

On Holy Saturday morning, as we await the first announcement of the Resurrection of Christ, we hear three prophecy readings. The first is from the book of Genesis, and is about the Creation of the world. The Church takes us all the way back to the beginning, as the world was when it was created by God. Because through the Cross and Resurrection, the world has been re-created by God. God created the world perfect. The world fell through the sin of mankind. The world is re-created and redeemed through the death and Resurrection of Christ.

The second prophecy is from the book of Jonah. Jonah was asked by God to go to Nineveh and he refused. So he boarded a ship and journeyed in a different direction. When the seas became rough and threatened to sink his ship, Jonah told the men on board that he was the cause of the wind and waves. He was then thrown overboard. A giant fish (sometimes depicted as a whale) swallowed Jonah. He spent three days in the belly of the fish, before the fish spit him out and then he went to Nineveh as he was asked. Though he didn't go without complaint. The journey of Jonah is the journey of the human race. Told by God what His hope was for us, we nonetheless headed in a different direction (the Fall). In the stormy seas that ensued, one man had to be cast overboard (Christ). Swallowed by the fish, He remained for three days in its belly (prefigures the three days in the tomb). Coming out of the fish (the Resurrection), He went to preach to Nineveh (all those who do not know God). While the church continues to preach, it is certainly not without complaints, just like Jonah.

The third prophecy is from the book of Daniel. It is the story of three youths who refused to bow down to a golden statue set up by King Nebuchadnezzar. Nebuchadnezzar was so angry with these three young men—Shadrach, Meshach and Abednago—that he ordered them cast into a fiery furnace. (Their original Hebrew names were Hananiah, Azariah, and Mishael). In the midst of the flames, Azariah opened his mouth and offered the prayer quoted above. After offering this prayer, the Lord drove the fire out of the furnace, sending dew upon the flames, so that the three men were untouched by the fire.

This prophecy is the final step of the Christian journey. If the first step is seeing the signs and the second step is committing to them, then the third step is spreading the good news. Nebuchadnezzar represents all those who hate Christianity, all those who are ignorant of the truth. The fire is our world—its struggles, temptations, and even the persecution of Christians we are seeing today. Who is Azarias? The one who stands up for Christ.

So, the questions are: Who is going to stand up for Christ? Who is going bring the hope of Christ in the midst of the flames? We know that Christ will protect us from the world, as he protected the three holy children from the fire. We need people to stand up with confidence, to those who build the golden statues, and not bow down to them. The golden statue is fame and fortune, gold and riches, the things that our world seems to bow down to, the things in our world that run counter to the message of Christ. Will we bow down as well? Or will we be different.

The prayer reminds us that there is *"no prince, or prophet, or leader, no burnt offering or sacrifice, or oblation or incense, no place to make an offering before Thee or to find mercy."* The only place we can go for deliverance is CHRIST. So, we need to resist the temptation to bow down at the golden statues that our secular world has set up. We need to not be afraid of being cast into the furnace of ridicule if we stand up for Christ. Many people, ourselves included, stand up in anger every day—on the roads, at the mall, on television. One cannot seem to find success unless he causes another to fail. Our world has made it all about ourselves. The journey of the Christian is to make it all about God. Heaven will be all about the Lord. In heaven we will behold God's glory, all the time. It will be *all* about Him. We need people to share this message because this is the message of hope and love, which will endure all things, including life's hardships, so that one day, when we enter our earthly tomb, we can emerge in a heavenly Resurrection.

We've made the preparations. Now is the time to begin the journey of Holy Week. The next week of reflections, beginning tomorrow, will offer one scriptural highlight of each day of the Holy Week journey, culminating in the Resurrection of Christ on Pascha. Make this journey with an idea of what you'll do after Pascha. Will you stay committed? Will you help others find Christ? Will you allow this experience to renew you? Will you allow it to change you? Will you step forward? By God's grace, I hope we, myself included, will answer *yes*.

> *Blessed are You, O Lord, the God of our fathers; the most praised and most exalted to all ages; and blessed is the Name of Your Glory, the Holy and most praised, and exalted above all, to the ages. Blessed are You in the Holy Temple of Your Glory; the most praised, and exalted above all, forever. Blessed are You, Who looks over the depths, and are seated on the Cherubim; the most praised and exalted above all forever. Blessed are you on the Throne of Your Kingdom, the most praised and exalted above all, forever. Blessed are You in the firmament of Heaven, and praised and gloried to all ages. (The Hymn of the Three Youths, from Vesperal Liturgy on Holy Saturday Morning, Trans. by Fr. George Papadeas, found in Daniel 3:52-26 of the Septuagint, and in the Song of the Three Young Men 1:29-34)*

Have a blessed and meaningful Holy Week journey!

PART THREE—THE GREAT AND HOLY WEEK

Palm Sunday-The Last Supper-The Entombment of Christ

Thru the hand of Fr. Anthony Salzman, www.imageandlikeness.com

Saturday of Lazarus

I AM the Resurrection and the Life

Jesus said to her, "I am the resurrection and the life; he who believes in Me, though he die, yet shall he live, and whoever lives and believes in Me shall never die.
John 11:25-26
(Gospel on the Saturday of Lazarus)

A few years ago, an older parishioner passed away. She had liveda long life, and she was a person of great faith. The night before she passed away, I visited her in a nursing facility. She was suffering from dementia and had long ago lost her ability to carry on conversation. She came to church rarely and only with great difficulty. I will always remember that last visit because I wanted her to receive Holy Communion and had hoped that she was conscious enough to do it. I remember singing a few hymns and this seemed to wake her up enough so that I could offer Holy Communion to her. This beautiful lady was a life-long church-goer. She had some pretty tough stuff thrown at her in her life, but she also had a deep and abiding faith. As I was about to leave, I decided, since I knew this was going to be the last time I ever saw her alive, that I should sing her favorite hymn, "Christ is Risen," even though we were not in the Paschal season. As I sang the hymn, she started to sing with me. This was truly amazing, as she couldn't remember my name, much less carry on a conversation, but she recognized Christ and she sang this most joyful hymn as she lay dying. In fact, she passed away very shortly after I left.

The next day, I started writing out a notice to send to our parishioners informing them of the funeral arrangements. As I wrote my customary "It is with great sadness that I inform you that _____ has passed away, " I paused and thought to myself, "Am I really sad about this?" Of course, I was sad on a human level, this was someone I really loved. As a priest, and certainly as a Christian, how could I not be anything but happy about this? I decided that day to begin all funeral notices with these two verses above from the Gospel of John, read in the Gospel on the Saturday of Lazarus. I also changed how I described the event of death, from "passed away" to "fell asleep in the hope of the Resurrection to eternal life."

Indeed, today's event of the Saturday of Lazarus is a reminder to all that there is life after death, and this is possible because of, and only because of, the power of Jesus Christ. He is Lord of the living and the dead.

In the raising of Lazarus, Jesus shows both His humanity and His divinity. He shows His humanity because when He goes to the tomb of Lazarus, He pauses to weep, a very human emotion. This is why it is not inappropriate to weep when someone dies. If the Son of God shed tears for His friend, it is totally acceptable for us to shed tears as well. In fact, there are two times in the Bible that we read that Jesus wept. The first was at the tomb of Lazarus and the second time was in the Garden of Gethsemane, as He wept about His own impending death.

Being scared of dying is okay too. To fear the pain that often goes with the dying process is something to be concerned with. Physical death, however, is the necessary "rite of passage" to attain eternal life. So when one "passes away in the hope of eternal life," meaning when one has lived a life that has honored God, then our spiritual emotion for them should be one of joy.

Perhaps the healthiest way to look at death is a passage to everlasting life. For the person who is going there, we have joy. For us who are left behind, we have human sorrow. For the person who is leaving, there is sadness to leave others behind. There is spiritual joy for what is to come.

Our church, I believe, has a healthy view of death. Not only do we have memorial services to remember and honor those who have passed away. We even consider them to remain part of the church. We call the church on earth the "church militant," the fighting church, still working its way to salvation. We call the church of heaven "the church triumphant," meaning the segment of the church whose earthly battle has been won, whose members are now beginning their heavenly reward and waiting for us to join them. These two segments of the church—the church militant and the church triumphant—are shown in a visible way on the stole that the priest wears for every liturgical act. Each stole has two layers of fringe on the bottom, one for the church militant and one for the church triumphant, as a reminder that even those who pass away remain part of our church, and when we gather to pray, even TWO people (the priest and one other person, as in confession), that we gather with the WHOLE of the church—church militant and church triumphant—to pray.

Let's change some terminology—we define "life" as the time we spend on earth. We define "death" as the time when "life" ends. In the eyes of God, "life" means being in the presence of God, and "death" denotes the absence of God. One who is "dead" is absent from God. That's why those who are in heaven are said to inherit "eternal life," and those who are in hell are the ones who are truly "dead." "Life" as we call it, should be redefined as "preparation." Our time on earth prepares us for the life to come. "Death," is our "passing" away from earth. So, using these new terms, we "prepare" during our time on earth. At the end of that time, we "pass away" and go to God for judgment, after which we enter either "death" (Hell) or "life" (Heaven). This is why Jesus says, *"he who believes in Me, though He die, yet shall He live, and whoever lives and believes in Me shall never die."* Because if physical death is merely a passing to an eternal life with God, the person who passes continues to live and can never die. This is cause for spiritual joy indeed.

This doesn't mean we don't have the right to grieve, especially when a person dies young. It also doesn't mean we don't have the right to scratch our heads or even question God's plan especially when someone dies suddenly or in an accident. There are things that happen in life that will leave us scratching our heads and even questioning God. It is especially in these times, when we have to have the faith of Martha, who even though she was saddened by the death of her brother, who was young, still found faith to say to the Lord, *"I believe that You are the Christ, the Son of God, He who is coming into the world"* (John 11:27). In these times we need spiritual support from others. The Christian life is not an easy one, but remember that this life, whether it be good or terrible, is just a preparation for the time that will count, because it will be permanent and eternal, it will either be life or death.

O Lord, even as You said to Martha: I am the Resurrection; so You fulfilled Your word in action by calling back Lazarus from Hades. Resurrect me, also, for I am dead through passions. I beseech You, compassionate One who loves mankind. (From the Praises of Saturday of Lazarus, Trans. by Fr. Seraphim Dedes)

Work toward eternal life today!

Palm Sunday

Fear Not Daughter of Zion—Your King is Coming on a DONKEY

And Jesus found a young ass and sat upon it; as it is written,
"Fear not, daughter of Zion; behold, your King is coming, sitting on an ass's colt!"
His disciples did not understand this at first; but when Jesus was glorified, then they
remembered that this had been written of Him and had been done to Him.
John 12:14-16
(Gospel of the Divine Liturgy on Palm Sunday)

When you think of the word "King," what is the first thing that comes to mind? Maybe a crown, a castle, loyal subject, flowing robes, rich banquets, a large army, trumpets and banners. I'm sure that the word "donkey" is not the first word that comes to mind.

Perhaps this is why after the crowded scene in Jerusalem on Palm Sunday ended, everyone was left wondering what it meant. The Gospel of John even says that the Disciples didn't understand the significance of what had happened. The people of Jerusalem were confused. Even the Temple elite were perplexed. How could anyone interpret a man riding on a donkey as the sign of an impending military overthrow?

What do you think of when you hear the word "Glory"? I think of brightness, majestic mountains, powerful waterfalls, crashing waves, millions of stars in a cloudless sky. I don't think of holding a screaming baby, or comforting someone who is sad, or helping a frustrated child with his homework, or visiting an intensive care unit to see someone who is seriously sick.

Christ made a statement on Palm Sunday. That statement is that being a King or a leader is not about the strength of an army or being a conqueror. It was that His "kingship" was not to lead His followers to political freedom, but to spiritual freedom. The path to glory was not going to be lined with material victory, but with material poverty. Christ could have ridden into Jerusalem on the most expensive chariot, surrounded by armies of angels, yet He chose to ride a simple donkey, not even a championship racehorse.

The path to God's glory does not wind through big houses, loud restaurants or exciting athletic contests. The path to God's glory winds through humility—taking care of those who need help, and doing good not for the sake of material reward, but for the purpose of eternal life, doing it for the Lord.

Palm Sunday "turned the tables" on everything society taught then and still teaches. We ride our children to be great students, so that they will get great jobs and make great money. We coach them to be good athletes with the hope that they might become professional athletes with the fame and fortune that follow. We occupy ourselves with the pursuit of the almighty dollar so that we can build on our material wealth. We forget sometimes to instill humility in our children, or seek it ourselves.

There is nothing wrong with having a nice home, or having a nice job, or taking a nice trip, or having your child get into a nice college. In the midst of all of this, let us not forget the image of our Lord riding on a simple donkey. Let us not forget that the path to His glory is not found by achieving our own glory, but in taking His path, one of humility and servitude.

"Fear not, daughter of Zion; behold, your King is coming, sitting on an ass's colt!" We need to fear not, we the children of God, that our "King" calls us to humility. Fear not to comfort a child. Fear not to refrain from encouragement to sin. Fear not to visit the sick. Fear not to love your neighbor.

Remember that fear and love cannot co-exist. Growing in God's love necessitates ignoring fear of the consequences of following God, and ignoring the fear of stepping outside of our comfort zone which calls us to greater sense of self, in order to have a greater sense of Him!

> *Blessed is He who comes in the name of the Lord. God is the Lord, and He revealed Himself to us. Save us, O Son of God, who sat on a donkey's colt, we sing to You Alleluia. (Hymn of the Entrance of Palm Sunday, Trans. by Fr. Seraphim Dedes)*

Never fear humility!

Holy Monday

Stop Living an Old Testament Christianity

"Woe to you, scribes and Pharisees, hypocrites! For you tithe mint and dill and cumin, and have neglected the weightier matters of the law, justice and mercy and faith; these you ought to have done, without neglecting the others.
Matthew 23:23
(From the Gospel of the Bridegroom Service on Holy Monday Evening)

One day, when my son was about seven years old, we were driving somewhere and from the backseat, my son asked me, "Daddy, if the speed limit sign says '55,' why are you driving '65'?" Wow! How could I answer that question? If I said, "Son, that is just a guideline," then when I tried to enforce a rule at home, he could give me the same answer, "That's just a guideline." Or I could say, "That's just a suggestion, no one really does that." Except then, how could I enforce getting homework done? So, I politely thanked my son for bringing this to my attention and I pay careful attention to drive the speed limit, at least, hypocritically, when he is in the car.

Now, I confess that the reason I obey the traffic laws has nothing to do with my concern for the other drivers on the road. I don't want to pay for a ticket and I don't want to damage my car. Truth be told, I wish all other drivers stayed home and I had the road all to myself.

I guess if Jesus were to critique my driving, He would say that I am an "Old Testament" driver and maybe most of us are. For the New Testament driver cares more for the other drivers on the road. He is eager to let people change lanes in front of him. How many of us do that? The New Testament driver also maintains a safe driving distance and follows all the rules out of a genuine concern for the other drivers on the road, rather than because they are the rules. He has in his consciousness, a strong desire for everyone to get home in one piece.

There are many people who live according to the letter of the Law and have lost its spirit. Such were the Pharisees and Priests of the Temple. Jesus ridiculed them for their hypocrisy. They had made themselves gods and along with that had ruled with an iron hand. In Matthew 23:2-4, Jesus said to them and the multitudes, "*The scribes and the Pharisees sit on Moses' seat; so practice and observe whatever they tell you, but not what they do; for they preach, but do not practice. They bind heavy burdens, hard to bear, and lay them on men's shoulders."*

One of the "traps" in the Orthodox Church is that we are so "ritual heavy." Many people think that lighting a candle will get you into the Kingdom of Heaven or checking food for ingredients to make sure it doesn't contain any oil or dairy during the fasting periods. Every year, people will call the office asking what time Communion is offered on Holy Saturday, rather than asking what time the service starts. We can easily become focused on rituals and not faith, on form rather than substance.

Rituals help provide consistency and comfort to us. They are aids in expressing our faith, but we don't worship fasting, icons, vestments, or hymns sung in the right key. We worship Christ. He is at the center of everything.

If anything, Old Testament Christianity is very "comfortable." Imagine going to college and you have the opportunity to take one of two different classes—one that has a syllabus that tells you day by day what is expected and that's what you'll be graded on. The other says, "You'll be graded by how much you learn and how much you love the class," but doesn't offer a syllabus. Which class would you take? Most people would probably sign up for the first one.

I recently met with our women's Bible study group. We sat in a circle, had nice discussion, people eagerly shared feelings and stories, some even shed a few tears. It was very nice, comforting and supportive. I mentioned to the group, what would happen if we brought a group of violent gang members into the church and told them to have a Bible study group that would also function as a spiritual support group. Obviously, they would be nowhere near able to do this. First, we'd have to make some rules to keep everyone safe. We might even have to phrase the rules using profanity and slang, if that's the language they understand. We wouldn't worry initially about what they were learning. We'd be preoccupied with keeping everyone safe and we'd be focused on rules and safety. That, however, would not be the end goal. The end goal would be studying God's word in an encouraging and supportive environment and care would have to be taken to not lose sight of that goal while bringing them around to a more peaceful way of thinking.

Many of us are still stuck in Old Testament Christianity. We're all about rules and fairness, and we often forget about love and mercy. We still live in more of the "eye for an eye" mentality (Exod. 21:24) rather than the "forgive seventy times seven" mentality (Matt. 18:22). People are hesitant to admit wrong and ask forgiveness for fear of retribution or litigation. This is why we don't forgive as easily as we once did.

Christ shows us the ultimate example of mercy when He forgave those who crucified Him. So, while we don't necessarily need rules, in our churches and in society, we definitely need to show more mercy and have more faith and love. We cannot neglect these.

The Old Testament was all about rules. The New Testament is all about love.

The Bridegroom, surpassing all in comeliness, has called us to the spiritual wedding Feast. Through sharing in Your sufferings, remove the blotched raiment of my sins, and adorning me with a robe of glory of Your comeliness, make me a radiant guest of Your Kingdom, as a Merciful God. (From the Aposticha of the Bridegroom Service of Holy Monday Night, Trans. by Fr. George Papadeas)

Live a New Testament Christianity today!

Holy Tuesday

Wise or Foolish, Which are You?

Jesus said, "Then the kingdom of heaven shall be compared to ten maidens who took their lamps and went to meet the bridegroom. Five of them were foolish, and five were wise. For when the foolish took their lamps, they took no oil with them; but the wise took flasks of oil with their lamps. As the bridegroom was delayed, they all slumbered and slept. But at midnight there was a cry, 'Behold, the bridegroom! Come out to meet him.' Then all those maidens rose and trimmed their lamps. And the foolish said to the wise, 'Give us some of your oil, for our lamps are going out.' But the wise replied, 'Perhaps there will not be enough for us and for you; go rather to the dealers and buy for yourselves.' And while they went to buy, the bridegroom came, and those who were ready went in with him to the marriage feast; and the door was shut. Afterward the other maidens came also, saying, 'Lord, lord, open to us.' But he replied, 'Truly, I say to you, I do not know you.' Watch therefore, for you know neither the day nor the hour.
Matthew 25:1-13
(Gospel from the Pre-Sanctified Liturgy on Holy Tuesday Morning)

Most of us are familiar with the Parable of the Ten Maidens. This is another parable that is very rich in meaning, which has an application to life even today.

The Bridegroom is Christ. The marriage feast is the inheriting of everlasting life. The ten maidens are us. The lamps are our souls. The hour of the feast is unknown.

When the call came to "meet the bridegroom," the wise maidens had enough oil in their lamps to keep them lit. The foolish did not. They wrongly assumed that either they had enough oil, the other maidens would share their oil, or there would be enough warning to give them time to go out and buy oil.

When I was a child, I always thought that the wise maidens were mean because they wouldn't share their oil. After all, are we not supposed to share with those who have little? Why were those "mean" maidens rewarded and the poor ones punished?

As I have gotten older, and have come to a deeper understanding of the Bible, I now know that the oil represents our faith. While I can "share" my faith with you and you can "share" your faith with me, in the sense of telling one another about our faith, one cannot "cut his faith in half" and give half of his faith to someone else, the way someone can cut a sandwich in half and share it. Faith is something that is personal to each individual. Either one has faith, or he doesn't. Faith is something that we can learn about from others. It is certainly something we should share with others, but faith is a personal thing that is "possessed" by each individual.

Merely "being around" Godly people doesn't make one a Godly person, no more than hanging out in a garage makes one a car. Just "talking" about the faith doesn't do it either. There have been many occasions in my ministry where someone has died and when the family comes to make the funeral arrangements, they will say something like, "Uncle Joe was really a spiritual person, I know he didn't come to church often, but he was always here for Easter." I wonder if they think they sound silly justifying something like that to me. I wonder what Uncle Joe will feel like when he says that to the Lord.

Faith is not just knowledge. It is action. James 2:17 reads *"so, faith by itself, if it has no works, is dead."* Works do not save us without faith. Faith and works go together in concert with God's grace in order for one to attain salvation.

Allow me to share an analogy of faith, works, and grace, compared to a cup, rocks, and water. The cup represents faith, the structure of what we believe; however, the empty cup is of little use, just like the faith that has no works is an empty faith. The rocks represent the works, but works done without faith are like rocks without a place to collect them. They scatter randomly and are ends to themselves.

Fill a cup with rocks and the cup still has empty spaces. That is because the water represents God's grace, which heals what is infirm and completes what is lacking in us. It fills the empty spiritual spaces. We receive grace through prayer and the sacraments, a little bit at a time. The idea is for our cup to be strong and large—to have a strong faith and for it to be filled with rocks, our good works. Then, filling the cup with water makes the cup truly full. This is the ideal Christian life—faith, works, and grace.

Going back to the Parable of the Maidens, the wise maidens not only had faith, but they had joyful expectation of the arrival of the Bridegroom. They slumbered and slept, confident that when the cry came to meet the Bridegroom, they would have sufficient oil in their lamps. No one knows the day or the hour when the Bridegroom will come for each of us. That is why the "smart" Christian is vigilant about his or her lamp, to keep it filled with faith, works and grace.

The desire of Christ is for all to enter into the feast. However, only those who prepare will be admitted. Just like in the Parable, some of the maidens are wise and some are foolish. Which are you?

I see Your Bridal Chamber adorned, O my Savior, and I have no wedding garment, that I may enter therein; O Giver of Light, make radiant the vesture of my soul, and save me. (Exapostelarion, from the Service of the Bridegroom, Trans. by Fr. George Papadeas)

Fill your cup today!

Holy Wednesday

Holy Unction and Our Need For Spiritual Cleansing

Jesus, knowing that the Father had given all things into His hands, and that He had come from God and was going to God, rose from supper, laid aside His garments, and girded Himself with a towel. Then He poured water into a basin, and began to wash the disciples' feet, and to wipe them with the towel with which He was girded. He came to Simon Peter; and Peter said to him, "Lord, do you wash my feet?" Jesus answered him, "What I am doing you do not know now, but afterward you will understand." Peter said to him, "You shall never wash my feet." Jesus answered him, "If I do not wash you, you have no part in Me."
John 13:3-8
(From the Gospel of the Vesperal Liturgy on Holy Thursday Morning)

The focus of Holy Wednesday is the spiritual cleansing that we will receive through the Sacrament of Holy Unction. Holy Unction is one of the sacraments that we are supposed to receive on a frequent basis, like Holy Communion and Confession. Because there wasn't a set time for Holy Unction to be offered during the Church year (some churches had it once a month, others once a week, others once in a "blue moon"), the Church decided that Holy Unction should be put on the liturgical calendar on Holy Wednesday, to make sure that each Orthodox Christian received Holy Unction at least once a year. Holy Unction is connected closely with the Institution of the Holy Eucharist on Holy Thursday morning, since Christ washed the feet of the Disciples shortly before instituting the Eucharist with them.

Ritual washing of feet was a common practice of the Jews at the time of Christ. Because most people wore sandals and because the roads were dirty, it was a ritual to wash the feet upon entering into a home. Many Jews had servants; some even had slaves, so most certainly the master of the house would not be washing the feet of the guests. In the case of the Last Supper, Jesus was the host; the Disciples were the invited guests. Most certainly the host would not have performed this duty. So Jesus again went against the grain of conventional behavior, stopping to wash the feet of the Disciples in another example of humility and servitude. It is interesting to note the sheer number of these humble acts, as well as teaching on love, offered by the Lord to His followers, to leave no doubt that the two greatest expressions of faith are humility and love.

Peter initially resisted this act of the Lord. Jesus reassured Peter that it was okay not to understand, but that He needed to participate. This is perhaps the most poignant thing to take away from not only this scripture reading, but from the sacrament of Holy Unction in which we will participate in today.

Holy Unction is offered for the healing of soul and body. However, Holy Unction is not going to heal a broken leg. That's why we have medical doctors. However, with every physical injury, there is a spiritual challenge. When we are wounded in body, many times we are wounded also in spirit. A broken leg at an inopportune time may cause us to feel despondent or hopeless. Just ask the athlete who breaks his leg before the Superbowl. Holy Unction helps to heal a wounded soul that is beaten down by the unrelenting battle of temptations that are part of life. Holy Unction helps to cleanse a soul that has been tainted by sin. Holy Unction helps to soothe the pain of a mind that is often times filled with sadness and doubt.

There is certainly a ritual aspect to Holy Unction, in that we are anointed with oil, but it is not just the oil that has the healing power. It is praying over the oil that gives this sacrament power. The Sacrament of Holy Unction consists of seven Epistles, seven Gospels, and seven prayers. Done properly, it is celebrated by seven priests. After each Gospel, there is a prayer that is offered. I sometimes imagine what it must be like to have seven priests offer this service, and in small groups, for the faithful to kneel under the stole of a priest seven times. What a comforting scene that is, like the father who embraced the Prodigal Son, to be embraced under the stole of the priest.

The words of the prayers are very powerful. They ask for those *"who are about to be anointed with it, unto complete remission of their sins, and unto inheritance of the Kingdom of Heaven."* *(First Prayer)* They remind us that, *"Yea, O Lord, Who are easy to be entreated; You alone are merciful and loves mankind; you are sorrowful for our evil deeds . . . You do not desire the death of a sinner, but rather that he should repent and live."* *(Second Prayer)* They ask the Lord for, *"cleansing and deliverance form every infirmity, illness, malady, and every defilement of body and soul."* *(Third Prayer)* They remind us that the Lord is, *"plentiful in mercy, rich in beneficence, the Father of mercies and God of all comfort."* *(Fourth Prayer)* They entreat the Lord to, *"remember not the sins of our youth,"* *(Fifth Prayer)* not only those made with the immaturity of age, but the mistakes we make because we are still spiritually immature. We are comforted with the thought that, *"You are the Good Shepherd, Who came in search of the wandering sheep; You give consolation to the faint hearted and life to the broken-hearted.* *(Sixth Prayer)* Finally, *"You have not created man for destruction, but for the keeping of Your commandments and for the inheriting of life incorruptible.* *(Seventh Prayer—All Prayers are quoted from the Holy Unction Service, Trans. by Fr. George Papadeas)*

These prayers are all offered over the oil, now sanctified into Holy Unction and given to us through anointing. As you pray this service, identify the things in the prayers that speak directly to you, and after you are anointed with the oil, sit for a few minutes in the pews and rub it into your skin, praying to God that as the oil goes into you, that the thoughts of these prayers will also come into you, healing the specific illnesses of spirit that you suffer from.

It has been said that the Church is a spiritual hospital. There are two kinds of people in hospitals—the ones who need healing and the ones who offer the healing. At some point, we will all be patients in a hospital. So, come to the church for Holy Unction, as a patient, who honestly affirms the need for healing in your life and humbly receives the Sacrament of Holy Unction. As you find healing in your life, become a healer yourself, aiding in the cure of God's people who suffer from hardship.

Christ told His Disciples as He washed their feet, that today the Master would stoop to wash the feet of His servants, but tomorrow, they would wash the feet of one another, and wash the feet of others. Tonight, allow the Master to cleanse you by Holy Unction, and tomorrow, bend your knee to wash the feet of another, by humbly serving those around you.

With washed feet, and they themselves purified by participation in the Divine Mystery, Your servants, O Christ, now come together from Zion to the great mount of Olives, and praise You, O Merciful Lord." (From the 5th Ode of the Service of the 12 Gospels on Holy Thursday Evening, Trans. by Fr. George Papadeas)

Accept healing tonight! Seek to be a healer tomorrow!

Holy Thursday

Do THIS in REMEMBRANCE of Me

For I received from the Lord what I also delivered to you, that the Lord Jesus on the night when He was betrayed took bread, and when He had given thanks, He broke it, and said, "This is My Body which is for you. Do this in remembrance of Me." In the same way also the cup, after supper, saying, "This cup is the new covenant in My Blood. Do this, as often as you drink it, in remembrance of Me." For as often as you eat this bread and drink the cup, you proclaim the Lord's death until He comes.
1 Corinthians 11:23-26
(From the Epistle of the Vesperal Liturgy on Holy Thursday Morning)

On Holy Thursday, we commemorate the Institution of the Eucharist. The Lord took two very ordinary things, bread and wine, and "consecrated" them to be His Body and Blood. Then He gave these two ordinary things, now "extra-ordinary," to His Disciples, to partake of them.

In our church, we celebrate the Eucharist often. We bring the same "ordinary" gifts, bread and wine, and offer them in the service. There is nothing extraordinary about bread and wine. They can be purchased in any store. They can be made in any home. They are rather ordinary substances, but when they are brought into the church, prayed over and "consecrated," these ordinary substances become "extraordinary." Because *the* Holy Spirit touches them, they become "extraordinary," they become "holy." "Holy" means "set apart." They become "Holy," in the sense that they are no longer mere bread and wine, they are *the* Body and *the* Blood of Jesus Christ. When we receive these "extraordinary" Gifts, we become "extraordinary" by association. Just like when you are dirty and take a shower and use a cleaning agent, soap, you become clean. So, when we touch what is "extraordinary" and "Holy," we become those things. The challenge comes after we receive what is "extraordinary." Do we leave church and act "extraordinary" and "holy" or do we revert back to being "ordinary."

We receive Holy Communion for many reasons. First, it is a command. "Take eat." "Drink of this all of you." "Do this in remembrance of Me." Second, it allows God to come into us, and it affords us the opportunity to touch the Divine God.

There is a third reason that we often forget. We receive Holy Communion in order to *remember* what Christ did for us. In celebrating the Divine Liturgy, we not only partake of Christ, but we get a refresher course in what it means to be a Christian. We remember that Christ died for our sins. We remember that He was Resurrected from the dead. We remember His teachings. We remember that He came from God and returned to God, and that we can follow the same path.

In bringing "ordinary" gifts and making them "extraordinary," we remember that WE can become "extraordinary" through partaking of Holy Communion. We remember that we cannot be content being "ordinary" because we have witnessed and partaken of the "extraordinary." In receiving Holy Communion, we remember that the Gifts are Holy, they are set apart, and in receiving the Gifts, we are to become Holy and set apart, set apart for God and His purposes for our lives.

In receiving Holy Communion we are sustained in our lives until we meet the Lord, because we have Him in our minds, our hearts and our lives, with regularity. This is why Saint Paul intentionally chooses the word "often," encouraging us to receive Holy Communion on a frequent basis, so that there isn't sufficient time to forget Christ and what He did for us.

We tell our spouses and our children often that we love them. Is that because if they don't hear it every day, they might doubt that we love them? I suppose if they only heard these words once a year, they might. We tell people we love them often because hearing that you are loved is a great source of encouragement. It is always a positive thing.

In the Eucharist, we are reminded that God loves us, so much that He died for us. He loves us so much that He is preparing a Heavenly Kingdom for us. He loves us so much that He has given us a pathway to follow to get us from here to there.

In receiving the Eucharist, we tell God that we love Him. We tell Him that we want to be "extraordinary" and "holy." So the Eucharist is not just some ritual where we bring "ordinary" gifts and a "show" is performed over them. The Eucharist is an opportunity to partake of the "extraordinary" to remind us that we are "extraordinary." It is the opportunity to stand in the presence of the Divine God in this life in preparation for living with Him in the next. It is an opportunity to partake of what is holy to remind us to be holy. It is an opportunity to remember all that God did and still does for us, so that we can go forth and live for Him.

> *Do this in remembrance of me. For as often as you eat this Bread and drink this Cup, you proclaim my death, and you confess my resurrection. Therefore, Master, we also, remembering His saving passion and life giving cross, His three day burial and resurrection from the dead, His ascension into heaven, and enthronement at Your right hand, God and Father, and His glorious and awesome second coming. (From the Anaphora of the Liturgy of St. Basil, Trans. by Holy Cross Seminary Press)*

Allow the Eucharist to help transform you from "ordinary" to "extraordinary" each time you receive! Receive often!

Great and Holy Friday

Condemned by a tree, Saved by the Tree

When Jesus had received the vinegar, He said, "It is finished";
and He bowed His head and gave up His spirit.
John 19:30
(Gospel of the Ninth Hour on Good Friday Morning)

In Genesis, we read that God created the world in "seven days." We also know that God's time doesn't move according to our concept of time. So, the world wasn't created in seven "literal" days, meaning seven 24-hour periods of time. Specific things were created on each "day" of Creation. At every step of the Creation, at the end of every "day," God looked upon what He created, "and saw that it was good" (Gen. 1:4, 12, 18, 21, 25). On the "sixth" day, God created man in His image and likeness. After creating the human race, then, and only then, did God assess what He created and, "*Behold, it was **very** good*" (1:31). Mankind was the "crowning jewel" in the Creation because only the human being was created in the image and likeness of God.

In Genesis 2, we read that God "*planted a garden in Eden, in the east*" (Gen. 2:8). In the Garden of Eden, mankind lived in a state of "paradise," in perfect harmony with God, with one another and with the environment. In the midst of the garden were two trees, the "tree of life" and the "tree of the knowledge of good and evil" (Gen. 2:9). God commanded mankind, saying, "*You may freely eat of every tree of the garden; but of the tree of the knowledge of good and evil you shall not eat, for in the day that you eat of it you shall die*" (Gen. 2:17). After Adam and Eve partook of the fruit of the tree of the knowledge of good and evil, God said to them, "*'Behold, the man has become like One of Us, knowing good and evil; and now, lest he put forth his hand and take also of the tree of life, and eat, and live forever'—therefore the Lord God sent him forth from the garden of Eden . . . He drove out the man; and at the east of the garden of Eden He placed the Cherubim, and a flaming sword which turned every way, to guard the way to the tree of life*" (Gen. 3:22-24).

God gave Paradise to humankind, and humanity lost Paradise by partaking of the "tree of knowledge of good and evil," which also cost us the "tree of life," which is eternal life. However, in God's abiding love for us, He wanted to give us a way back to Paradise, to again put the human being into a state of union with Him. The only way this would be possible would be for God to take on OUR human image and likeness and live like one of us, to show us the way back to Paradise. This is the reason why it was necessary for Jesus Christ to come to earth in the first place.

Remember how our demise came because of the "tree of knowledge of good and evil"? Well, our salvation also came through a tree. A tree was made into a cross, upon which was hung the Son of God, and for us, THAT tree is now the "tree of life," because through the cross, we have a gateway back to the Garden of Eden. Because of the cross, we now have the opportunity to partake of the "tree of life" and live forever. In fact, there is no other way to attain Paradise than by partaking of the "tree of life," the cross of our Lord.

The words of Christ, "*It is finished,*" are not a statement of defeat, but rather a statement of triumph. If Christ came to "re-create" the world, to again be in the image and likeness of God, the "re-creation" was now complete, it was finished. "*It is finished*" is the call to all people that the gateway to Eden is now open. We now all have access to the "tree of life." I'm reminded of a hymn of the Nativity, which is also the first prayer offered by a priest when he prepares the Gifts for Holy Communion:

> *O Bethlehem, prepare, Eden is opened unto all. And be ready, Ephrata, for the Tree of life has in the grotto blossomed forth from the Virgin. Indeed her womb is shown to be spiritually a Paradise, in which is found the God-planted Tree. And if we eat from it we shall live, and shall not die, as did Adam of old. Christ is born, so that He might raise up the formerly fallen image. (Trans. Fr. Seraphim Dedes)*

Indeed, Eden is now open to all. If we eat of the "tree of life," if we partake of Christ's Divine Nature through Holy Communion and through our faith, and if we honor His Divine Nature through acts of service to one another, then we also will "live" and not die, as did Adam of old.

When Jesus ended His earthly life, He suffered an earthly death. There is one more very significant thing that He did as He expired on the cross. "*He bowed His head and gave up His Spirit*" (John 19:30). In most movie scenes where someone dies, they give up their spirit and then their head falls. Christ's death was the opposite. Because His decision to die was voluntary, He chose to lay His life down for us, out of love for us. He remained Lord even in death—for no one can kill God. God chose to die for us.

The human race was condemned because of a tree. The Son of God, allowed Himself to be nailed to the Tree, in order to save us from our sins by opening a path back to Paradise. The "tree" in the Garden of Eden condemned us. The "Tree" of Christ's cross on Golgotha saved us.

Today is hung upon the Cross, He Who suspended the Earth amid the waters. A crown of thorns crowns Him, Who is the King of Angels. He, Who wrapped the Heavens in clouds, is clothed with the purple of mockery. He, Who freed Adam in the Jordan, received buffetings. He was transfixed with nails, Who is the Bridegroom of the Church. He was pierced with a lance, Who is the Son of the Virgin. We worship Your Passion O Christ. Show us also, Your glorious Resurrection. (From the Fifteenth Antiphon of the Service of the 12 Gospels on Holy Thursday Evening, Trans. by Fr. George Papadeas)

May the Lord our God remember us in His Kingdom, now and forever and to the ages of ages. Amen.

Holy Saturday

And God "Rested"

In the beginning God created the heavens and the earth. The earth was without form and void, and darkness was upon the face of the deep; and the Spirit of God was moving over the face of the waters. And God said, "Let there be light" and there was light.
Genesis 1:1-3
(From a Prophecy at the Vesperal Liturgy on Holy Saturday Morning)

Have you ever wondered why the Crucifixion happened on a Friday, as opposed to another day of the week? Going back to Genesis 2, on the "sixth" day, *"the heavens and the earth were finished, and all the host of them,"* and on the "seventh" day, *"God rested on the seventh day from all His work which he had done. So God blessed the seventh day and hallowed it, because on it God rested from all His work which He had done in creation"* (Gen. 2:1-3). The "seventh" day, the day God rested, was called the Sabbath, a day of rest from all labor, a day dedicated to God.

The crucifixion occurred, and Jesus said, *"It is finished"* (John 19:30), on a Friday, the 6th day of the week. On the Sabbath, He "rested" in the tomb. It was the Jewish Law for all work to cease on the Sabbath. Jesus did not come to abolish the Law, but to supersede the Law. In Matthew 5:17, Jesus said, *"Think not that I have come to abolish the law and the prophets; I have come not to abolish them but to fulfill them."* So, even in death, He fulfilled the Law. On that Sabbath, on what would be the last of the "Old Testament" Sabbaths, the world waited and wondered. What would happen on the "third day?" Would He really rise from the dead as He had foretold?

In the Gospel of Matthew, we read what was going on amongst the chief priests and the Pharisees:

> *Next day, that is, after the day of Preparation, the chief priests and the Pharisees gathered before Pilate and said, "Sir, we remember how that imposter said, while He was still alive, 'After three days I will rise again.' Therefore order the sepulcher to be made secure until the third day, lest His disciples go and steal him away, and tell the people, 'He has risen from the dead,' and the last fraud will be worse than*

the first." Pilate said to them, "You have a guard of soldiers; go, make it as secure as you can." So they went and made the sepulcher secure by sealing the stone and setting a guard (Matt. 27:62-66).

The sun set on Jerusalem that Saturday night with a lot of uncertainty in Jerusalem. The disciples were scared and hidden. The women wondered whether it would be safe to go and anoint the body of Jesus when the Sabbath had passed. The followers of Jesus wondered if He would really rise from the dead. The Jewish authorities worked hard to prevent the theft of the Body, wondering if some kind of conspiracy would be afoot to have the Body stolen. The Roman soldiers were probably tired of the whole thing. A nervous tension must have been over the whole city wondering, "What will tomorrow bring?"

For us, today marks the end of the Lenten journey. In the Divine Liturgy of Holy Saturday morning, we hear the beautiful hymn "*Arise O God, and judge the earth; for you shall take all nations to Your inheritance.*" (Trans. by Fr. George Papadeas) Leaves are scattered around the church, announcing the Resurrection of Christ. The Lenten colors are removed and the Paschal decorations put up. As the sun sets, we will prepare to go back to church to celebrate the Resurrection of Christ. Unlike Jerusalem on that Saturday night, we know what will transpire in the night—a beautiful service, a joyous celebration.

Just like Jerusalem on that Saturday night, we also have some uncertainty. Some perhaps even feel some fear and sadness. For those who put a lot into the Lenten journey, we wonder, will we continue the good habits we've started, or will we regress into our pre-Lenten lifestyle? For those who have attended services every day of Holy Week, perhaps we fear that we are in for a big letdown. For all of us, will we see Pascha more as an end or as a new beginning?

The sun is setting on our Lenten journey, but it is not setting on the Prayer Team. A new set of reflections is about to begin. For the past seventy days, we have focused on the scriptures of Triodion, Lent and Holy Week. For the next fifty days, we will focus on the scriptures of the Resurrection, the Ascension, and Pentecost. We will focus on the joyful event of the Resurrection, the reaction of the various witnesses of this event, and our own reaction to the Resurrection. There will be some challenges to us as we seek to integrate our Lenten goals into our Post-Resurrection lives. I hope that the Prayer Team reflections will encourage and challenge you to make this Pascha different. Today, the Lenten journey ends. Tomorrow the joy of the Resurrection begins. Monday, the challenges of life will return, with us ready to meet them with joy and renewed commitment to living a Christ-centered life, with the Cross and Empty Tomb serving as our sources of hope and motivation. Joy came to the world through the Resurrection. The Resurrection was made only possible through the Cross. Our Resurrection is possible when we have faith, and when we carry our crosses and follow as well—through the struggles and tribulations of life, to the joy and ecstasy of eternal life!

> *The great Moses mystically foreshadowed this day, saying: "And God blessed the seventh day." For this is the blessed Sabbath; it is the day of rest, in which the*

Only-Begotten Son of God rested from all His works, and through the dispensation of death, in body He rested. And having returned to it again through the Resurrection, He granted us Life eternal, as the only Good and merciful Lord. (Doxastikon of the Praises at the Lamentations Service on Good Friday Evening, Trans. by Fr. George Papadeas)

Kali Anastasi! A blessed Resurrection to all!

PART FOUR—THE JOY OF THE RESURRECTION

The Resurrection of Christ

Thru the hand of Fr. Anthony Salzman, www.imageandlikeness.com

PASCHA

The Paschal Homily of St. John Chrysostom

"He has risen."
Mark 16:6

Whosoever is a devout lover of God, let him enjoy this beautiful bright Festival. And whosoever is a grateful servant, let him joyously enter into the joy of his Lord. And if any be weary with fasting, let him now receive his reward. If any has toiled from the first hour let him receive his just debt. If any came after the third let him gratefully celebrate. If any arrived after the sixth, let him not doubt; for he too shall sustain no loss. If any have delayed to the ninth, let him come without hesitation. If any arrived only at the eleventh hour, let him not be afraid by reason of his delay; for the Master is gracious and receives the last, even as the first. He gives rest to him who arrives at the eleventh hour, as well as him, who has labored from the first. He is merciful to the one who delays and nourishes the first. He gives also to the one, and to the other He is gracious. He accepts the works, as He greets the endeavor, He honors the deed, and the intent He commends.

Let all of you then enter into the joy of your Lord. The first and second enjoy your reward. You rich and poor, rejoice together. You temperate and you heedless, honor the day. You who fasted, and you who did not, rejoice today. The table is richly laden. All of you, fare sumptuously on it. The Calf is a fatted one; let no one go away hungry. All of you enjoy the banquet of faith. All of you enjoy the riches of His goodness. Let no one grieve poverty; for the universal Kingdom has been revealed.

Let no one grieve over sins; for forgiveness has dawned from the tomb. Let no one fear death; for the Death of our Savior has set us free. He has destroyed it by enduring it. He despoiled Hades, when He descended thereto. He embittered it, having tasted of His flesh. Isaiah foretold this when he cried out: "You, O Hades, have been embittered by encountering Him below." It was embittered, for it was abolished. It was embittered, for it was mocked. It was embittered, for it was slain. It was embittered, for it was annihilated. It was embittered, for it is now made captive. It took a body, and, lo, it discovered God. It took earth and, behold! It encountered Heaven. It took what it saw, and was overcome by what it could not see. O death, where is your sting? O Hades, where is your victory? Christ is risen, and You are annihilated. Christ is risen, and the demons have fallen. Christ is risen, and the Angels rejoice. Christ is risen, and life is liberated. Christ is risen, and the tomb is emptied of the dead; for Christ, having risen from the dead, has become the first fruits of those who fall asleep. To Him be the glory and the dominion to the Ages of Ages. Amen. (Paschal Homily of St. John Chrysostom, read at the Liturgy on Pascha, Trans. by Fr. George Papadeas)

Come, receive the Light from the unwaning Light, and glorify Christ, Who has risen from the dead. (From the Resurrection Service, Trans. by Fr. George Papadeas)

Bright Monday

The Icon of the Resurrection

Peter said, "Brethren, I may say to you confidently of the patriarch David that he both died and was buried, and his tomb is with us to this day. Being therefore a prophet, and knowing that God had sworn with an oath to him that he would set one of his descendants upon his throne, he foresaw and spoke of the resurrection of the Christ, that He was not abandoned to Hades, nor did His flesh see corruption. This Jesus God raised up, and of that we all are witnesses.
Acts 2:29-32

Christ is Risen!

For the next forty days, the icon of the Resurrection will be displayed in our churches. The icon of the Resurrection depicts not what happened on Easter Sunday. It actually reflects what happened on Holy Saturday. It does not show Christ coming out of the tomb, like a superhero, carrying a banner that says "I cheated death." It shows our most Merciful Lord, descending into Hades, and raising all those who had fallen through death.

The icon depicts Christ wearing all white garments, because He is the Light of the world. The wounds in His hands and feet are visible. Christ is often shown carrying His cross, because only through the cross is the Resurrection possible. Sometimes instead of showing a Cross, the icon depicts Christ holding a scroll. In either case, the cross or the scroll, both represent the message that Christ preached to the captives He found in hell when He descended there. Christ is standing on two doors, which are the brass gates of Hades, now broken down because of the Resurrection. They are in the shape of a cross. Scattered near the gates are the locks and keys that bound humanity to Hades.

The most prominent figures in the icon, after the Lord, are Adam and Eve, the first human beings that God had fashioned, the symbols of a human race created in God's image and likeness, who distorted that image through sin. Adam and Eve are now given a new chance and a restored image. For Christ, who in many places is called "the Second Adam," has come to earth and done what the first Adam could not. He showed that it is possible to live a life in unity with

God, demonstrating faith and love, and avoiding temptation. The reward for this life is eternal life, Resurrection from the dead.

The icon depicts many of the righteous figures who preceded Christ. A young man is often depicted in the icon. This is Abel, the first person to die, killed by the hand of his brother Cain, the first person to suffer death as a result of the Fall (Gen. 4). Moses, the one whom God spoke through to give the people the Law is shown. It was Moses who instituted the first Passover. It is very appropriate that he is present for the "new Passover," the Resurrection. David and Solomon, both kings, both ancestors of Christ, are depicted in the icon. John the Baptist, the forerunner and last of the prophets is also usually depicted.

Christ is shown grabbing the wrists of Adam and Eve. This is an important part of the icon. When people greet one another and shake hands, this denotes a position of equality, you might even say that symbolically it means meeting one another halfway. The depiction of Christ grabbing the wrist of Adam tells us that we are not equal with God. We cannot even meet God halfway, but if we reach out to God, He is ready to grasp us by the wrist to take us with Him to Paradise. This is the most hopeful part of the icon. It reminds us that we have to reach out to God in faith, and let Him take care of the rest.

In some icons of the Resurrection, Eve is depicted behind Christ, waiting her turn for her Resurrection. In some depictions her wrists are covered. In the icons where Christ is grabbing only the hand of Adam, with the other hand, Adam is gesturing toward Eve, as if asking Christ to take care of his helpmate and to save her as well.

The Resurrection was made possible only because of the crucifixion. An earthly death was required in order for the Resurrection to occur. In our lives, an earthly death is required in order to inherit eternal life and enter into the Kingdom of Heaven. The depiction in the icon assures us that those who fall through death will be raised to eternal life because of the Resurrection of the Lord. The righteous figures of the Old Testament died with faith that something greater was coming. They did not immediately go to heaven, because Jesus had not yet come and died for them, as He did for us. Through the Resurrection, when we fall through death, we are raised to Paradise by the power and the mercy of Christ.

Jesus did not "cheat" death—He destroyed the power of death. We will not cheat death either. Each of us will eventually die an earthly death, but because the Resurrection destroyed the power of death over us, when we die on this earth, we will be resurrected with Christ. The power "death" has over us will indeed be destroyed.

The service celebrated Holy Saturday morning is affectionately known as the "proti-Anastasis," the First Resurrrection. This is not a correct sentiment. There was only one Resurrection, and it occurred after the Sabbath passed. The event of Holy Saturday morning is the "First Announcement of the Resurrection," which came to those in hell. What an announcement it must have been! A hymn from the Matins (Orthros) of each Sunday (also chanted on Good Friday) says:

The assembly of the Angels was amazed beholding You numbered among the dead, O Savior, destroying the power of Death; with Yourself You raised up Adam, and freed everyone from Hades. (Evlogetaria of Sunday Orthros, and of the Orthros of Holy Saturday, Trans. by Fr. George Papadeas)
May we be so fortunate to hear this announcement when we pass away from our earthly life.

Today Hades cried out groaning: "My power has been trampled on; the Shepherd has been crucified, and Adam He raised up. I have been deprived of those, over whom I ruled; and all those, I had the power to swallow, I have disgorged. He, who was crucified has cleared the tombs. The dominion of death is no more." Glory O Lord, to Your Cross and Resurrection. (From the Vesperal Liturgy on Holy Saturday Morning, Trans. by Fr. George Papadeas)

May we one day be raised from the dead by the Lord!

Bright Tuesday

The Most Joyful Hymn

Remember Jesus Christ, risen from the dead, descended from David, as preached in my gospel, the gospel for which I am suffering and wearing fetters like a criminal. But the word of God is not fettered. Therefore I endure everything for the sake of the elect, that they also may obtain salvation in Christ Jesus with its eternal glory. The saying is sure:
If we have died with Him, we shall also live with Him;
if we endure, we shall also reign with Him.
2 Timothy 2:8-12

Christ is Risen!

The marquee hymn of the Orthodox Church, is the hymn of the Resurrection, known as "Christos Anesti" or "Christ is Risen." This hymn is about twenty words in length, and yet it encapsulates what we believe about the Resurrection and its significance for our lives. The hymn provides history from the past, theology for the present and direction for the future:

Christ is Risen from the dead, by death trampling down death and to those in the tombs He has granted life. (Translation by the Greek Orthodox Archdiocese, 2013)

We will sing this hymn multiple times at every divine service until the Feast of the Ascension. If an Orthodox Christian knows only one hymn, this is the hymn. More important than knowing how to sing it, however, is knowing what it means:

Christ is Risen from the dead—This is a statement of triumph and one of faith. None of us was there at the Resurrection. We put our faith in the writings of the scriptures, the eye-witness accounts recorded for us in Scripture and Tradition, and we put our faith in the history of a church that for 2,000 years has spread this message of hope.

By death trampling down upon death—Through His death and Resurrection, Christ destroyed the power of death. He proved that God can have dominion even over death.

To those in the tombs He has granted life—To the one who has died, the death is only of a body. The soul inside of that body leaves from the body and goes back to God for judgment, and if the soul has lived in faith, then it goes into everlasting joy, heaven.

This beautiful hymn neither praises God, nor asks God for anything. Rather it states for us in very encouraging language, the whole goal of life, which is to live as a person of faith, so that we can conquer death and attain eternal LIFE. We sing it hundreds of times during the Paschal season, so that we can retain its important message. If anyone asks you why the Resurrection is necessary or important, you can answer this complicated question in twenty-one words, the words of this hymn.

It is not only this hymn that is front and center to our Paschal observance. We are also supposed to greet one another with the words "Christ is Risen," and the response is "Truly He is Risen!" In Greek, we say "Christos Anesti," with the response being "Alithos Anesti!"

Why greet one another with these words? First, because it's good news! On Christmas, everyone wishes each other "Merry Christmas!" When it's someone's birthday, we wish them "Happy Birthday!" Well, the most significant thing that has ever happened in the history of the world and in our lives is that Christ is Risen from the dead. So, we should greet each other with these words and with great JOY. This statement is one of triumph and also one of encouragement. Many times when we are down in the dumps and someone says, "Well, think of it this way, it could be worse." Well, when you are down in the dumps, remember "Christ is Risen" and this is cause for hope even in the worst of times. Because Christ is Risen, there is eternal hope for me. There may not be hope on a given day or in a given circumstance, but speaking in God's eternal terms, there is always eternal hope and this is so because Christ is Risen!

Finally, these words serve as a good conversation starter. We all have caller ID on our phones. I challenge you to answer your phone with these words "Christ is Risen" for 40 days. Even if the person calling is not Orthodox, it will be a great way to witness your faith. You don't have to stand on a street corner holding a sign, or go to a third world country to tell others about Christ. It can be as simple as answering your phone! Begin all correspondence with this greeting as well!

Let us greet one another with these words, and let us sing this hymn with joy and with purpose. Christ is Risen! There is hope for me to be risen with Him.

> *Having beheld the Resurrection of Christ, let us worship the Holy Lord Jesus, Who alone is without sin. We venerate Your Cross, O Christ, and we praise and glorify Your Holy Resurrection. For You are our God, and we know no other, except You, and we call on Your Name. Come, all you faithful, let us worship Christ's Holy Resurrection; for lo, through the Cross, joy has come to the whole world. For, at all times, blessing the Lord, we praise His Resurrection. Having endured the Cross for us, He destroyed Death by death. Having risen from the grave, as He foretold, He has given us Eternal life and the Great Mercy. (Resurrection Ode at the Resurrection Service, Trans. by Fr. George Papadeas)*

Christ is Risen! Truly, He is Risen!

Bright Wednesday

The Resurrection—From the Gospel of Matthew

Now after the Sabbath, toward the dawn of the first day of the week, Mary Magdalene and the other Mary went to see the sepulcher. And behold, there was a great earthquake; for an angel of the Lord descended from heaven and came and rolled back the stone, and sat upon it. His appearance was like lightning, and his raiment white as snow. And for fear of him the guards trembled and became like dead men. But the angel said to the women, "Do not be afraid; for I know that you seek Jesus who was crucified. He is not here; for He has risen, as He said. Come, see the place where He lay. Then go quickly and tell His disciples that He has risen from the dead, and behold, He is going before you to Galilee; there you will see Him. Lo, I have told you." So they departed quickly from the tomb with fear and great joy, and ran to tell His disciples. And behold, Jesus met them and said, "Hail!" And they came up and took hold of His feet and worshiped Him. Then Jesus said to them, "Do not be afraid; go and tell my brethren to go to Galilee, and there they will see Me."
Matthew 28:1-10
(From the Gospel read at the Vesperal Liturgy on Holy Saturday Morning)

Christ is Risen!

The four Gospels each have an account of the Resurrection, and for the next four days, we will examine them. There are slight differences between each Gospel account, but that doesn't make the Resurrection any less true. If any four people describe an event, there are going to be differences in their accounts. For instance, if four people describe the Resurrection service in the Orthodox Church, one might write, "It was dark and we lit candles." Another might say "We went outside and sang 'Christ is Risen.'" Another might say, "We lit candles and then we went outside." The fourth might say, "We heard a Gospel reading and then we sang." All four versions will be truthful because all of those things happened. This is how one accounts for four similar, but distinctly different accounts of the Resurrection, one told in each of the four Gospels.

The first account that we hear read in the church is from the Gospel of St. Matthew. It is read on Holy Saturday at the Vesperal Liturgy. Saint Matthew's account is the only one that gives a description of the actual moment of the Resurrection. It is the only account that mentions an earthquake and an angel coming down from heaven and rolling back the stone.

The tomb was being guarded by a detachment of Roman soldiers. The stone that had been rolled over the entrance to the tomb was very large and very heavy. It had also been sealed over the tomb. There was a great earthquake. An angel came and rolled away the stone. The purpose of the angel rolling the stone was not so Christ could walk out of the tomb. In His Divinity, He could have and would have passed right through the stone. (In John 20:19, which we will examine in a later reflection, we read that Jesus passed through the doors to encounter the Disciples later that day. He most certainly would have been able to pass through the stone over the door of the tomb.) The purpose of the angel rolling the stone back was to show that the tomb was empty.

As we will read in the other Gospel accounts, it was the women who were the first witnesses to the Resurrection of Christ. There is only one angel in the account from Matthew. The angel tells the women not to be afraid. He refers to the crucifixion—"You seek Jesus who was crucified." There is no shying away from the heinous manner in which Jesus was killed. This points to the "glory" of the cross, rather than seeing it as a sign of shame. In Matthew's account, the women leave the tomb and run to tell the disciples. In other accounts, they are afraid and tell no one immediately.

While on the way, the women are met by Jesus. They immediately recognize Him and worship Him. He directs them to tell the Disciples that He is going to Galilee. Interesting that He would go there, since Galilee was primarily Gentile territory. He chooses Galilee because the Resurrection was for the salvation of all peoples, not only the Jews.

Finally the Resurrection is necessary. Saint Paul writes in 1 Corinthians 15:17, that "If Christ has not been raised, your faith is futile and you are still in your sins." Dying on the Cross for our sins was necessary, but death is only conquered through the Resurrection of Christ.

> *Even though You descended into the grave, O Immortal One, You destroyed the power of Hades; and You arose as a victor, O Christ our God, saying to the myrrh-bearing Women, "Hail!" and to Your Apostles granting peace; You also grant resurrection to the fallen. (Kontakion of the Paschal Season, Trans. by Fr. George Papadeas)*

Continue to rejoice in the Resurrection today!

Note: In the Orthodox Church, there is no fasting the week after Pascha. You can eat anything all week and still receive Communion provided you do not eat breakfast the morning you receive.

Bright Thursday

The Resurrection—From the Gospel of Mark

And when the Sabbath was past, Mary Magdalene, and Mary the mother of James, and Salome, bought spices, so that they might go and anoint Him. And very early on the first day of the week they went to the tomb when the sun had risen. And they were saying to one another, "Who will roll away the stone for us from the door of the tomb?" And looking up, they saw that the stone was rolled back—it was very large. And entering the tomb, they saw a young man sitting on the right side, dressed in a white robe; and they were amazed. And he said to them, "Do not be amazed; you seek Jesus of Nazareth, who was crucified. He has risen, He is not here; see the place where they laid Him. But go, tell His disciples and Peter that He is going before you to Galilee; there you will see Him, as He told you."
Mark 16:1-7
(From the Gospel Reading at the Resurrection Service on Pascha)

Christ is Risen!

The account of the Resurrection from the Gospel of Mark is the account that is read at the Resurrection Service at midnight on Pascha. In this account, three women—Mary Magdalene, Mary the Mother of James and Salome—went to the tomb.

The hour of the Resurrection is not known. *"When the Sabbath was past"* can refer to any time after sunset on Saturday, the Sabbath. The Jewish (and later Byzantine and Orthodox) day ended and the new day began with the sunset each evening. So, the Sabbath, for instance, lasted from sunset on Friday until sunset on Saturday. This is why the Body of Jesus needed to be removed from the Cross and buried before the sun set on Friday. The women came before the dawn of the first day of the week. So the Resurrection occurred sometime after sunset on Saturday before the dawn of the first day of the week. This puts it between 9:30 P.M. on Saturday and prior to 6:00 A.M. on Sunday. The Resurrection Service in the Orthodox Church is traditionally held at midnight, with the calendar day of Saturday passing and before the dawn of Sunday morning.

The women take great courage, walking through a hostile city in the dead of night. Imagine the most hostile part of your city, then imagine walking through it at night with one or two friends, or even by yourself. That would be a courageous act indeed. There was also some faith involved. The women realized that the stone covering the door of the tomb was very large and they weren't sure how they would roll it aside. Would God give them strength? Would the Roman soldiers guarding the tomb show some kindness and compassion and remove it for them? Faith is when you don't know the outcome of something, but you do it anyway and believe you will have success. The journey of the women that morning was most certainly an act of faith.

The purpose of the journey of the women was to go and anoint the Body of Jesus. It was the Jewish custom that spices were put over the body, as part of the burial process. This also showed great respect to Jesus in death. Because the burial had happened so quickly on Good Friday, and all work had to stop on the Sabbath for the required day of rest, it is likely that the women were going early in the morning with the spices in order to anoint the body to complete the burial process.

When they arrived at the tomb, they found the stone rolled back. The Gospel passage does not say how this happened. They entered the tomb and found a young man sitting on the right side, dressed in a white robe. The Gospel of Matthew refers to the person at the tomb as an angel. St. Mark calls him a young man. St. Luke says that there were two men. St. John has no one at the tomb.

There is a tradition in the Orthodox Church that during the Orthros (or Matins) service on most Sundays, one of the eleven post-Resurrection Gospel passages are read. Since most Sundays commemorate the Resurrection of Christ, these Gospel passages are read on a rotating basis every eleven weeks. The priest who reads the Gospel reads from the right side of the altar table, representing the young man from the Gospel of Mark who sat at the right side of the tomb to proclaim the good news of the Resurrection.

In this Gospel account, as in Matthew, the women are afraid, and the young man they encounter who encourages them to go tell the Disciples that Jesus is going before them into Galilee comforts them. The lesson from this passage is that the faith of the women won out over their fear and uncertainty. They wanted to do the right thing for Christ and ventured into the darkness, undaunted by the hostile city or the large stone, in their desire to do the right thing.

> *The Myrrh-bearing maidens anticipated the dawn, and sought as those who seek the day, their Sun, Who was before the sun, and Who now had set in the Grave. They cried to each other, "Come, let us anoint with spices His Life-bearing and entombed Body, raising the fallen Adam lying in the tomb. Let us go, hastily like the Magi, let us worship, and bring myrrh as a gift to Him, Who is wrapped now not in swaddling bands, but in a sheet. Let us weep and cry aloud, 'O Master, arise! You, who grants to the fallen resurrection.'" (Oikos, read at the Orthros of the Pascha, Trans. by Fr. George Papadeas)*

May our faith always win out over fear and uncertainty!

Bright Friday—Feast of the Life-Giving Fountain

The Resurrection—From the Gospel of Luke

But on the first day of the week, at early dawn, they went to the tomb, taking the spices which they had prepared. And they found the stone rolled away from the tomb, but when they went in they did not find the Body. While they were perplexed about this, behold, two men stood by them in dazzling apparel; and as they were frightened and bowed their faces to the ground, the men said to them, "Why do you seek the living among the dead? Remember how He told you, while He was still in Galilee, that the Son of Man must be delivered into the hands of sinful men, and be crucified, and on the third day rise." And they remembered His words, and returning from the tomb they told all this to the eleven and to all the rest. Now it was Mary Magdalene and Joanna and Mary the mother of James and the other women with them who told this to the apostles; but these words seemed to them an idle tale, and they did not believe them. Luke 24:1-11
(From the Fourth Eothinon Gospel of Sunday Orthros)

Christ is Risen!

Continuing our study of the accounts of the Resurrection told in each of the Gospels, we encounter similar passages with subtle differences. Beginning with the first people to encounter the empty tomb, again it is the "women" who discovered the empty tomb. The "women" are not identified in the Gospel of Luke until the whole episode of the Resurrection has been told. In Luke 24:10, we learn that it was Mary Magdalene and Joanna and Mary the mother of James and the "other women" with them who gave the good news to the Apostles. We do not know how many women there were in total, nor do we know if only Mary Magdalene went to the tomb, as is told in the Gospel of John and then told the other women who told the disciples. All of these are possibilities.

The encounter at the tomb takes place at early dawn, again in the context of taking spices to go and anoint the Body of Jesus.

As in the Gospel of Mark, the women find the stone rolled away, though there is no explanation of how this happened. They encounter TWO men rather than the one described in Matthew and Mark. As in the Gospel of Mark, the women entered the tomb and then encountered the two men. In Matthew, the angel was sitting outside the tomb.

The men ask the women "Why do you seek the living among the dead?" (In certain manuscripts the words, "He is Risen, He is not here," are recorded.) The men recall for the women the words of Christ, *"Remember how He told you, while He was still in Galilee, that the Son of Man must be delivered into the hands of sinful men, and be crucified, and on the third day rise"* (Luke 24:6-7). Their memory now recollected, they went and told what they had seen to the eleven disciples (with Judas gone from their number, the disciples numbered eleven), and to "all the rest" presumably the other myrrh-bearing women.

The response of the disciples was that their words seemed to be like an "idle tale" and the disciples did not believe the women. Some manuscripts add in a verse (v. 12) which reads *"But Peter rose and ran to the tomb; stooping and looking in, he saw the linen cloths by themselves; and he went home wondering at what had happened."* Peter had both faith and uncertainty. He didn't completely dismiss the claims of the women, in that he ran to the tomb to see for himself, but even he was perplexed by what he had seen and what it meant and he went home uncertain of what to make of it.

You can see a pattern developing here in the three Gospel accounts we have examined thus far. It is the women who go to the tomb. They exhibit great courage to make the journey. Despite all the foreshadowing Jesus did, telling them He would rise from the dead, when they actually see the empty tomb, the reaction of the women is fear, astonishment, and uncertainty. Even when the women are bold enough to tell the Disciples, the reaction of the Disciples is one of skepticism. There is no reaction of, "That is awesome! Just how He said it would happen!" The fact that it had happened just as He said it would happen, still brings doubt and skepticism.

On the positive side, both the women and the disciples are eager to see more. They want to believe. They want more signs. Like Joseph of Arimathea, whom we discussed before, they are "seekers," who haven't found exactly what they are looking for, and perhaps aren't even sure what they are looking for, but they are looking. This is the first step of faith—to seek knowledge of something you don't completely know. These accounts of the Resurrection in many ways reflect our reaction to the Resurrection we have just celebrated. Some of us are still skeptical. Some are still confused. Some are still trying to figure it out. If you are "still in the game," still reading, still searching, then you match the women and the Disciples at the Resurrection. They still had a ways to go in their faith—and so do we. They glorified God and are recognized as saints, even though they were once skeptics and seekers. The glory of God and sainthood are still very much on the table for us as well.

> *The Myrrh-bearing Women, at early dawn drew near to the Tomb of the Giver of Life, and found an Angel sitting on the stone. And speaking to them, he said: "Why do you seek the Living among the dead? Why do you mourn the Incorruptible one, amid corruption? Go, and proclaim it to His Apostles." (From the Praises of the Resurrection Orthros, Trans. by Fr. George Papadeas)*

Reflect on God in some way today!

Bright Saturday

The Resurrection—From the Gospel of John

Now on the first day of the week Mary Magdalene came to the tomb early, while it was still dark, and saw that the stone had been taken away from the tomb. So she ran, and went to Simon Peter and the other disciple, the one whom Jesus loved, and said to them, "They have taken the Lord out of the tomb, and we do not know where they have laid Him." Peter then came out with the other disciple, and they went toward the tomb. They both ran, but the other disciple outran Peter and reached the tomb first; and stooping to look in, he saw the linen cloths lying there, but he did not go in. Then Simon Peter came, following him, and went into the tomb; he saw the linen cloths lying, and the napkin, which had been on His head, not lying with the linen cloths but rolled up in a place by itself. Then the other disciple, who reached the tomb first, also went in, and he saw and believed; for as yet they did not know the scripture, that He must rise from the dead.
Then the disciples went back to their homes.
John 20:1-10
(From the Seventh Eothinon Gospel of Sunday Orthros)

Christ is Risen!

Today we examine the Resurrection as told in the Gospel of John. In John's account, it appears that Mary Magdalene comes to the tomb alone. Though in verse 2, she uses the word "we," that "we do not know where they have laid Him." It would seem that there could have been other women there, with Mary as the spokesperson for the group, or perhaps Mary was there alone. There is no mention of taking spices to the tomb, so we do not know if Mary was going there just to mourn, or to work.

She finds the stone has been taken away from the tomb, though again we are not told how that happened. Mary does not enter the tomb in John's account, nor does she encounter an angel or a young man. Instead, she runs away and finds Simon Peter and the other Disciple, the one whom Jesus loved (this is John, also called the "beloved Disciple"). We are not told if Mary had to go a great distance to find them, if they were in a house, or if they were near her, also going to the tomb in the darkness.

The reaction of both Disciples is to run toward the tomb, certainly more out of curiosity than confidence. John reaches the tomb, but does not go in. Peter comes quickly afterward and goes into the tomb. John waiting for Peter is perhaps deference to Peter's position as the "rock" of the Apostles. When Peter enters into the tomb, he sees the linen cloths lying, and the napkin, which had been placed over Jesus' head, not lying with the linen cloths, but rolled up in a place by itself. This is significant, because it shows a scene of order. Grave clothes rolled up nicely and folded depict an orderly scene. Had there been some kind of robbery of the grave, the robbers most certainly wouldn't have taken the time to roll up clothes.

Then John entered the tomb and we are told that he saw and believed, yet the very next verse points to the Disciples' lack of understanding of the scriptures. They believe at the moment in the Resurrection, but perhaps not in the context of everything else that had happened. We are told that the Disciples went back to their homes. Later in the day and later in John's Gospel, we will read about how they gathered behind closed doors.

> *They who were with Miriam came before dawn, and finding the stone rolled away from the Tomb heard from the Angel "Why do you seek as man among the dead, Him, Who dwells in Light Eternal? Behold the shroud of the grave; make haste and proclaim to the world, that the Lord is risen, putting to death, Death; for He is the Son of God, the Savior of mankind." (From the Divine Liturgy on Pascha, Trans. by Fr. George Papadeas)*

As the Disciples ran to the tomb, let us run to Christ today!

Thomas Sunday

Have You Seen the Lord? Does it Make You Glad to See Him?

On the evening of that day, the first day of the week, the doors being shut where the disciples were, for fear of the Jews, Jesus came and stood among them and said to them, "Peace be with you." When He had said this, He showed them His hands and His side. Then the disciples were glad when they saw the Lord.
John 20:19-20
(From the Gospel Reading at the Divine Liturgy on Thomas Sunday)

Christ is Risen!

The Sunday after Pascha is affectionately known as "Thomas Sunday." For the next few reflections, we'll be examining the story of Thomas, as well as Christ's first encounter with His Disciples after the Resurrection. On Pascha, at the Agape Vespers, we read from John 20:19-25, Christ's first encounter with the Disciples. On Thomas Sunday, we read John 20:19-31, which includes both the encounter on the evening of Pascha and the second encounter eight days later, when Thomas was present.

On the evening after the Resurrection, which took place on the first day of the week, the Disciples had gathered behind doors that were locked for fear of the Jews. Jesus came and stood among them. He miraculously appeared in their sight. He didn't knock on the door or announce that He was coming. He just "appeared."

He spoke with them, to show that not only was He God, but that He was still human. He had experienced a human death and now He had been resurrected from the dead and was appearing to them not as a ghost, not in a dream, but as a human being. His first words to them are, "Peace be with you." Among His last words before His Passion concerned peace as well: *"Peace I leave with you; my peace I give to you"* (John 14:27). It is interesting to note that when Orthodox Christians assemble to celebrate the Divine Liturgy, the first three petitions center on peace. The introductory petition invites us, "*In peace let us pray to the Lord.*" This reflects the first words of Christ to His disciples after the Resurrection, "Peace be with you."

Sensing that His Disciples will want some kind of proof that He is actually the same Jesus they saw crucified, He shows them the mark of the nails in His hands, and the mark of the spear that pierced His side. This erases all doubt in their minds that this is the same man whom they saw crucified two days earlier.

The reaction of the Disciples becomes one of joy, not of skepticism. Of course, that is easy for them, for they stand face to face with Christ. We have not stood face to face with Christ yet. Or have we?

Every time we celebrate the Divine Liturgy and receive Communion, we have the opportunity to touch the Living God. We "*taste and see*" (Ps. 34:8) the Lord in the Eucharist. After all have partaken, we sing a hymn: "*We have seen the true Light; we have received the heavenly Spirit; we have found the true faith, worshipping the undivided Trinity, for the Trinity has saved us.*" (From the Divine Liturgy, Trans. by Holy Cross Seminary Press) Does this make us glad? Does this encounter send us away with joy? Or are we skeptical? Or has it even become part of a "routine"?

In the parable of the sower, Jesus says to His disciples, "*To you it has been given to know the secrets of the Kingdom of God; but for others they are in parables, so that seeing they may not see, and hearing they may not understand*" (Luke 8:10). This means that some "see" the Lord and yet they don't see Him. Others are looking and they "see" the Lord, and they see Him with the joy that the Disciples saw Christ that evening in Jerusalem.

How, then, do we see Christ? We see Him through the eyes of faith, which are sharpened through the eyes of vulnerability. Make yourself in some way vulnerable to the Lord, whether it is in the spiritual intimacy of prayer, or the difficult task of forgiveness, the humility needed in the sacrament of confession, or in the selfless act of service to others. Make yourself vulnerable to the Lord and you will "see" Him and have the joy that the Disciples had when they saw the Lord.

Of course, as the saying goes, you will only find what you are looking for. If you are not looking for God, you are not likely to find Him. Which goes back to the question posed many reflections ago, "Are you a seeker?" We need to be looking for Christ, and we need to look for Him through vulnerability. When we find Him, let us pray for our reaction to be one of joy.

As You came and stood among Your disciples, O Savior, and gave them peace, come and be with us also and save us. (Hypakoe from Orthros of Thomas Sunday, Trans. by Fr. Seraphim Dedes)

May today, His day, be filled with joy, and may you be glad in the time you spend with Him in worship today!

Monday of the 2nd Week of Pascha

The First Ordination

Jesus said to them again, "Peace be with you. As the Father has sent Me, even so I send you." And when He had said this, He breathed on them, and said to them, "Receive the Holy Spirit."
John 20:21-22
(From the Gospel Reading at the Divine Liturgy on Thomas Sunday)

Christ is Risen!

In all of the Gospel accounts, Jesus "commissions" the Disciples to go out into the world and spread the Good News. In the Gospels of Matthew, Mark and Luke, this "commissioning" takes place at the time of the Ascension, when Jesus went up to heaven forty days after the Resurrection. In the Gospel of John, this "commissioning" takes place on the day of the Resurrection, at the first encounter that Jesus has with His Disciples.

After appearing to them through closed doors, and sharing in their joy with them, Jesus "got down to business" again, so to speak. He again offered them His "peace." Then He commissioned them: *"As the father has sent Me, even so I send you."* God the Father sent His Only-Begotten Son into the world to do a specific thing, *"For God sent the Son into the world, not to condemn the world, but that the world might be saved through Him"* (John 3:17). Jesus now has a specific task for the Disciples, to bring His message to others, and to bring others to Christ.

The "commissioning" includes the bestowing of the Holy Spirit on them. This verse is the "genesis" of the Orthodox Sacrament of Ordination. Because when a man is ordained into the Holy Priesthood of the Orthodox Church, the ordaining Bishop invokes the grace of the Holy Spirit upon Him so that he can become a deacon, priest or bishop. The words of ordination are as follows:

The divine grace, which always heals that which is infirm and completes that which is lacking, ordains the most devout (Subdeacon, Deacon or Priest) to the office of (Deacon, Priest or Bishop). Let us, therefore, pray for him, that the grace of the All-Holy Spirit may come upon him.

The word "grace" in Greek is the word "Haris." "Haris" is closely aligned with the word "Hara" which means, "joy." Thus, grace and joy are closely related. Grace is the God-given quality bestowed on someone or something that, "heals what is infirm and completes what is lacking" in that person or thing. In the case of Holy Communion, "Grace" comes upon bread and wine, two ordinary materials, and transforms them into the extraordinary Gifts of the Body and Blood of Christ. In the case of ordination, the Holy Spirit comes down on the person being ordained and "completes what is infirm and heals what is lacking" in that person, to allow them to step into the lofty office of deacon, priest, or bishop, whatever they are being ordained to do.

One of the Traditions of the Orthodox Church, is our Tradition of Apostolic Succession. This means that the Bishops of the church can trace "their lineage" back to the Apostles, who received their commissions from Christ Himself. If the Bishop stands as the "typos Christou," or "type of Christ," in order to do so, the Bishop must be connected to Christ through Apostolic Succession. There is no way that one can proclaim himself a Bishop, because a Bishop must be related to all other Bishops through the tradition of Apostolic Succession.

The Bishops then ordain the priests and deacons, who represent the Bishops in their respective parishes. An interesting side note, only one Bishop is required to ordain a deacon or priest, but at least three Bishops are required in order for another Bishop to be ordained, which along with Apostolic Succession, preserves the authenticity of the Bishop.

Apostolic Succession is established through the commissioning of the Disciples as told in these verses. When Christ bestowed the Holy Spirit on them, they in turn bestowed the Holy Spirit on others, who continue to bestow the Holy Spirit through the sacrament or ordination to the bishops, priest and deacons who serve to this day.

While the text of the sacrament of ordination is not found in scripture, and while the word "ordination" itself is not used in this passage, this is where the idea of ordination comes from. Our "Traditions" then are all based in scripture, "codified" or accepted by all Orthodox Churches through Tradition and Canon Law.

> *O Life, You rose from the sepulcher, even though the tomb was secured with a seal, O Christ God. And though the doors had been bolted, You came to Your disciples, O Resurrection of all. Through them You renew a right spirit in us, according to Your great mercy. (Apolytikion of Thomas Sunday, Trans. by Fr. Seraphim Dedes)*

Receive the Holy Spirit as it comes upon you at the Divine Liturgy today, and pray that He heals what is infirm and completes what is lacking in you!

Tuesday of the 2nd Week of Pascha

One of Christ's Greatest Gifts to Us— One of the Greatest Gifts You Can Give Yourself

And when He had said this, He breathed on them, and said to them, "Receive the Holy Spirit. If you forgive the sins of any, they are forgiven; if you retain the sins of any, they are retained.
John 20:22-23
(From the Gospel Reading at the Divine Liturgy on Thomas Sunday)

Christ is Risen!

In yesterday's reflection, we examined the sacrament of ordination, which has its genesis in John 20:22. In the very next verse, we have the genesis of the sacrament of Confession. Christ knows that life is hard. It's hard to always have our focus on Him. He watched His Disciples, His closest friends, fail again and again to trust in Him, and to do the right thing. So, He created this sacrament as a way of "encouraging" His followers, by giving them a means to eliminate sins and guilt in this life, and not lose hope if the sins were great!

Christ gave His Disciples both a gift and a responsibility when He said to them, *"If you forgive the sins of any, they are forgiven; if you retain the sins of any, they are retained."* Only God alone forgives sins, but through this gift, God's servants—His Disciples, Bishops and now Priests—are given the opportunity to "loose" sins of the faithful, so that the faithful are not beset with guilt.

We spoke about the concept of Apostolic Succession, which means that Christ ordained the Apostles, endowing them with the Holy Spirit. The Apostles then ordained the next generation of church leaders, whom we call "Episkopoi" or "bishops." Later on, the office of Presbyter was added.

As an aside, the first office of the clergy to be created was the rank of Bishop. These were the Apostles who founded the churches in the various cities where they spread the Gospel. When a "new" church was established in a new city, a new bishop was ordained to shepherd the new church. Deacons were ordained to assist the Bishops. In Acts 6, we read about the ordination of the first deacons:

Now in these days when the disciples were increasing in number, the Hellenists murmured against the Hebrews because their widows were neglected in the daily distribution. And the twelve summoned the body of the disciples and said, "It is not right that we should give up preaching the word of God to serve tables. Therefore, brethren, pick out from among you seven men of good repute, full of the Spirit and of wisdom, whom we may appoint to this duty. But we will devote ourselves to prayer and to the ministry of the word." And what they said pleased the whole multitude, and they chose Stephen, a man full of faith and of the Holy Spirit, and Philip, and Prochorus, and Nicanor, and Timon and Parmenas and Nicolaus, a proselyte of Antioch. These they set before the Apostles, and they prayed and laid their hands upon them. (Acts 6:1-6)

Later, the office of Presbyter was created so that as more churches were established in each city, and the Bishop could not preside over all of them, the Presbyter was representing the Bishop in the satellite parishes, with the Bishop presiding over the Cathedral parish and occasionally visiting the others. (This practice is still followed in our church to this day.)

The Bishops were given the authority to bind and loose sins through their Apostolic Succession. The Presbyters (who we now call priests) are given this authority through their Bishop through a prayer of elevation to the office of Confessor. Not every priest has this responsibility. In fact, a priest usually serves for a period of time before being given this awesome responsibility. (A deacon does not hear confessions, he is not given this responsibility).

It is one of the greatest feelings in the world to be told that you can live your life "without any anxiety" about the things you brought to confession. It is one of the greatest gifts God has given to His Church. It is one of the greatest gifts we can give ourselves. This gift is possible through the sacrament of confession. God really has taken care of the needs of His faithful. He has given us a great way to feel encouraged and hopeful by giving us a mechanism to be released of past guilt.

The choice to "forgive" or "retain" a sin is given over to the "discernment" of the priest or bishop hearing the confession. Why would a priest "retain" a sin that someone has confessed? I can't answer for all priests, but let me give you my personal reason. At the end of confession, there is a prayer called the "prayer of absolution" that is offered over the person who has confessed their sins. The prayer includes the words "Have no further anxiety about the things you have confessed, depart in peace." Sometimes I ask the person who has confessed if they still feel "anxiety" about what they've confessed and many times, the answer is "yes," they still do. Instead of offering a prayer that **they** are not ready to accept, I ask them to do a "penance." Many people associate penance with punishment, after all "penance" and "penalty" share the same root. I look at penance more like a project. For instance, I might ask someone to read a Psalm for 40 days, like Psalm 50/51 that speaks about "create in me a clean heart," and then after 40 days to check in to see if the anxiety has subsided. For someone who hasn't received Communion in a long time, perhaps a "penance" might be that they receive for a period of time. (Some priests ask people to not receive Communion for a period of time, I do not do that because I don't think it is spiritually healthy to do that to someone). For someone who has had an abortion, who still carries sadness over this sin, I ask them to write a letter to the child they didn't keep and this has always helped bring healing to the wounded heart and soul. **Again, I use "penance" very infrequently.** What I "discern" when I listen to a confession, is the "contrite" heart that says "I want to come back." Then it is with great joy that I offer the prayer of absolution, granting each person who comes to confession, the new start and unburdening of sin they so desire. (Another important suggestion for confession, you should go to a priest whom you know, or have some familiarity with, and feel comfortable with.)

Today's verses represent one of God's greatest gifts to us, the ability to start over again, granted to us from Christ, to the Apostles, through the Bishops, and to the priests, who impart it to the faithful. Receiving absolution through the sacrament of confession is one of the greatest gifts you can give yourself!

> *O Giver of Life, You did not break the seals that secured Your tomb. And likewise after Your awesome rising from the Sepulcher, You unhindered entered the room where Your glorious Apostles were, the doors being shut, O Christ, and cause them to rejoice. And You granted them Your governing Holy Spirit, for mercy immeasurable. (From the Praises of Orthros, Thomas Sunday, Trans. by Fr. Seraphim Dedes)*

If you didn't go to confession during Lent, make an appointment with your priest so you can receive this gift! It's available all year!

Wednesday of the 2nd Week of Pascha

Unless I see, I will not believe

Now Thomas, one of the twelve, called the Twin, was not with them when Jesus came. So the other disciples told him, "We have seen the Lord." But he said to them, "Unless I see in His hands the print of the nails, and place my finger in the mark of the nails, and place my hand in His side, I will not believe."
John 20:24-25
(From the Gospel Reading at the Divine Liturgy on Thomas Sunday)

Christ is Risen!
"Unless I see, I will not believe!" This is one of the most honest and relatable statements in the Bible. We call Thomas, "Doubting Thomas" and sometimes I wonder if we say that in an affectionate way or in a derogatory one. "Doubting Thomas" is all of us at some point, which is why it is so refreshing that his story is told in the Bible.

Faith is believing without fully seeing or comprehending. There are a lot of things in life that require us to have "faith." Getting married is an act of faith—no one who gets married knows what it will be like to live with someone for decades, have children with them, go through life's ups and down with them—so getting married is an act of faith. Having children is an act of faith—until you have a child, you don't know what it is like to raise one. The same can be said for starting a new job, moving to a new city, going to college, buying a new home, having a serious surgery, and many other things.

None of these examples I mentioned require "blind faith," in the sense of knowing NOTHING and still going forward. An arranged marriage, where you do not know the person you are marrying at all, if you meet them for the first time at the altar, that would require "blind faith." If you get married to someone you know well, as most people do, you don't know everything about them, but you know a lot, you certainly know enough to pledge to marry them. No one knows exactly what it is like to have a child until you have one, but we've all seen children and what they do at various ages and stages, so we know "something" of what it is like to have a child. We all know people who have started new jobs, many of us have as well, so starting a new job isn't totally foreign either.

Just about every time we "take a leap of faith," that leap is accompanied by some doubts. Who has a child and has never wondered "what did I do?" Who hasn't ever questioned "Why did I marry THIS person?" Or "Why did I buy this car?" or "this house" or "why did I move to this city?" Doubts are part of life.

Unfortunately, the devil seizes upon our doubts and causes us to lack confidence in ourselves and others. It is one of his tricks. Doubt and distraction go hand in hand, and many times these lead to levels of destruction.

How do we defeat doubt? Well, doubt leads to lack of confidence, which leads to fear. The antidote to fear is love. In I John 4:18, we read: *"There is no fear in love, but perfect love casts out fear."* Love is built through vulnerability. When you want to grow in your relationship with anyone—a friend, your spouse, your child—when you make yourself more vulnerable, that's when love grows. It definitely takes some faith to be vulnerable. Sometimes one gets burned when he or she makes himself or herself vulnerable. More often, I think, when one is vulnerable, the result is positive. What I know is that without being vulnerable, there is no way that a deeply loving result is possible.

Most of us have probably had doubts about the faith. We have wondered, "Is there really a God?" "Is this whole story of Jesus as told to us in the Bible true?"

Many of us have doubts about OUR personal faith—"Do I believe enough?" "Do I really believe at all?" "If my life were to end today, do I really believe in eternal life?"

Probably all of us have doubts about God's plans for our lives and the lives of others. Many times I'm scratching my head and wondering why certain things happen in the world, and why certain things happen to me. These doubts again are cured with vulnerability—in my times of doubt, I increase my efforts to pray. I increase my efforts to worship and be involved in things of faith. I go to confession or talk to my spiritual father and talk it over with him.

There are certain things about the Christian faith that I can say for certainty. First of all, I have "seen" enough of the "things of God" that I know there is a God. Looking out at the creation, seeing clouds in the sky, feeling the gentle breeze, there is no way that these things are man-made. I have seen enough beautiful things in my life that defy any human logic or human ingenuity that I know that these things have to be from God. Even if I had no personal experience of God, I've known enough people who have had experiences of God that either the message of Christ is true, or there are a lot of people walking in this life whose lives are a fraud. I've read stories of saints who have given their lives for Christ, who died because they loved Him. Who is going to die for a fraud? No one.

Doubts are normal! Thomas was really a lot like us. We aren't likely to see Jesus walk into our office today and show us His hands and His side. We can see Christ in so many things—in nature, in our own gifts, in beautiful things that defy rational explanation, and in the lives of many who are faithful to Him.

Thomas, who was also called the Twin, was not there when You appeared to the Disciples, O Lord, and therefore he did not believe that You resurrected. Thus emphatically he cried aloud to those who saw You, "Unless I put my finger in His side and the wounds created by the nails, I will not believe that He indeed arose." (From the Praises of Orthros, Thomas Sunday, Trans. by Fr. Seraphim Dedes)

When in doubt, pray it out!

Thursday of the 2nd Week of Pascha

Jesus is My _____ and My _____

Eight days later, His disciples were again in the house, and Thomas was with them. The doors were shut, but Jesus came and stood among them, and said, "Peace be with you." Then He said to Thomas, "Put your finger here, and see My hands; and put out your hand, and place it in My side; do not be faithless, but believing." Thomas answered him, "My Lord and my God!"
John 20:26-28
(From the Gospel Reading at the Divine Liturgy on Thomas Sunday)

Christ is Risen!

As with many figures in the Bible, Thomas redeemed himself. After initially doubting the Resurrection of Christ, when he saw Christ eight days later, he offered the "highest confession" of Christ's divinity in the Bible. He called Him "My LORD and my GOD!" Thomas went on to found the church in India. He was ultimately martyred for his faith by being run through with a spear. After it was "all said and done," Thomas got it right, despite his doubts.

Thomas' story is one of the most comforting in the Bible. Because it shows how a man can change and strengthen his beliefs. It shows how the Lord is patient and loving as He waits for us to "find ourselves."

There are two things to take away from today's scripture passage. The first is that when Jesus appeared to the disciples eight days after His first appearance, that Thomas had missed, Thomas was with them. They had shared the great news that they had seen the Lord, yet he was filled with doubts. He stayed "in" with the disciples. He kept "showing up." He wasn't so filled with doubt and discouragement that he left. This is an important lesson for all of us, when we have doubts about our faith, or about God's plan for our lives. It is important that we keep "showing up"—to worship, to pray, to try. A dear friend once told me, "eighty percent of life is just showing up." When you "show up" things happen. When you don't, nothing happens. When you have the inevitable "crisis" of faith that just about everyone goes through, it is really important to keep "showing up" for church, for prayer, and for the Lord, because in showing up, there is an opportunity to grow in faith and erase doubt. "Staying away" lessens, if not eliminates, that opportunity.

Allow me to share that there have been a number of occasions in my ministry when a young person has passed away. I have told the families, "please make sure you are in church the following Sunday, please 'show up.'" It is important as a witness for others. It is important for a person when he or she stands before the Judgment Seat of Christ that one is able to say, "on a Sunday that I was filled with pain and doubt, I still 'showed up.'"

The other lesson to take away from today's scripture is if you were to make the same "confession" that Thomas made to the Lord, how would you fill in the blanks? Thomas said "My Lord and my God." How do you fill in those blanks? How do you "confess" the Lord?

My "insurance policy" on Christmas and Easter?
My "rock" and my salvation?
My strength and my hope?
My joy and my purpose?
My challenge and my struggle?
My beginning and my ending?

Think seriously on how you "confess" Christ. Because how you fill in these blanks says a lot about Christ's place in your life, the strength of your faith and what you think of your salvation. Indeed, Thomas' confession provides us with the most profound way to think of our own confession of faith.

> *After eight days from Your resurrection, O Jesus our King, and the Father's only-begotten Word, You appeared to Your Disciples, the doors being shut; and You granted them Your peace. And to the disbelieving Disciple You showed the marks on Your body. "Come and touch My hands and My feet, and My uncorrupt side. "And he believed and cried to You, "My Lord and my God, glory to You." (Doxastikon from Orthros of Thomas Sunday, Trans. by Fr. Seraphim Dedes)*

Fill in the blanks of this statement, directing it to the Lord: My _____ and my _____.

Friday of the 2nd Week of Pascha

Believing without Seeing—Our Greatest Challenge

Jesus said to him, "Have you believed because you have seen me? Blessed are those who have not seen and yet believe."
John 20:29
(From the Gospel Reading at the Divine Liturgy on Thomas Sunday)

Christ is Risen!

I've never been to China, but I know people who have been there. I've never flown in outer space, but I have had the opportunity to meet someone who has.

There are a lot of things I've never seen and places that I've never been. Do I ever doubt there is a China? Do I ever doubt that the world isn't really round? I've never seen either with my own eyes. However, there is so much evidence from people who have done these things that they must be true. Even though I haven't personally experienced them, I accept them as truth. I believe, even though I have not seen them.

Believing without seeing is what faith is all about. When I got married, I didn't have a crystal ball to tell me the future. When we had a child, we didn't have a crystal ball either. Did we believe we could be successfully married? Or successfully have a child? We did, or we wouldn't have done either. Will we ultimately be successful? Do I know that? No, I don't. I have faith in God, faith in the person I am married to, and faith in myself that what I can't see are still things I can put my faith and my confidence in.

The most worthwhile things in life require faith. If one knows all the variables and never "risks" anything, then there is no real reward in life. If no one takes a chance on anything, there is no success. Perhaps there isn't as much failure or pain, but for sure there is no success, and no success IS failure and is painful.

There are many things in life that we take on "faith." There is a difference between "knowing" and "believing." "Knowing" is based on scientific or exhaustive knowledge. "Believing" is taking something on faith, with partial or sometimes virtually no knowledge. Did you "know" that you went to the right college when you started college? Unless you checked out every college in the world, the answer would have been "no." When I was checking out colleges, I checked out three of them and then picked the one I went to "believing" it was the right choice. Do I know it was the right choice? I think so, because I had a good college experience, but perhaps I might have chosen differently and still had a good experience. So, I "believe" I made the right choice.

When a person gets married, do they marry based on knowledge or faith? The answer is both—people have some knowledge of the person they are marrying. No one has dated everyone in the world, or even many people, so the decision to marry someone is based in large part on faith.

The choice to follow the Lord is based on both knowledge and faith. It is not based solely on faith. Everyone has some knowledge of the Lord. That might come through reading the scriptures, through the experience of worship or prayer, through life experiences where God is present, and even through the experiences of others. We don't follow the Lord based on knowledge alone. There are many aspects to Christianity where one has to have faith and that faith has to be a personal faith—remember the parable of the Maidens? We can talk to one another about the faith, but a person's faith can't be divided into parts and shared. Faith is something that has to be personal to each individual. I've never been to heaven, but I believe there is a heaven. I believe that there will be a judgment before Christ when I die. I believe that He will be merciful, but also judging. How much of each, I don't know. What I do know is that He has blessed me with some talents that He expects me to use and I will do my best to use them. I know that God is "glorious" because I've seen His glory in ways large and small throughout my life. I ask God, to "show me His glory in ways large and small" and then I keep my eyes open so that this prayer can be answered.

The other thing about faith is that it is a continuous action, not a destination or accomplishment. Going back to the example of marriage, I was married at a finite moment in time, I am married now and hopefully I will still be married many years from now. I took the first step of marriage at a finite moment in time. Marriage is something that I have to work on every day. It's the same thing with faith. We take our first steps of faith in a finite moment in time. There was a finite moment of time when you realized that you believed "something" about God. Each day, then, there should be work to build on that faith through acquiring knowledge and experience. Thus, even what you can't see, you still have confidence in because your faith is not a "blind faith" where you know nothing, but a knowledgeable faith, where you know something and crave to know more.

> *"O Thomas, according to your wish, handle Me," said Christ to him. "Put out your hand, and be cognizant that I have flesh and bones, and an earthen body. Be not one who disbelieves. But rather with the others be confident." And he in turn cried out, "You, O Jesus, are my Lord and God, and my Savior. Glory to Your resurrection." (From the Praises of Thomas Sunday, Trans. by Fr. Seraphim Dedes)*

Blessed are those who have "seen" and want to see more!

Saturday of the 2nd Week of Pascha

Being a Christian Requires a Soft Heart

And they went out and fled from the tomb; for trembling and astonishment had come upon them; and they said nothing to any one, for they were afraid. Now when He rose early on the first day of the week, He appeared first to Mary Magdalene, from whom He had cast out seven demons. She went out and told those who had been with Him, as they mourned and wept. But when they heard that He was alive and had been seen by her, they would not believe it. After this He appeared in another form to two of them, as they were walking into the country. And they went back and told the rest, but they did not believe them. Afterward He appeared to the eleven themselves as they sat at the table; and He upbraided them for their unbelief and hardness of heart, because they had not believed those who saw Him after He had risen.
Mark 16:8-14
(From the Second and Third Eothinon Gospels of Orthros)

Christ is Risen!

It's interesting to see the reactions of various witnesses to the Resurrection. Even though it all unfolded as Jesus said it would, reactions varied from astonishment to fear to doubt. Joy would come much later. The first women who went and found the empty tomb, according to the Gospel of Mark, were both trembling and astonished and they said nothing to anyone for they were afraid. What were they afraid of? That no one would believe them? That they too might be punished by the Jewish leaders, after all they were Jews as well? Were they afraid to actually believe themselves?

Mary Magdalene was not afraid to share the news, but no one believed her. Two of the disciples were walking in the country (we will talk about the encounter on the road to Emmaus in a couple of days) and they told the rest of the disciples that they had encountered the Lord. No one believed them either. Eventually, Jesus appeared to the eleven disciples and chastised them for not believing the testimony of the others.

In some ways it is a scary thing to be a Christian. Because a Christian is called to a great degree of accountability. If we stand in the presence of Christ in prayer, or in worship, or if we partake of Him in Holy Communion, we are in a place of accountability. We have heard the good news. We have partaken of Christ. Then what?

There are a few times in my life that I can honestly say I wished I lived in ignorance of Christianity. Then I wouldn't have accountability. People have often asked me the question, "What happens to people who have never heard of Christ, who haven't had a chance to believe in Him, like someone living in a remote village in a third world country?" My answer to this question is, "I truthfully don't know what will happen to a person like this. I'd like to believe that Christ will give them an additional chance to believe, since they went through this life without that chance." I sometimes add, "I'm not worried as much about the person in the remote village, I'm worried about me. Because I can't plead ignorance, and sometimes I wish I could." I have heard the message of Christ. In many ways, I have seen the power of Christ at work in the world. I sometimes wonder am I more like Mary Magdalene, going and sharing the news? Or am I more like the Disciples, who have heard the news and still have unbelief and hardness of heart?

Unbelief and hardness of heart go hand in hand. For those who live with hardened hearts, who go from "zero to sixty" in seconds when it comes to losing their temper, who make others nervous and uncomfortable around them, it leads to wonder whether they truly believe. Because one who truly believes has a softened heart and one who is trying to grow in faith is working on softening their heart. I have to remind myself of this during the times when I have a short temper.

For those who follow sports, many times we hear the phrase, related to many athletes, "that he/she has soft hands," and that's why they handle the ball so well. A person who plays baseball with stiff hands is not going to be able to play as well as someone who plays with soft hands. Being a Christian is similar. It's not the one with the hard heart or hard head that is the most effective Christian or ambassador for Christ. It is the one who has the soft heart that is ready to be filled with Christ. It is the one who has the soft voice that speaks with love, not with force.

Every time we worship in church, we "sit at the table" with the Lord, whether we are concentrating fully or even just going through the motions. We sit at the table with the Lord. When we pray to Him, we are "sitting" with Him as well. If perfect love casts out all fear, then it is the soft heart that grows love and faith. The Lord understands that there is fear. Mary Magdalene was one of the women who fled from the tomb with astonishment and fear, but she also had faith because she eventually went and told the good news. So, having some fear in your Christian life is fine. What we want to seek in our lives though, is a soft heart that witnesses Christ with love.

When Mary Magdalene announced the good news of the Savior's resurrection from the dead and His appearance, the disciples did not believe her and were reproached for their hardness of heart. But armed with signs and wonders, they were sent to preach. You, O Lord, were lifted up to the Father, the source of light, while they preached the word in all places supported by miracles. We, therefore, enlightened by them glorify Your resurrection from the dead, O loving Lord. (Doxastikon of the 3rd Eothinon, Trans. by Holy Cross Seminary Press)

Have a soft heart today!

Sunday of the 2nd Week of Pascha

Mary Magdalene—Talk About a Turnaround

But Mary stood weeping outside the tomb, and as she wept she stooped to look into the tomb; and she saw two angels in white, sitting where the body of Jesus had lain, one at the head and one at the feet. They said to her, "Woman, why are you weeping?" She said to them, "Because they have taken away my Lord, and I do not know where they have laid Him." Saying this, she turned round and saw Jesus standing, but she did not know that it was Jesus. Jesus said to her, "Woman, why are you weeping? Whom do you seek?" Supposing Him to be the gardener, she said to Him, "Sir, if you have carried Him away, tell me where you have laid Him, and I will take him away." Jesus said to her, "Mary." She turned and said to Him in Hebrew, "Rabboni!" (which means Teacher). Jesus said to her, "Do not hold Me, for I have not yet ascended to the Father; but go to My brethren and say to them, I am ascending to My Father and your Father, to My God and your God."
Mary Magdalene went and said to the disciples, "I have seen the Lord"; and she told them that He had said these things to her.
John 20:11-18
(From the Eighth Eothinon Gospel of Sunday Orthros)

Christ is Risen!

The first person to see Jesus after He rose from the dead was Mary Magdalene. In all of the Gospel accounts, she is among the first to go to the empty tomb. In the Gospels of Matthew, Mark and Luke, Mary goes to the tomb in the company of one or two other women. In the Gospel of John, she goes alone. In all four Gospels, she witnesses the tomb empty of the Body of Jesus. In the Gospel of John, she encounters Jesus at the tomb, but supposes that He is a gardener. She doesn't immediately recognize Him. He then reveals Himself to her. He reveals Himself to Mary Magdalene in the other Gospels as well. It is Mary who is the first to run to tell the disciples that she has seen the Lord, risen from the dead. Mary Magdalene has the title "equal to the Apostles," because an apostle spreads the good news, and Mary was the "apostle to the Apostles," she was the one who shared the good news of the Resurrection with them.

So, who was Mary Magdalene? It is probably first appropriate to answer who she wasn't. Mary Magdalene was not the sister of Martha and Lazarus. She was also not the woman who anointed Jesus' feet and wiped them with her hair at the home of Mary and Martha.

We read about Mary Magdalene first in the Gospel of Luke, 8:1-3: *"Soon afterward Jesus went on through cities and villages, preaching and bringing the good news of the Kingdom of God. And the twelve were with Him, and also some women who had been healed of evil spirits and infirmities: Mary, called Magdalene, from whom seven demons had gone out, and Joanna, the wife of Chuza, Herod's steward, and Susanna, and many others, who provided for them out of their means."*

Mary Magdalene was present at the cross of Christ, as we read in the Gospel of Matthew 27:55-56: *"There were also many women there, looking on from afar, who had followed Jesus from Galilee, ministering to Him; among whom were Mary Magdalene, and Mary the mother of James and Joseph, and the mother of the sons of Zebedee."*

Mary was present at the tomb when it was sealed: *"And Joseph took the body, and wrapped it in a clean linen shroud, and laid it in his own new tomb which he had hewn in the rock; and he rolled a great stone to the door of the tomb, and departed. Mary Magdalene and the other Mary were there, sitting opposite the sepulcher"* (Matt. 27:59-61).

Little is known about her life after the Resurrection, though it is believed that she went to Ephesus and worked with St. John the Theologian to establish the church there.

Mary Magdalene is another example, amongst countless others, of people who had some significant life challenges whom Christ chose to have important roles in spreading His message of salvation. Once demon-possessed, she is now considered "equal to the Apostles." There are lots of examples of people whom God has allowed to have significant challenges—blind men, paralytics, Lazarus (whom he allowed to die) and these afflictions were overcome by the power of God and used for His glory.

Every person carries a cross, and every person's cross can be used to further the message of the Gospel. I'm reminded of the healing of a blind man in John 9:1-3: *"As Jesus passed by, He saw a man blind from his birth. And His disciples asked Him, 'Rabbi, who sinned, this man or his parents, that he was born blind?' Jesus answered 'It was not that this man sinned, or his parents, but that the works of God might be made manifest in him.'* God doesn't cause our misfortunes. Our misfortunes can be turned into a positive witness for Him. Mary Magdalene is another great example of that.

> *Seeing two angels inside the tomb, Mary was struck with wonder and not recognizing Christ, she asked Him supposing Him to be the gardener: "Where, O Lord, have you laid the body of my Jesus?" But recognizing by His call that He was the Savior, she heard: Touch me not; tell the brethren I go to My Father.* (Exapostelarion of the 8th Eothinon, Trans. by Holy Cross Seminary Press)

Glorify God in your challenges today!

Monday of the Third Week of Pascha

The Resurrection Didn't Bring Joy to Everyone

While they were going, behold, some of the guard went into the city and told the chief priests all that had taken place. And when they had assembled with the elders and taken counsel, they gave a sum of money to the soldiers and said, "Tell the people, 'His disciples came by night and stole Him away while we were asleep.' And if this comes to the governor's ears, we will satisfy him and keep you out of trouble." So they took the money and did as they were directed; and this story has been spread among the Jews to this day.
Matthew 28:11-15
(From the Gospel of the Vesperal Liturgy on Holy Saturday)

Christ is Risen!

The Resurrection elicited various responses from the different people affected by it. Initially, it brought fear and uncertainty to the women who went to the tomb and found it empty. Thomas had his doubts. Fear quickly turned to amazement and joy for the women and the disciples. To this day, there is great joy in the hearts of all who truly believe in the Resurrection of Christ.

The Resurrection didn't bring joy to everyone. Both the Jews and the Romans were perplexed, confused, fearful and angry. The Romans looked embarrassed. How could soldiers place a stone over the tomb, seal the tomb and have a detachment of soldiers guarding the tomb only to have Jesus "escape" without any explanation! The Jewish leaders who had pulled all the strings to set up the crucifixion and the guarding of the tomb had their worst fears realized—the body was gone. Christ had risen from the tomb as He had said He would, and now their power was threatened. Indeed, Jesus was the Christ, the Messiah. Their reign of terror over the Jewish people had ended with the Resurrection of the Messiah.

Both Jews and Romans had to act fast to concoct a story that would breed doubt and confusion among the people. The chief priests arranged to pay off the Roman soldiers. The Roman soldiers would tell people that the Body of Jesus was stolen in the night. The Jewish leaders would protect the Roman soldiers from punishment. The story would then spread among the people that there was no resurrection, but rather a theft. In this way, all parties would be spared.

Lies continue to be told about Christ to this day. I remember reading many years ago, a newspaper article that said that eighty percent of Christians believe in the Resurrection. Which led me to wonder what do the other twenty percent believe? Have twenty percent of Christians been convinced that there was no Resurrection of Christ? Since the time of Christ up until present day, there have been many perversions of Christianity, people working in the name of Christ, but doing all manner of unChristian things. Even well-meaning people have focused on "doing" church rather than "being" the church—they've put up beautiful buildings, but haven't worked to spread the message!

Sadly, it seems that not a day goes by that Christianity does not come under some kind of attack. Christians are pressured to water down the message of Christ and many are doing so. Christians who stick up for what Christ really said are now being attacked. The authentic message of Christ that calls for taking up one's cross and following Him is being lost amidst calls that any kind of behavior is okay and taking up a cross and following Christ makes one either weak or narrow minded. Christ makes it very clear that the path to salvation is both narrow and a path of choice, not coercion, but one has to make the choice to follow. Today's climate of political correctness says the door is open to everyone, no matter what they choose to believe or do in life. This sentiment is completely unsupported by Scripture.

As for the "payoff" of the guards, there are, to this day, people who are paying off the politicians, the media and anyone else with influence to spread lies about Christ, and to stop the truth from being spread. In some corners, it works, just like it did two thousand years ago. In many others, it doesn't work. Now, as then, people are still willing to carry the authentic Christian message. Now, as then, there is becoming the increasing potential of harm toward the genuine believer. Now, as then, the followers of Christ are faced with not only the choice to believe, but to do so in the face of potential persecution. Now, as then, love will always win out over hate. That may not always ring true in material terms or even in one's earthly life, but in spiritual terms, love conquers all. In the span of eternity, those whose lives are centered on the love for Christ, are the ones who will inherit the Kingdom of Heaven. Unfortunately, anger has surrounded the Resurrection from the day it happened to the present day, but anger has not won. Joy has won because anger couldn't cover up the Resurrection. There are countless people who believed back then and up to the present. Joy is what has spread this message. Joy is what this message is all about.

So, if there is any advice for the Christian today—don't focus on the world's negativity toward the Christian message. Focus on your joy about being a Christian.

> *The guards that kept watch over You, O Lord, related all the wonders that had come to pass. But the vain assembly of the Sanhedrin filled their hands with bribes, thus thinking to hide Your resurrection which all the world glorifies. Have mercy on us. (From the Praises of Orthros, Tone 3, Trans. by Holy Cross Seminary Press)*

Focus on *your* Christian joy today!

Tuesday of the Third Week of Pascha

There Will Still Be Moments of Confusion

That very day two of them were going to a village named Emmaus, about seven miles from Jerusalem, and talking with each other about all these things that had happened. While they were talking and discussing together, Jesus himself drew near and went with them. But their eyes were kept from recognizing Him. And He said to them, "What is this conversation which you are holding with each other as you walk?" And they stood still, looking sad. Then one of them, named Cleopas, answered Him, "Are you the only visitor to Jerusalem who does not know the things that have happened there in these days?" And He said to them, "What things?" And they said to Him, "Concerning Jesus of Nazareth, who was a prophet mighty in deed and word before God and all the people, and how our chief priests and rulers delivered Him up to be condemned to death, and crucified Him. But we had hoped that He was the one to redeem Israel. Yes, and besides all this, it is now the third day since this happened. Moreover, some women of our company amazed us. They were at the tomb early in the morning and did not find His body; and they came back saying that they had even seen a vision of angels, who said that He was alive. Some of those who were with us went to the tomb, and found it just as the women had said; but Him they did not see." And He said to them, "O foolish men, and slow of heart to believe all that the prophets have spoken! Was it not necessary that the Christ should suffer these things and enter into His glory?" And beginning with Moses and all the prophets, He interpreted to them in all the scriptures the things concerning Himself. So they drew near to the village to which they were going. He appeared to be going further, but they constrained Him, saying, "Stay with us, for it is toward evening and the day is now far spent." So He went in to stay with them. When He was at the table with them, He took the bread and blessed, and broke it, and gave it to them. And their eyes were opened and they recognized Him; and He vanished out of their sight. They said to each other, "Did not our hearts burn within us while He talked to us on the road, while He opened to us the scriptures?"
Luke 24:13-32
(From the Fifth Eothinon Gospel of Sunday Orthros)

Christ is Risen!

Just because one chooses to be a Christian doesn't mean that there are never any moments of confusion. There are certainly moments in my own life as a priest where I am confused about the things I believe. Certain passages of the Bible are still confusing to me, no matter how many times I read them. Sometimes I am confused by God's plan for my life. Sometimes I am confused about God's plan for the world, why He allows certain things to happen.

When I was a little boy, I used to like to do dot-to-dot's. I would see a paper filled with hundreds of dots and then I'd connect the numbers and eventually a beautiful picture would emerge. When I would get to one dot, I would find the next dot and continue. I wouldn't see the whole picture until all the dots were connected.

I recognize in my life that I won't see the picture of my whole life until it's over, until all the dots are connected. I accept that. I even have faith that God has put all the dots together on my paper, so that I have the potential for a beautiful life. It may not be a long life necessarily. It may not even be a totally joyful life. There is the potential for me to live a life that is beautiful in His eyes.

There have been times, though, that I have felt lost, where I have gotten to one dot and can't seem to find the next dot. It's as if on my dot-to-dot sheet, the dots end and the picture is not complete. I wonder, "Where is the next dot?" "Is there a next dot?" "Why can't I seem to find the next dot?" Most frequently, "I think the next dot should be 'here,' so why isn't it?"

Many times I feel like the Disciples on the road to Emmaus. I'm hearing the message, but I do not understand it. I may even see Christ right in front of me and not recognize Him. More often, I see His plan unfolding right in front of me and I don't recognize it. To the credit of Cleopas and Luke, their "hearts burned" within them enough that they stayed with the conversation. They didn't cynically dismiss Christ. In fact, they wanted Him to stay with them, so that they could learn more.

This is the lesson for today. Many times I am confused about Christianity—both the message and God's plan for my life. There is a burning in my heart to know more, so I stay on the road with Christ, and I keep the dialogue going. When you are confused about the Christian message or God's plan for your life, keep the dialogue going, keep the fire in your heart burning until you have a moment of clarity. Don't leave the conversation. Invite Christ to stay with you. *This* is one of the reasons why we pray every day, to keep the conversation going with Christ, to keep the fire burning, especially in those moments when life is more confusing than clear.

> *Christ, the life and the way, risen from the dead, accompanied Cleopas and Luke and became known at Emmaus at the breaking of the bread. Their souls and hearts burned with ardor when He spoke to them on the way and interpreted what He had endured by the Scriptures. Let us cry with them: He is risen and has appeared to Peter. (Exapostelarion of the 5th Eothinon, Trans. by Holy Cross Seminary Press)*

Keep your dialogue with God going today!

Wednesday of the 3rd Week of Pascha

Communion Is How We Stoke the Fire

And they rose that same hour and returned to Jerusalem; and they found the eleven gathered together and those who were with them, who said, "The Lord has risen indeed, and has appeared to Simon!" Then they told what had happened on the road, and how He was known to them in the breaking of the bread.
Luke 24:33-35
(From the Fifth Eothinon Gospel of Sunday Orthros)

Christ is Risen!

We've all sat around a campfire. In my experience of campfires, it seems to take a lot of effort to get them going, some effort to keep them going, and little effort to put them out. I'm reminded of the Protestant song, *"It only takes a spark to get a fire going, and soon all those around can warm up in its glowing; that's how it is with God's love, once you've experienced it; you spread His love to everyone, you want to pass it on."*

It's true that in very dry and parched terrain it only takes a spark to start a forest fire, but that's not how it works with a campfire. It takes some work to put together small "kindling" like newspapers and pine needles, and once those are set aflame, you have to keep the fire going until the larger pieces of wood catch fire and your camp fire is established. Once you have a nice size fire going, throwing on another log occasionally is all the work you have to do. However, not throwing on additional logs will allow the fire to go out in a very short amount of time.

When the fire is about to go out, what it needs is the addition of another log. When the spiritual fire is about to go out, what it needs is the addition of Christ. The best way we add Christ to our lives is through Holy Communion. He is "made known to us in the breaking of the bread." Looking back at the journey to Emmaus, the disciples were at first sad because Jesus had died. Then they were confused by what the unidentified man was saying as they walked with him. Obviously, that man was Christ, but they didn't recognize Him. They couldn't quite put together what He was saying to them, but their hearts were burning and they wanted to know more. So, they invited Him to stay with them, and when He came and sat with them, and "broke the bread" in the same way He did at the Last Supper, this is when all their doubts were erased, and they knew He was the Risen Christ. This truth came to them in the breaking of the bread, in the Holy Eucharist. Because, as St. Paul tells us in 1 Corinthians 11:26, *"For as often as you eat this bread and drink the cup, you proclaim the Lord's death until He comes."* The Eucharist is the "log" that stokes the fire that burns in our hearts.

Going back to the Emmaus experience, the "spark" that got the fire going was the *interest* of Luke and Cleopas in engaging in the conversation. This is what got their hearts to burn. The breaking of the bread is what set them afire. The spark needed to get us going is interest, but that is not enough to keep the fire going. We need the Eucharist to both set our hearts aflame and to keep the fire from going out. We need the Eucharist on a regular basis. Remember the campfire—you have to throw a new log on every 30 minutes or so, or the fire burns out. Throw a log on every 30 minutes and the fire stays ablaze. Once the fire is going, the regular maintenance by throwing in logs keeps the confidence high that the fire will continue to burn, providing light and warmth.

In our spiritual lives, we need the Eucharist on a frequent basis, so that the Light of Christ stays ablaze in our hearts, and so that we have confidence that His Light will continue to burn in us, providing Light and warmth in our hearts and souls.

Our liturgical tradition of lighting a candle at the Resurrection service illustrates this point. We use a small flame from a single candle to ignite our hearts again with the warmth of Christ. The Light of Christ is enough to get our hearts to burn within us once again. We keep that fire going through the Holy Eucharist, for He is made known to us continually in the "Breaking of the Bread."

The Communion Hymn of the Paschal season presents the Eucharist as a spring that quenches a thirsty soul. So, whether we see the Eucharist as a fire to warm the heart or a spring to quench the thirsty soul, what is most significant is that the Eucharist is the gift that grows and sustains the faith that strengthens the heart and soul for the journey to everlasting life.

Receive the Body of Christ; and taste of the Immortal Spring. Alleluia. (Communion Hymn of the Paschal Season, Trans. by Fr. George Papadeas)

Make sure your plans for this coming Sunday include "Breaking bread" with Christ in the Eucharist!

Thursday of the 3rd Week of Pascha

Proof of the Resurrection

As they were saying this, Jesus Himself stood among them. But they were startled and frightened, and supposed that they saw a spirit. And He said to them, "Why are you troubled, and why do questionings rise in your hearts? See My hands and My feet, that it is I Myself; handle Me, and see; for a spirit has not flesh and bones as you see that I have." And while they still disbelieved for joy, and wondered, He said to them, "Have you anything here to eat?" They gave Him a piece of broiled fish, and He took it and ate before them.
Luke 24:36-42
(From the Sixth Eothinon Gospel of Sunday Orthros)

Christ is Risen!

Can we prove the Resurrection actually happened? There are many cynics who argue that there was no Resurrection of Christ. The Bible testifies to "many proofs" (Acts 1:3) that Jesus rose from the dead. We read these in the Gospel accounts—First, there is the empty tomb, and as we are told in the Gospel of John (20:6-7), the grave clothes were neatly folded. There was not a scene of chaos at the tomb.

There were multiple appearances to the Disciples. He appeared to them on the evening of the day of the Resurrection. Thomas was not with them. He appeared to them a week later and Thomas was with the Disciples. (John 20:19-29) He appeared to Luke and Cleopas on the road to Emmaus. (Luke 24:13-35)

In today's scripture, Jesus appeared to the Disciples and stood among them. He entered a scene where they were frightened and mistook Him for a "spirit." In His perfected and Resurrected Body, He had no need for food. Nevertheless, He ate before them, much as He would have before the Resurrection. (Incidentally, it is the Orthodox tradition after funeral services that there is a "mercy" meal, sometimes called a "makaria" and traditionally fish is served at such a meal. This custom comes from this scriptural account, that after the Resurrection, Christ ate fish. If the end of a person's earthly life is their Resurrection in Christ, then when we gather to remember them, we also eat fish.)

Back to the proofs of the Resurrection, Jesus walked the earth for forty days after the Resurrection and appeared to many people. Saint Paul testified that Jesus, "*appeared to more than five hundred brethren at one time, most of whom are still alive*" (1 Cor. 15:6). Many people were giving oral history testifying to the Resurrection of Christ. During the same time frame, there is no evidence of anyone saying that the Resurrection was not true.

We know that the Gospel accounts of the Resurrection were written during the middle to end of the first century. There are historic documents that have been dated to this time period. In other words, the first written records of the Resurrection are from the years immediately after it happened. There is no disputing that.

Then there is the behavior of the Disciples, who all of a sudden went from scared and hiding to boldly proclaiming the Gospel everywhere. What could have motivated them to do so? The TRUTH of the Resurrection.

There is the behavior of the untold number of people who have died for Christ, the martyrs who were tortured and killed, who refused to renounce their faith in Jesus Christ in the face of death. Could all of them have died because of a lie?

Then there are the untold billions of people whose lives have been centered around their faith in Jesus Christ. Did they all perpetuate a fraud?

Finally, there is the work of Christ in this world today. I can't tell you how many "miracles" I have seen where I walk away not only amazed at the power of God in the world today, but of the utter truth that there is no way that there can't be a God at work in the world.

I recently read somewhere that the definition of a lie is "rewriting history." Contemporary society is trying to rewrite history in order to write the truth of the Resurrection out of it. The facts simply don't support this.

There is no question that a man named Jesus walked the earth two thousand years ago. There is no question that He taught in synagogues, worked miracles and made the Jewish Temple leadership uncomfortable. There is no question that He demonstrated many of the "Messianic" signs that were foretold in the Old Testament. There is no doubt that He was crucified on a Friday afternoon outside of Jerusalem. Even in the Nicene Creed, we say "Crucified for us under Pontius Pilate" in order to put a specific period of time on the Crucifixion. Pontius Pilate is an undisputed figure in history. The crucifixion is also undisputed.

Which leads us to the Resurrection. The Resurrection is true. And the reason is the billions of people who have testified and who continue to testify to this day through their Christ-centered lives that indeed Christ rose from the dead. Christ is either the most incredible person who ever lived or the greatest fraud ever perpetuated. Not only have I studied the historical evidence, but I have experienced the spiritual evidence; watching people die in the hope of eternal life, and more importantly, watching people live, and living myself, with this same hope every day.

Revealing Your human nature, O Savior, You partook of food after You rose from the tomb and standing in their midst preached repentance. Then You ascended immediately to Your heavenly Father and promised to send the Comforter to Your disciples. O most Divine God-man, glory to Your Resurrection. (Exapostelarion of the 6th Eothinon, Trans. by Holy Cross Seminary Press)

Let your experience of Christ, as well as the experience of others, strengthen your faith in Him today!

Friday of the 3rd Week of Pascha

Going Fishing? Now Is Not the Time to Let Up

After this Jesus revealed Himself again to the disciples by the Sea of Tiberius; and He revealed Himself in this way. Simon Peter, Thomas called the Twin, Nathanael of Cana in Galilee, the sons of Zebedee, and two others of His Disciples were together. Simon Peter said to them, "I am going fishing." They said to him, "We will go with you." They went out and got into the boat; but that night they caught nothing.
John 21:1-3
(From the Tenth Eothinon Gospel of Sunday Orthros)

Christ is Risen!

I remember a professor I had at the Seminary used to joke, when talking about the reactions of various people to the Resurrection of Christ each year, that many people quote St. Peter and say "I am going fishing" and don't show up for church for many weeks or months after Holy Week. The truth is that there is quite a "let down" after the journey of Lent and the intensity of Holy Week. Now nearly three weeks removed from Pascha, have you made good on your Lenten goals or have you regressed back into pre-Lenten habits you were working to change? Are you still working? Or have you "gone fishing?"

Many times we feel like the Disciples did when they had a bad fishing day. We feel that we are putting in the work, but are catching nothing. Every year someone tells me after Holy Week that they didn't get a lot out of the experience. Which leads naturally to the question: how much did you put into it? There are people who attend church regularly, who are "doing the work," and are still not getting anything out of it. Here is where one of the greatest challenges to Christianity comes in: DO-ing church versus BE-ing the church. There is a critical difference.

There are plenty of people who buy nice clothes to wear to church, who wear nice crosses around their necks, who have beautiful Bibles on their shelves, and if they are Orthodox may even have expensive icons on the walls. One can have nice clothes and "go" to church each Sunday and not worship. One can wear a cross around his neck and still be dishonest and act unChristian. One can have a large collection of Bibles and not read them. One can have beautiful and expensive icons and not pray in front of them. A Church community can even have a full house on Sundays, but neglect the poor, not welcome the visitor, and not be in tune with the parishioner who might really need some help. These are all examples of "DO-ing" church rather than "BE-ing" the church.

The goal of the Lenten and Holy Week journey was not to "do" church, in the sense of "putting on" good services. It was to re-energize us to BE the church. It was to re-energize us to pray, to read the scriptures, to worship with purpose, to commune with renewed joy and to live the Christian life with greater enthusiasm.

In our church, we greet each other for forty days with the words "Christ is Risen" or in Greek, "Christos Anesti." Are you still greeting people with these words? The response to this greeting is "Alithos Anesti" in Greek, or "Truly He is Risen" in English. I was at a church event recently and I was greeting people "Christos Anesti" and the response was "Alithos!" Alithos? That is the equivalent of saying, "Christ is Risen" and the response being "truly." Truly, what? The Resurrection of Christ merits more than a ho-hum response. It demands more than an "I'm going fishing" attitude. The Resurrection of Christ demands a response. It demands a standing up with joy, with purpose. It calls us to action, not complacency.

The actions are two: individual action and community action. The individual action is development of one's personal spiritual life. Make sure that you are praying every day, even if it is for a short period of time. Feed yourself with the Scriptures. Again, you don't have to read chapters, read only a few verses and really meditate on them. The verse that comes to my mind as I'm writing is Psalm 23:1: *"The Lord is my Shepherd, I shall not want."* Meditate on this verse today if you are frustrated in any way with your life. If the Lord is your Shepherd, and you want for Him, and are satisfied with Him, then life's disappointments will be short-lived, since He is leading you to the "sheep pen" of heaven. Meditate and prepare daily for your next encounter with Christ in the Eucharist.

As for the community action, make a gesture of love toward a neighbor in some way each day. This can be something as simple as opening a door for someone, being a courteous driver, sitting with someone who has no one to talk to at lunch, or being the sympathetic ear for someone who needs to talk.

There is nothing wrong with going fishing, or taking in a baseball game, or enjoying a pizza, but don't let the fishing, the baseball, or the pizza become the primary focus of your life. I'm reminded of the words of 1 Chronicles 16: 9-11, *"Sing to Him, sing praises to Him, tell of all His wonderful works! Glory in His Holy Name; let the hearts of those who seek the Lord rejoice! Seek the Lord and His strength, seek His presence continually!"*

> *After Your descent into Hades, the disciples despaired of Your resurrection, as might be expected in Your absence, O Christ. They returned to their work; to their boats and nets, but they caught nothing. But You, O Savior, have been revealed as Master of all and commanded them to cast their nets on the right side. Immediately the*

word became deed, and they caught a great multitude of fish and found an unexpected meal on shore, of which they partook. Now make us worthy to enjoy the same food spiritually, O Loving Lord. (Doxastikon of the 10th Eothinon, Trans. by Holy Cross Seminary Press)

Keep working on those Lenten goals!

Saturday of the 3rd Week of Pascha

We Are All Supposed to Become Fishermen

Just as day was breaking, Jesus stood on the beach; yet the disciples did not know that it was Jesus. Jesus said to them, "Children, have you any fish?" They answered Him, "No." He said to them, "Cast the net on the right side of the boat, and you will find some." So they cast it, and now they were not able to haul it in, for the quantity of fish. That disciple whom Jesus loved said to Peter, "It is the Lord!" When Simon Peter heard that it was the Lord, he put on his clothes, for he was stripped for work, and sprang into the sea. But the other disciples came in the boat, dragging the net full of fish, for they were not far from the land, but about a hundred yards off.
When they got out on land, they saw a charcoal fire there, with fish lying on it, and bread. Jesus said to them, "Bring some of the fish that you have just caught." So Simon Peter went aboard and hauled the net ashore, full of large fish, a hundred and fifty-three of them; and although there were so many, the net was not torn. Jesus said to them, "Come and have breakfast." Now none of the disciples dared ask Him, "Who are You?" They knew it was the Lord. Jesus came and took the bread and gave it to them, and so with the fish. This was now the third time that Jesus was revealed to the disciples after He was raised from the dead.
John 21:4-14
(From the Tenth Eothinon Gospel of Sunday Orthros)

Christ is Risen!

When Jesus called the first Disciples, He called common fishermen. Why fishermen? First, Jesus called "common men" to be His Disciples. He didn't choose from the extremely educated, extremely wealthy, or extremely popular. He chose from the extremely common, because His message is for all. In fact, the fishermen he chose weren't even very good fishermen. Several times in the Scriptures, they had to admit to Jesus that they were toiling at their nets and not catching anything.

Fishermen, however, had a few special attributes. First, they were not afraid to work in adverse conditions—at night, in the dark, in the cold, because that's when the fish were biting.

Second, they were not afraid to fail. Every time they told Jesus that they had caught nothing, they were still out on the sea working, they were not on the dock complaining or moping. Third, they were open to suggestions for improvement. Every time Jesus told them to cast the net again, or cast it on the right side of the boat, they never questioned Him. Each time they did what He suggested, their faith was rewarded. Jesus told them when He first called them from their boats that He was going to make them *"fishers of men"* (Matt. 4:19). Never did they ask "what is that?" Nor did they think the idea of leaving everything and following for this new job was an absurd idea. Finally, when they did as Jesus suggested, they found that their nets were filled with fish, more so than they were even prepared to handle. When Jesus sent them out into the world to catch fish, after Pentecost, they found their nets were filled with new Christians on a regular basis.

We would do well to learn from the example of these "fishermen." The first thing we need in order to be a "fisher of men" is humility. If education, wealth or popularity is the end goal, we are not going to make it as a "fisher of men." As we learn from the disciples, it is not *hard* work that God is after. It is **"heart"** work that God wants.

Second, we need to put aside fear and be ready to work for Christ even in adverse situations—like when it isn't popular, or when the "fish" (other people) are not biting (encouraging or coming to the Christian message). Third, we can't be afraid to fail. Being a disciple is going to have its moments of success, but it is also going to have its moments of failure. There will always be people who do not want to hear the message, so we have to get used to not having it be easy. Fourth, we have to continually work to "improve our craft." There are many people who don't have the desire to better themselves when it comes to their understanding of the Christian faith. The Bible and the church through the priests, through other people, through other circumstances, continually encourages us to become stronger in our faith, so that we can become not only more committed Christians, but more effective fishermen.

> *On the Sea of Tiberias, the sons of Zebedee, Nathaniel and Peter, and two other disciples of old were fishing with Thomas. At Christ's command they cast their nets on the right side and drew in a multitude of fish. Then Peter recognized Him and cast himself after Him. When He appeared to them a third time, He showed them bread and fish upon live coals. (Exapostelarion of the 10th Eothinon, Trans. by Holy Cross Seminary Press)*

Go "fishing" today!

Sunday of the Paralytic

The Meaning of the Word "Love"

When they had finished breakfast, Jesus said to Simon Peter, "Simon, son of John, do you love Me more than these?" He said to Him, "Yes, Lord; you know that I love You." He said to him, "Feed My lambs." A second time He said to him, "Simon, son of John, do you love Me?" He said to Him, "Yes, Lord; you know that I love You." He said to him, "Tend My sheep." He said to him the third time, "Simon, son of John, do you love Me?" Peter was grieved because He said to him the third time, "Do you love Me?" And he said to Him, "Lord, you know everything; you know that I love You." Jesus said to him, "Feed My sheep."
John 21:15-17
(From the Eleventh Eothinon Gospel of Sunday Orthros)

Christ is Risen!

One of the biggest drawbacks in the English language is that we have only one word for "love." With the same word that we use to say, "I love my spouse," we also say, "I love pizza." In the Greek language, there are many different words for "love." There is the word "agape," which means "sacrificial love," the kind of love that one has for a spouse, a child, a parent or a close friend. This is the kind of love we are also supposed to have for God, and this is the kind of love God has for us. This is the kind of love where one is willing to do anything, including dying, for someone else.

The word "eros" refers to romantic love. This is where we get the word "erotic." The word "filia" refers to a more "friendship" love. This is where we get the word "philanthropy." In case you were wondering how one talks about love for pizza in Greek, there is a phrase "mou aresi," which means "pleasing to me." This is the phrase one uses when talking about his favorite sports team or a piece of pizza. I certainly enjoy pizza and sports. I am not willing to sacrifice my life for either of them. Maybe a few dollars!

In today's scripture reading, Jesus speaks with Peter and asks him, "Do you love Me?" They have this exchange three times. After the third time, the Gospel says, "Peter was grieved," because Jesus asked Peter this basic question, "Do you love Me?" three times. Why three times? Most people would guess because Peter denied Christ three times, so he was "restored" by saying three times "Yes, Lord, You know that I love You." Another reason might be the redundancy. "Certainly I love You Lord and You know that, so why ask me three times?"

The real reason has to do with the word "love" and what Jesus is asking Peter. The first time Jesus asks Peter, "Do you love me?" He uses the Greek word "Agape" and asks "Agapas Me?" In other words, "Do you love Me with Agape love, the kind of love that you would die for Me?" Peter answers, "Yes, Lord, You know that I love You," but uses the word "Filia," meaning, "I love You like a friend."

So, Jesus asks a second time, "Agapas Me?" meaning "Do you love Me with Agape?" Peter answers a second time, "Yes Lord, You know that I love You like a friend." Again, Peter uses the word "Filia."

Jesus asks a third time "Filis Me?" "Do you love Me like a friend?" (Jesus uses the word "filia" the third time). Then Peter is grieved because he realizes that Jesus has been asking him "Do you love Me to die for Me?" and he has been answering, "I love You like a friend." Then Peter finally gets it right—He says that he loves Christ, and then Christ says that indeed Peter will die for Him. (More on this in the next reflection.)

If we are disciples of Christ, all of us who have been baptized into Christ, then Jesus asks the same question of us: "Do you love Me with Agape love?" "Do you love Me like you would die for me?" What is our answer? "I love you like a friend?" Or "I love you with 'Agape,' to die for You?" Or, "I love You like I love football, I fit You into a compartment on Sundays."

When we use the word "love" to describe our relationship with family and also our relationship with the word "pizza," it actually cheapens or "dumbs down" the concept of love. While I am not a linguist, I would agree that our concepts of love should be guided by these Greek words. We should not be giving "agape" to our favorite sports teams, and "filia" to our families and to the Lord. Christ has given us "Agape" love in dying for us. What kind of love do we have for Him?

> *Appearing after the Resurrection to Your disciples, O Savior, You gave Peter the tending of Your sheep as recompense for his love, asking him to tend them with care. Therefore You said: If you love Me, O Peter, feed My sheep, tend My lambs. He immediately displayed his affection and inquired about the other disciple. By their prayers, O Christ, preserve Your flock from ravaging wolves. (Doxastikon of the 11th Eothinon, Trans. by Holy Cross Seminary Press)*

Meet Christ's "Agape" with your "Agape."

Monday of the 4th Week of Pascha

Peter Really Got it Right When It Counted

Truly, truly, I say to you, when you were young, you girded yourself and walked where you would; but when you are old, you will stretch out your hands, and another will gird you and carry you where you do not wish to go." (This He said to show by what death He was to glorify God.) And after this He said to him, "Follow me."
John 21:18-19
(From the Eleventh Eothinon Gospel of Sunday Orthros)

Christ is Risen!

The Apostle Peter provides us yet another (there have been so many of these!) example of a follower of Christ who was devout in his faith, who took a few wrong turns, but in the end got it really right.

In Matthew 16:13-18, we read:

> *Now when Jesus came into the district of Caesarea Philippi, He asked His disciples, "Who do men say that the Son of man is?" And they said, "Some say John the Baptist, others say Elijah, and others Jeremiah or one of the prophets." He said to them, "But who do you say that I am?" Simon Peter replied, "You are the Christ, the Son of the living God." And Jesus answered him, "Blessed are you, Simon Bar-Jona! For flesh and blood has not revealed this to you, but My Father who is in heaven. And I tell you, you are Peter, and on this rock I will build My church, and the powers of death shall not prevail against it. I will give you the keys of the kingdom of heaven.*

When Jesus asked the Disciples who they thought He was, it was Peter who jumped up first to confess Jesus as the Christ, the Son of the Living God. In the very next few verses of scripture, Jesus chastised the same Peter who He had just told would be the rock of the church:

> *From that time Jesus began to show His disciples that He must go to Jerusalem and suffer many things from the elders and chief priests and scribes, and be killed, and on the third day be raised. And Peter took Him and began to rebuke Him, saying, "God forbid, Lord! This shall never happen to You." But He turned and said to Peter, "Get behind me, Satan! You are a hindrance to Me; for you are not on the side of God, but of men"* (Matt. 16:21-23).

At the Last Supper, Jesus told His Disciples *"You will all fall away because of Me this night; for it is written, 'I will strike the Shepherd, and the sheep of the flock will be scattered.' But after I am raised up, I will go before you to Galilee"* (Matt. 26:31-32). Immediately, Peter rose from the Disciples and declared, *"Though they all fall away because of You, I will never fall away." Jesus said to him, "Truly, I say to you, this very night, before the cock crows, you will deny Me three times." Peter said to Him, "Even if I must die with You, I will not deny You"* (Matt. 26:33-35).

Just as Jesus predicted, Peter denied Jesus three times. Unlike Judas, who betrayed Jesus and who killed himself, Peter went out and wept bitterly tears of repentance and stayed with the company of the Disciples.

In restoring Peter, Jesus not only forgave Him and restored Him to his place as the leader of the Disciples, Jesus told Peter that eventually he would "get it right," predicting that Peter would indeed show "Agape" love for Christ in dying for Him as a martyr.

Peter shows us the best example of a devout follower of Christ who made his share of mistakes and still got it right. St. Paul didn't start off as a follower of Christ. He was making many mistakes, persecuting and killing Christians, but when he was converted to Christianity, he started living right. We aren't told that St. Paul made many (or any) gaffes after He became a Christian. Peter, on the other hand, became a devout follower of Christ and still made many gaffes. There is no doubt that Peter was devout in his following of Christ. After all, he left his fishing business and followed. There is also no doubt that Peter struggled at times, both to understand and to follow the teachings of Christ.

Peter provides us an example of what it is to believe and then to fall, and then to get up, and then fall again, and then get up, and repeat this cycle many times, but in the end to get it right. At the end he stood up for Christ, was killed for his faith, and received a heavenly crown from the Lord. At the end he got it right. This is what the Lord's hope is for each of us. He wants us to follow. He doesn't expect us to get it right all the time. He expects us to repent and "stay with Him," to pick up ourselves when we fall down. In order to inherit eternal life, we need to make sure we have it right at the end. This is facilitated most specifically by striving to get it right throughout life, and picking ourselves up, repenting, and continuing in the Christian journey when we get it wrong.

The name of Rock have you worthily been given. On this rock the Lord of all confirmed the Church's faith which is unshaken; and He made you, O Holy Peter, the senior pastor of reason endowed sheep. Therefore the benevolent Master appointed you to hold the keys of the heavenly gates, and thus to open to every person approaching them with faith. And you were therefore counted worthy of imitating your Lord, being crucified. We entreat you to pray Him to illumine us and save our souls. (From the Orthros of the Feast of Saints Peter and Paul, June 29, Trans. by Fr. Seraphim Dedes)

Keep at it (your faith) today and if you get knocked down, get up again!

Tuesday of the 4th Week of Pascha

Don't Worry About the Other Guy!

Peter turned and saw following them the disciple whom Jesus loved, who had lain close to His breast at the supper and had said, "Lord, who is it that is going to betray You?" When Peter saw him, he said to Jesus, "Lord, what about this man?" Jesus said to him, "If it is My will that he remain until I come, what is that to you? Follow me!" The saying spread abroad among the brethren that this disciple was not to die; yet Jesus did not say to him that he was not to die, but, "If it is my will that he remain until I come, what is that to you?"
John 21:20-23
(From the Eleventh Eothinon Gospel of Sunday Orthros)

Christ is Risen!

Having just been restored in the eyes of the Lord, Peter made a mistake that we frequently make. Peter had been conversing with Jesus as they were walking, answering for his lack of "agape" love and being forgiven and restored by Jesus. He looked back and saw *"the disciple whom Jesus loved"* who is identified as the Apostle John (who would later write the Gospel of John) following Jesus and Peter. Peter asked, *"What about this man?"*

Why did Peter ask this question? Jesus had just told Peter that Peter was going to eventually die for Christ. He was eventually going to die a martyr's death and it was going to be in the same humiliating and painful way that Jesus died, by crucifixion. Undoubtedly, Peter wanted to know, "Is John going to suffer the same fate as me?"

Jesus, I believe, lovingly, did not answer Peter's question directly. He didn't say "No, John will not be martyred, he will outlive all of you and die peacefully in old age." What would have happened if Jesus had said that? Would Peter have declared "that's not fair," or "why does he get to live and I have to die violently?" Would a full answer have shaken Peter's faith?

Jesus said to Peter *"If it is my will that he remain until I come, what is that to you? Follow me!"* In other words, "Don't worry about him. *you* follow me!"

In our world, we are "conditioned" to be in competition with other people, even if we don't know them. We look at our neighbors with judgment when we think, "I'm older than them, but they have a better car, I should have the better car." Or, "I have more education, I should make more money." Or, "Why does a teenager have two children, but the married couple has none?" Or the proverbial, "Why do bad things happen to the good people?" Or, "Why do the good people die young?"

Christianity is not a competition by any means. While a community assists us in our journey, the choice to follow Christ is a personal choice, and the judgment in front of Christ will be an individual judgment. We won't stand in front of Him with our family, or our neighbors or our church community. The Lord has given each of us a different set of gifts and talents. Remember the parable of the talents? (Matt. 25: 14-31). No one got anything. God has a specific plan for each of our lives, and these plans are not in competition with one another. When I was "younger" I used to wonder, "Why don't I have a bigger parish, or a nicer home, or a higher level of material gain, compared to everyone else my age?" Now that I am older and more mature, I still have these thoughts at times, but certainly not as much as I used to. I try to be grateful for what God has given me. I try to do the best I can with what I have been given by Him. I try to not look at others, choosing to focus on my relationship with Christ. As I said, I try, and sometimes, I still fail. Sometimes I am still like Peter, wondering about the other guy.

Jesus' message to Peter is, *"Don't worry about the other guy. I have plans for him, just as I have plans for you. I have given talents to him, just as I have given talents to you. My plans for him and for you are different. So are the talents I have given both of you. But what is most important is you follow me."* That is what is most important to each of us, that each of us follows Him. Don't get fixated on what you don't have. Appreciate what you do have and don't get fixated on God's plans for the lives of others. Be faithful in following His plan for *you*!

> *After the divine Resurrection, the Lord asked Peter thrice: Do you love me? And thus put him forward as shepherd of His flock. But when Peter saw that he whom Jesus loved was following, he asked the Master: Why is he here? And He said, "If I wish that he should remain until I come again, what is this to you, beloved Peter?"*
> *(Exapostelarion of the 11th Eothinon, Trans. by Holy Cross Seminary Press)*

Keep your eyes on Christ today!

Wednesday of the 4th Week of Pascha—Feast of Mid-Pentecost

Let God Arise, and the Story of a Dear Friend Named Eva

Let God arise, let His enemies be scattered; let those who hate Him flee before Him!
As smoke is driven away, so drive them away; as wax melts before fire,
let the wicked perish before God! But let the righteous be joyful! Psalm 68:1-3
This is the day which the Lord has made; let us rejoice and be glad in it.
Psalm 118:24
(Verses sung with the Paschal Hymn "Christ is Risen" during Bright Week)

Christ is Risen!

Today, the church celebrates the feast of Mid-Pentecost. This day marks the half-way point between Pascha and Pentecost, falling on the 25th day of Pascha and 25 days before Pentecost. The Gospel lesson of the feast day is from John 7:14-30, and gives an account of Jesus speaking to the Jewish leadership in the temple. The icon of the feast depicts Jesus as a twelve year old teaching in the temple as told in Luke 2:41-52.

We learn everything that we know through repetition. Only in experiencing something over and over again do we retain it. Thankfully, the Church understands this and the Lord understands this. This is why the Lord created days and seasons, to give us starting and ending points. Can you imagine if a day lasted a week, a bad day would feel like an eternity! Thankfully at the end of each day, we rest and awake refreshed from many daily frustrations. Thankfully, we have many opportunities for new starts in our lives.

New starts are available at any time, through prayer, repentance and confession. One doesn't have to wait for Lent and Pascha to come in order to have a new beginning. However, one also doesn't have to go out of his way to create a new beginning because Lent and Pascha provide this opportunity for us each year. All we have to do is take advantage of it.

Every year, when we proclaim Christ is Risen at the empty tomb, we sing it ten times, with the above verses intoned before we sing each hymn. These verses refer to the triumph of God's people in the Old Testament, and they foretell of His rising from the dead in the New Testament.

They are a powerful reminder to us that in God rising from the dead, the greatest enemy—death—is vanquished. All enemies of God are invited to be scattered and flee. The Psalmist tells us that as smoke vanishes, the enemies of God will also vanish. They will melt in the same way wax does in the presence of fire. For the ungodly, there is reason to fear—they will perish at the sight of the Risen Lord. For the righteous, there is cause to rejoice.

Psalm 118:24 is also included with these Psalm verses, with the Paschal refrain of "*Christ is Risen from the dead, by death trampling down death and to those in the tombs, He has granted life.*" This verse reminds us that *this (today)* is the day that the Lord has made, let us rejoice and be glad in it. If every good and perfect gift is from Above, (James 1:17), then *this very day* is a gift. Because it is a gift from God, it is a cause to rejoice. Because every day brings us one day closer to our own resurrection in Christ, then each day is a day to rejoice. If nothing else good happens to you on a particular day, we are one day closer to the Kingdom of Heaven. For the ungodly, this is cause for fear. For the devout Christian, this should be cause for constant joy.

There was a woman in my parish many years ago named Eva. She was a very devout lady and a dear friend. On Holy Wednesday of 2004, she was the last person in line for Holy Unction. I remember that we had a beautiful conversation, even made plans to get together the week after Pascha to do some flower planting in her garden, Eva, my wife and I. The next evening, Holy Thursday evening, Eva came to church for the service of the Passion of Christ. During this service, after the fifth Gospel, we carried the life-size cross of Christ crucified through the church and placed it up in the front. I invited people to come up and venerate the cross and pray in front of it as the service continued. I remember that Eva came up and venerated the cross, and was waving to people, including me, which I thought was odd. I remember that it looked like she had a halo over her head, like she was an angel. After she venerated the cross and returned to her seat, she laid down on her pew and quietly passed away. Apparently, her heart gave out. It wasn't a traumatic event for her. It was for the rest of us who witnessed it, but for her it was the perfect ending to life—in church, with her friends, her last words were probably, "*Lord, remember me in Your kingdom,*" and she died at the same hour we commemorated the death of the Lord.

I remember that we held Eva's funeral on Bright Tuesday. The church had been filled on Holy Thursday night when Eva passed away. Since virtually the whole community witnessed this, the whole community came out to her funeral. The funeral during Bright Week is different from the funeral at other times of the year. We sang, "Christ is Risen," ten times with the Psalm verses, just like at the Resurrection service. I love these verses, because they speak of the power and majesty of God—*Let God arise, and let His enemies be scattered!*

As I stood at the head of her casket and offered the words of the Psalm, I looked down and saw my dear friend Eva who had such an unbelievably beautiful death. Then my eyes looked up to see the altar table, bathed in all white, and continued looking up to see the empty cross (the figure of Christ is removed from the Cross on Good Friday and the cross remains empty until the feast of the Ascension) and felt this awesome presence of Christ all around me. Here was this special lady, who had lived 77 years in expectation of her personal resurrection, which was made possible in the most beautiful and special way because of the empty cross and empty tomb. Looking back at that moment, I felt not only joy, but also euphoria and ecstasy. I have to say, that moment was one of the most joyful moments of my LIFE, and it happened at a funeral! On that day that the Lord made, even though I mourned the loss of a friend; I did it in the context of the Resurrection, that to those in the tombs Christ grants everlasting life. Even on a sad day, there was cause for joy.

> *We were illumined, O brethren, by the Resurrection of Christ the Savior. And now we have reached the middle of the feast of the Lord. Let us sincerely keep the commandments of God, so that we may become worthy to celebrate the Ascension as well, and witness the coming of the Holy Spirit. (Doxastikon from Orthros of Mid-Pentecost, Trans. by Fr. Seraphim Dedes*

TODAY is a day that the Lord made for you. Rejoice and be glad in it!

Thursday of the 4th Week of Pascha

Let's Go Back to the Beginning

In the beginning was the Word, and the Word was with God, and the Word was God.
He was in the beginning with God; all things were made through Him,
and without Him was not anything made that was made.
John 1:1-3
(From the Gospel at the Divine Liturgy of Pascha)

Christ is Risen!

At the Resurrection service, we read two Gospel passages. The first commemorates the Resurrection of Christ, taken from Mark 16:1-8. This is read at the Resurrection service, traditionally outside of the church, at midnight, a message to the entire world that Christ is risen from the dead.

The second passage is taken from John 1:1-17. The next several reflections will be on this Gospel passage, which is filled with theology and history. Why read this passage on Pascha? The reason is that Pascha represents both an ending and a beginning for us. Pascha is the end of the Lenten journey. It is also the end of the history of hopelessness of the human race. Through the Resurrection the path was opened to Paradise for every person of faith.

More than the commemoration of an ending, Pascha provides us with a new beginning. Pascha provides us with a renewed start, and an opportunity for a renewed commitment. We remember God's commitment to us to redeem us after we had fallen through sin. We remember this blessed event by recommitting ourselves to a renewed start. To mark this renewed start, the church takes us back to the very beginning, so that we can again understand not only where we are going, but where we came from.

In the beginning was the Word. In the beginning, when there was nothing, there was God. God is "without beginning" and "uncreated." God created everything. Nothing created God. Before anything was created, there was God. If a person wants to believe in God, the first thing one must believe is that God is uncreated and that He created everything. Because if God is created, then what makes Him different than us! God is greater than us because He created us. No one and nothing is greater than God because God created everything.

God existed, without beginning, in Trinity. Genesis 1:1-3 reads, *In the beginning God created the heavens and the earth. The earth was without form and void, and darkness was upon the face of the deep; and the Spirit of God was moving over the face of the waters. And God said, "Let there be light"; and there was light.*

In these first three verses of the Bible, in the account of creation, we see God present "as Trinity." "God" created refers to the Father. The "Spirit of God" moving over the waters refers to the Holy Spirit. "God said" refers to the voice of God, who is Jesus Christ. Christ is referred to by many names: Jesus, Christ, Son of God, Messiah, Savior. One of the names given to the "Son of God" is the "Word," or the "Logos."

So, when we read the term "Word" in John 1, this refers to Jesus Christ. Re-reading John 1:1-3 and inserting the name "Christ" into it, it would read as follows: In the beginning was Christ, and Christ was with God, and Christ was God. Christ was in the beginning with God (the Father and the Holy Spirit); all things were made through Christ and without Christ was not anything made that was made.

Working together—the Father, the Son and the Holy Spirit created everything that was created. God did not create the Son or the Spirit. Father, Son and Holy Spirit are pre-eternal. They are one God, in three persons—The Holy Trinity.

One way to explain the Holy Trinity is to take three candles, and hold them closely together and light them. From a distance, the three candles look like one candle, there is one light that is visible. You can then take the candles and separate them keeping one flame in the middle and showing that there are three distinct candles. This is how the Holy Trinity works—one God (one flame) in three distinct persons (three candles).

In the Resurrection, we declare that everything will "end" with Christ, since He grants life to those in the tombs. In going back to the Gospel of John, we declare that not only things end with Christ, but they begin with Him as well.

> *O Lord, midway through the feast, give drink to my thirsty soul from the waters of true religion. For to all You the Savior cried aloud, Let whoever is thirsty come to Me and drink. As the fountain of life, O Christ our God, glory to You. (Apolytikion of the Feast of Mid-Pentecost, Trans. by Fr. Seraphim Dedes)*

If Christ is the beginning and the end of us, make sure to keep Him in the center of your life today!

Friday of the 4th Week of Pascha

Darkness Can Never Defeat the Light

In Him was life, and the life was the light of men.
The light shines in the darkness, and the darkness has not overcome it.
John 1:4-5
(From the Gospel at the Divine Liturgy on Pascha)

Christ is Risen!

Allow me to share with you a view from the priest's perspective for a moment. Just before midnight on Pascha, all of the lights in the Orthodox churches are extinguished, save for one light that remains on the altar table. From that light, the priest lights a single candle. He then emerges from the royal doors of the altar with the one light and then that light is spread to the rest of the congregation, quickly illuminating what was a "darkened" church only moments before.

In our church in Tampa, we close a curtain over the gateway to the altar. This makes the church very dark, but in the altar, it is as if we are "bathed" in the glow of that one candle that sits on the altar. I can still see the faces of the altar boys, and the gold on the Gospel and the other furnishings shining with majesty. What might look like a space that is dark and gloomy actually feels "filled" with light and warmth.

One of the greatest feelings I experience as a priest is to turn around from the altar, holding that one candle, watching the curtain open and then stepping into the darkened church, and singing, "*Come, receive the light from the unwaning light, and glorify Christ, who has risen from the dead.*" Even though the church is darkened, this one flame seems to fill it with light. In my ministry, I have always had the tradition of asking three women to receive the Light from me. There were three women who went and found the empty tomb, so in remembering this event each year, three women come to receive the light. Our choir stands on either side of the solea (chancel area between the altar and the pews) and sings "*Come, receive the Light*" several times. The three women kneel in front of the altar step, and I kneel also to give them the Light. This moment, four people bathed in the light of the Resurrected Christ, with the voices of the choir in the background, to me, this moment is a foretaste of heaven. Christ at the center of four friends, with a choir of angels singing behind. There is no "noise," no "busy-ness" just the Light shining in the darkness, bringing peace and joy.

The world is busy. The sun is shining brightly outside as I write today. Outside the "sanctuary" of my office, the "light" of the world is filled with "darkness"—so much stress and strife that makes even the brightest of days sometimes seem "dark."

God's world is just the opposite—Among the times I feel closest to God is at the Resurrection service, because a little of *His* Light is what fills the dark spaces of life. We know that darkness is the absence of light. Where there is even a little light, there cannot be darkness. Where Christ's light shines, there is no darkness in life. I can be in the dark church and His Light makes me feel like I am in heaven. I can be having the worst day, and His Light, experienced through prayer, worship, and faith—the knowledge that He is Lord, and that I am His child—are enough to make me feel "light" in my worries.

The difference between a "light" life and a "strife" life is Christ. Christ is life and the opportunity for eternal life. This is what brings "light" to our stressful lives. The light of Christ's promise shines in the darkness, and no darkness can overcome it.

The greatest miracle in life is the potential for eternal life, to experience the "heaven" I described earlier—friends around the light of Christ with a choir of angels all around us—forever. This miracle is always on the table for us. Even when life is "dark"—when one has had a bad day, or lost a job, or had a death in the family, or has a serious illness, or is facing his or her own death, the Light of Christ and the potential of eternal life are always on the table. No "darkness" can overtake that. This is what gives joy on even the most stressful days. That miracle is on the table for all. There have been times when people who are seriously ill have asked me, "Do you think I am going to get a miracle?" Many times I answer, "You will either get a miracle of healing, or the miracle of eternal life. You will get a miracle either way."

In every Orthodox Church, there are supposed to be two things that remain constant. One is the tabernacle on the altar table, which contains the Body and Blood of Christ. So, Christ is present at all times in the church in the Eucharist. In front of the tabernacle is a vigil light that is supposed to burn at all times. It is called the "Akimiton Fos," the Light that never sleeps. Every year during Holy Week, the priest consumes the Eucharist that remains in the tabernacle and a new Reserved Sacrament is placed in the tabernacle for the upcoming year. The Light in front stays the same. Since I arrived in Tampa many years ago, I've changed the candle in front of the tabernacle every few days, but I've moved the flame from candle to candle, so that the flame, the Light, has stayed the same for all the years I've served here. It is indeed a flame that never sleeps. What's amazing is to think of how many things have changed in the world in the past years. One thing that hasn't changed is that Light of Christ. He was, and is and ever shall be, the same—our Light in the darkness, the Light that the darkness can never overtake.

It is the Day of Resurrection! O people, let us glory in splendor! Pascha, the Lord's Pascha! For Christ our God has transported us who sing the triumphal hymn from death to life, and from earth to Heaven. (From the Katavasias of the Paschal Season, Trans. by Fr. George Papadeas)

Remember your life has the Light of Christ in it, no matter how stressful today is!

Saturday of the 4th Week of Pascha

Are You Ready to "Testify" as a "Witness"?

There was a man sent from God, whose name was John. He came for testimony, to bear witness to the Light, that all might believe through him. He was not the Light, but came to bear witness to the Light.
John 1:6-8
(From the Gospel at the Divine Liturgy on Pascha)

Christ is Risen!

The Gospel of John doesn't begin with a story of the Nativity. Rather, it begins with a summary of all that came before the Incarnation, with only one verse about the Incarnation itself (check back in a couple of days for that), so that by the end of chapter one, we are already reading about the ministry of Christ. The Evangelist almost immediately deals with the person of St. John the Baptist. There are two purposes for this. The first is to state that John the Baptist was NOT "the Christ," as many had thought. The second is to state that John the Baptist was the Forerunner of Christ. John the Baptist would then eventually endorse Christ, the Messiah.

The purpose of John the Baptist was not to be the Light, but to bear witness to the Light. This is a reminder to us that our call is to do the same. Each of us has the Light of Christ in us, and each of us has the ability to witness to that Light.

John the Baptist *"came for testimony, to bear witness to the light, that all might believe through him."* When I hear the words "testimony" and "witness," I think about a court trial. "Witnesses" are people who "testify" about something they have seen or something they know related to a court case. So, imagine for a moment that you were called as a "witness" to give "testimony" to Christ, to Christianity, and to how being a Christian affects your life, what would you say?

I remember an amazing conversation that I had with my Dad, shortly before he died. My Dad was a lifelong Christian, he went to church every Sunday, sang in the choir every Sunday, helped to raise two sons who are very involved in the church. As he neared the end of his life, he told me that he had a fear of dying and was there any way that I could help him overcome his fear. I asked him "Do you believe in God?" He said "Yes." I then asked him "What do you believe about God?" He answered "I'm not sure."

This was a "light bulb going off" moment for me, as I realized that there are many people like my Dad who fill the pews of our churches, who even fill them with joy, but when it comes to "testimony" about the Lord, they really don't know what to say. I'm not sure if this is because we've been conditioned not to learn about the Lord or that we've been conditioned not to talk about what we've learned.

Part of being able to bear witness is to be able to talk about the Lord with others. The foundation of our witness is to be able to articulate what we believe to ourselves. If we don't know what we believe, then it has no power for us. We are either "mechanical" Christians, who go through the motions of Christianity, or we are frustrated mechanical Christians who lose interest in the motions.

Knowing our faith moves us to becoming "committed Christians" and the committed Christian not only feels the joy of Christianity at all times, but even as he is dying, he is able to share that joy with others.

I am thankful that my Dad was able to articulate the joy of his Christianity before he passed away. Because he had real joy, he was able to pass away with joy in the hope of the Resurrection.

If you were called as a witness to a trial where Christianity was on trial, what would you say in defense of Christianity? When you are called before God's awesome judgment seat to give a "defense" of your life, what will you say about your Christianity? That Christ was the source and center of your life and your joy? Or that Christianity was confusing and frustrating and that you never really "got it"?

I will always be thankful to God for the beautiful conversation I had with my Dad before he passed away. Because I know that before he passed on, that my Dad truly "got it"—he understood Christ, he understood that he was going to meet the Lord, and he knew that his lifetime of building faith was leading to an eternity of everlasting joy.

> *Let us arise in the early dawn, and instead of myrrh, offer a hymn to the Master; and we shall see Christ, the Sun of Righteousness dawning life to all. (From the Katavasias of the Paschal Season, Trans. by Fr. George Papadeas)*

Think about your "testimony" today!

Sunday of the Samaritan Woman

Everyone Has the Light

*He was not the light, but came to bear witness to the Light,
the true Light that enlightens every man was coming into the world.*
John 1:8-9
(From the Gospel at the Divine Liturgy on Pascha)

Christ is Risen!

Just like there is no one who does not have a talent that they've been given by God, there is no one who does not have the Light of Christ in them. The Light of Christ enlightens *every* person coming into the world. This includes even people who don't believe ostensibly in Christ.

In James 1:17, we read that, *"every good endowment and every perfect gift is from Above, coming down from the Father of lights."* This means that everything that is good comes from God. When we do something good, it is a blessing from God. So, when a doctor performs a surgery that saves a person's life, God has performed a miracle through the hands of the doctor. Even if the doctor is an atheist and does not believe in God, God can still work through the hands of anyone to bring good into the world.

Remember the story of the Last Judgment, Matthew 25:31-46. The Lord addressed the sheep at His right hand, lauding them for feeding the hungry, clothing the naked, welcoming the stranger and visiting the sick. The "righteous" answered Him, *"When did we see Thee hungry and feed Thee, or thirsty and give Thee drink? And when did we see Thee a stranger and welcome Thee, or naked and clothe Thee? And when did we see Thee sick or in prison and visit Thee?"* (Matt. 25:37-39). They were doing the right things; they didn't realize that they were doing them for Christ.

If something is not good, it is not from God. If something is good, it is from God. God works through all kinds of people and in all kinds of situations to bring good into the world. Goodness even shines in times of sadness and tragedy. Every good gesture that comes in a bad situation is from God. Even every good gesture that comes through a bad person is from God.

In fact, no matter what talent we've been given by God, we have been given a measure of His goodness, His light. So, not only will we answer to God, "What did you do with the *talent* I gave you?" We will also answer these questions from Him, "What did you do with the *goodness* I gave you? What did you do with *the Light* that I put into you? Did you use your light to help others shine their lights more brightly? Or did you let your light flicker and encourage others to do the same?"

I was walking somewhere and it started pouring down rain. Someone near me had a large umbrella and asked me if I wanted to walk with them under their umbrella, so that I could stay dry. As it was raining very hard and I would have gotten soaked in no time, I gratefully accepted the offer. The person carrying the umbrella remarked to me "I wish this umbrella was bigger, so we could fit even more people under it." Unfortunately, only two of us were able to stay dry under it.

The Light of Christ is similar to the umbrella. We can share it with others to keep them "bright," to help shield them from the storms and challenges of life. Unlike the umbrella that could only shield two people from the rain, we have the ability to share the Light of Christ with an unlimited number of people. There is no question that there is opportunity for us to do this. There is no question that there is need for people to do this. The variable is our desire (individually and collectively) to live in the Light and to share it with others.

The first thing God created was Light. We renew ourselves on Pascha with the Light of the Resurrected Christ. Light is what gives life in this world to allow things to grow. The Light of Christ is what illumines each person and lights the path to salvation. It is our purpose to live in the Light and to share it with others.

> *O Christ, the true Light, which illumines and sanctifies every man who comes into the world, let the Light of Your countenance leave its mark on us; that in it, we may behold the ineffable Light; and direct our steps aright, to the keeping of Your commandments; through the intercessions of Your All-pure Mother, and of all Your Saints. Amen.*

Walk in the Light today! Share the Light with someone today!

Monday of the 5ᵗʰ Week of Pascha

There Is Power in Being a Child of God

He was in the world, and the world was made through Him, yet the world knew Him not. He came to His own home, and His own people received Him not. But to all who received Him, who believed in His name, He gave power to become children of God; who were born, not of blood nor of the will of the flesh nor of the will of man, but of God.
John 1:10-13
(From the Gospel at the Divine Liturgy on Pascha)

Christ is Risen! Even though the Jewish world had been waiting for a Messiah and had been given specific signs to indicate how they would know that the Messiah was among them, and even though Jesus fulfilled all of these signs, still His own people rejected him. Jesus said in Matthew 13:57, *"A prophet is not without honor except in his own country and in his own house."* Jesus had come to call His people, the children of Israel, to salvation. The strongest rejection, the demand for His crucifixion, came from His own people.

Jesus came also to call the whole world to Him, to repentance, to salvation, to the Kingdom of Heaven. He gave the honor of becoming children of God to all those who received him. (We'll get to the word "power" used in this passage in a moment.) That goes for the Jews who received Him when He walked the earth, and the Gentiles who received Him, and to every person of every nation, from the time He walked the earth until now. All of us, no matter who we are or where we come from, or even what we've done, we all have the opportunity to become children of God, if we receive Christ. To become a child of God is something that is on the table at all times for all people. Even to the person who has committed the greatest sin, they too can become a child of God if they "receive" Christ.

An important caveat though, which is that while "receiving" Christ makes one a child of God, it is doing something with what we've received, doing something to honor Christ, not only in thought but in action, this is what allows one to attain the Kingdom of Heaven. Romans 10:9 says, *"If you confess with your lips that Jesus is Lord and believe in your heart that God raised Him from the dead, you will be saved."* This leads some to believe that just "receiving" Christ is enough. Just as with anything we receive, what we receive is not as important as what we DO with what we've received. So, we must receive Christ, but then we must DO something with the message of salvation we have received. Because it is not "having" Christ that saves us, but "living in Christ" and "living for Christ" that will get us to heaven.

Let's talk about power. There is great power that comes from the Lord. Christ had the power to raise the dead, to give sight to the blind, to heal the paralytic, etc. Christ has the power to change lives, to bring joy where there is sorrow, to bring hope where there is despair, to bring purpose where there is no focus. Those who have Christ have power. This power isn't material or political power. Rather it is the power to survive and sustain in the midst of difficulties. It is the power to meet the challenges of the human spirit. It is the power to forgive and restore. These things bring real power.

Think about the causes of human despair—sometimes we lose hope in relationships, sometimes we lose hope in ourselves, sometimes we lose hope in the goodness of people, we stress about the busy-ness of life. For any cause of human despair, there is a spiritual cure. Those who have Christ have the cure for life's despairing moments. There is real power in this.

I'm not naïve enough to think that just because I believe in Christ that I am immune to sickness, stress, sadness, etc. Because I have Christ, I believe that I have the strength to meet the challenges of life that come my way, because I face them with Him, I don't face them alone. Because I have Christ, I rarely feel like I'm at a deficit, because He fills the empty spaces. Because I have received the forgiveness, the patience, and the love of Christ, I want to offer the same to others. Because I see myself as a child of God, I have more love for God's other children, everyone else. Because I want to end up with Christ at the end of my life, I use this as motivation to keep me going even when life gets tough. I'm reminded of the words from Psalm 121:2, *My help comes from the Lord, who made heaven and earth.*

As for receiving Christ, we have a chance to do so daily through prayer, and (at least) weekly through the Holy Eucharist. One of the reasons we pray and receive Christ through Holy Communion is to be empowered as His children, to have joy and confidence. So that as we "receive Him," we feel endowed with purpose—that we are to see ourselves as His children, with the Lord as our benevolent Father, and if, we are His children, then we will inherit His Kingdom, the most "powerful" thing of all.

> *At the middle, O Lord, of the sacred feast, as You stood in the Temple amid the crowd, You proclaimed, "If anyone thirst, let him come unto Me and drink." And You said, "He who drinks this divine drink that I provide, from his heart will My dogmas like rivers flow out of him. Whoever believes in God the Father, who sent Me, will truly be glorified together with Me by Him." Let us therefore cry aloud, "Glory be to You, Christ God, for You poured out to Your servants abundantly the waters of Your love for humanity." (Kathismata, from the Feast of Mid-Pentecost, Trans. by Fr. Seraphim Dedes)*

Receive Christ in prayer today! Rejoice in being His child!

Tuesday of the 5th Week of Pascha

The Story of the Nativity in Nine Words

And the word became flesh and dwelt among us, full of grace and truth.
John 1:14
(From the Gospel at the Divine Liturgy on Pascha)

Christ is Risen!

We've all seen displays of the Nativity in our homes and churches during the Christmas season. Christmas plays and pageants highlight the story of the shepherds and angels, told in the Gospel of Luke, and the Magi, as told in the Gospel of Matthew.

In some sense, these Nativity scenes can cause confusion. We all know that babies are born at finite moments in time. For those of us who have children, there was a finite moment of time when you went from having no children to having a child. The "problem" if you want to call it that, with the way that the Nativity is told from the Gospels of Matthew and Luke, is that it leads some to think that, like our children, Christ was "born" at a finite moment in time, that before the event of the Nativity, there was no Christ. This "problem" is clarified most succinctly in the Gospel of John, which, as we have said, has no account of the Nativity.

The Gospel of John summaries the Nativity in nine words: *And the Word became flesh and dwelt among us.* Having established that the Word is God and has been with God from the time of creation, the Nativity is when the Word of God "took on flesh" (or in theological terms "became incarnate") and dwelt among us. The Nativity marks the day that the Creator came to live with His creation. St. Athanasius, in his treatise *On the Incarnation* offers a well-known saying, "*God became a man, so that man can become like God.*"

Years ago, on Christmas Eve, I gave a sermon where I asked three men from the congregation to come up and sit in three chairs that were side-by-side. The man in the middle represented "God the Father." The man to his right represented "Jesus Christ," who sits at the right hand of the Father. The man to the left represented the "Holy Spirit." Each man held a candle that was lit and each of the candles were held together so they came together at one point—one light, held by three people, the one God in three persons. I asked two other people to come up, one man and one woman. Each of them was given a candle and they united their candles with "the Holy Trinity." I then read the story of creation—that God (the Father), created the heavens and the earth, that the Spirit (the Holy Spirit) was moving over the waters and that God (the Word, Jesus Christ) said, "Let there be light." The man and woman represented Adam and Eve, created by God to live in union with God. This is why their candles touched the candles of the Holy Trinity, because before the Fall, mankind lived in harmony and union with God.

At the Fall, mankind fell away from God. At this point, I asked the man and woman to step away from the other three. They kept their candles lit, the "Light" did not go out in them, but their light wasn't "as strong" because it was separated from the power of the Trinity. I then had some people hold a large sheet, a wall of separation, in between "the Trinity" and "Adam" and "Eve." This was the consequence of the fall. The feast of the Incarnation was the day that the wall of separation came down. Mankind again had access to God, in the person of Jesus Christ. This is why the Incarnation is such an important feast, because God came to be with us. The Resurrection is the feast where Christ opened back the path to Paradise. This is also why Adam and Eve are depicted in the Icon of the Resurrection, to show that all people who come to know Christ, from the first to fall, up to the last, all those who know Christ will be with Him for eternity. All who receive Christ will have a chance to be like "Adam" and "Eve" in my sermon—each will have a chance to unite with God, in the same way that Adam and Eve were with God before the fall. This is why the Incarnation is important, because in the Incarnation, the Word (Jesus Christ), who existed forever, came to be with us, His creation, and to rescue us from our sins, by paying our debt for us.

Today's hymn is taken not from the Paschal season of the year, but from the Divine Liturgy. It is sung at EVERY celebration of the Divine Liturgy, and it speaks to us of the mystery of the Incarnation, and what God did for us:

> *Only-Begotten Son and Word of God, although immortal You humbled Yourself for our salvation, taking flesh from the Holy Theotokos and Ever-Virgin Mary and, without change, becoming man. Christ, our God, You were crucified but conquered death by death. You are one of the Holy Trinity, glorified with the Father and the Holy Spirit—save us. (From the Divine Liturgy of St. John Chrysostom, Trans. by Holy Cross Seminary Press)*

Celebrate the Incarnation not only on December 25, but every day!

Wednesday of the 5th Week of Pascha

Show Me Your Glory!

And the Word became flesh and dwelt among us, full of grace and truth;
we have beheld His glory, glory as of the only Son from the Father.
John 1:14
(From the Gospel at the Divine Liturgy on Pascha)

Christ is Risen!

How often do you think of the word "glory", specifically, God's glory? Have you ever wondered what "the glory of the Lord" might look like? Most of us probably don't think about this often, if at all. We live in a world that is super-crazy-busy. The pace of life usually does not allow for us to slow down and reflect on things like this. We should, but many times we don't. Also, because we are surrounded by the accomplishments of man, we forget about the accomplishments of God. For instance, as I sit in my office typing this message, I sit in a chair made by man, at a desk made by man, in a building built by man, using a computer made by man, typing on a keyboard with an arrangement of letters invented by man. Where is God's glory at this moment?

Many of us are familiar with the Old Testament story of Moses. Moses was a man who I can totally relate to. God called him to lead His people out of Egypt. Moses at times was filled with doubt, sometimes he lacked self-confidence, other times he was stubborn, and sometimes he had a short fuse—with both the people of Israel and with the Lord—but he kept at it. He sometimes went to the Lord and threatened to quit, but he never did. One day, Moses was exasperated and he came to the Lord in total desperation. The Lord saw Moses, in a state of panic and sadness and asked Moses what He could do to help him. Moses answered with one request: *"Show me Thy glory"* (Exod. 33:18).

> Moses said, "I pray Thee, show me Thy glory." And He (God) said, "I will make all my goodness pass before you, and will proclaim before you My name 'The Lord'; and I will be gracious to whom I will be gracious and will show mercy on whom I

will show mercy. But," He said, "you cannot see My face; for man shall not see Me and live." And the Lord said "Behold, there is a place by Me where you shall stand upon the rock; and while My glory passes by I will put you in a cleft of the rock, and I will cover you with My hand until I have passed by; then I will take away My hand, and you shall see My back; but My face shall not be seen" (Exod. 33:18-23).

Reading further we see that Moses was profoundly impacted by the experience:

When Moses came down from Mount Sinai, with the two tablets of the testimony in his hand as he came down from the mountain, Moses did not know that the skin of his face shone because he had been talking with God. And when Aaron and all the people of Israel saw Moses, behold, the skin of his face shone and they were afraid to come near him (Exod. 34:29-30).

Later in the Old Testament, we meet Elijah, a prophet of God who was respected by some, feared by others, and hated by others. Again, Elijah is easy to relate to, as most of us can say that we, too, are respected by some, feared by others and hated by others. One day Elijah was afraid, because he was running for his life from Jezebel, who had promised to kill him. In his great anxiety, he asked God to just go ahead and take his life. As he lay down to sleep, an angel came to him and provided him food and water to strengthen him. Then God brought Elijah to a cave, and God passed by, then there was a strong wind, then an earthquake and then a fire. God was neither in the wind, the earthquake or the fire. He was in the small and still voice. His glory was not experienced in the power of the wind, or the force of the earthquake or the intensity of the fire, but in the peace of a small, still voice (1 Kings 19:1-12).

Christ Himself was scared in the Garden of Gethsemane. With the exasperation of Moses and the fear of Elijah, Jesus begged the Father to take away His cup of suffering. Ultimately, though, He submitted to God's will for Him at that moment. In His surrender, in the stillness of His prayer, an angel came and strengthened Him (Luke 22:43).

Back to the example of the office I am sitting in, if I didn't give it much thought, I might wonder if there is a God in the midst of all my man-made stuff. If I sit and reflect, I realize that God made the tree, from which the wood came to make my desk. God made the metal that was mined from the earth to make the chair. God made the mind of the man who created the computer and invented typing. If I stop long enough to reflect, I am surrounded by God's glory, even in my man-made office.

We see—in prayer, in faith, in stillness, in trust—that Moses, Elijah and Christ felt the glory of God. If we want to experience God's glory, we need the same attributes of prayer, faith, stillness, and trust.

Psalm 46 reads in part, *God is our refuge and strength, a very present help in trouble, therefore we will not fear though the earth should change... The Lord of hosts is with us... Come, behold the works of the Lord... Be still and know that I am God.* Yes, there have been moments of majesty when I have seen the glory of God—overlooking the Grand Canyon comes to mind. On a daily basis, I do not visit the modern marvels of the world. I seek after God's glory in stillness and in prayer. Part of my daily prayer is to ask the Lord to "show me Your glory in some way large or small today." Then I wait for Him to reveal Himself. Every day, something happens, sometimes large, usually small, that helps me to see God's glory and to strengthen my faith.

> *With the streams of Your blood, water my soul parched by unlawful offenses, and show it to be fruitful in virtue. For you have said to all, to approach You, all-holy Word of God, and to draw the water of incorruption, which is alive and washes away the sins of those who extol Your glorious and divine Resurrection. O Good One, You grant those who know You to be God the power of the Spirit that truly came down from on high to Your Disciples. You are the fountain and source of our life, O Lord. (Oikos, Feast of Mid-Pentecost, Trans. by Fr. Seraphim Dedes)*

Ask God to show you His glory in some way large or small today, and spend some time being still, so that you can know that He is God.

Thursday of the 5th Week of Pascha

Grace Molds Us Gradually and Continually

(John bore witness to Him, and cried, "This was He of whom I said,
'He who comes after me ranks before me, for He was before me.'")
And from His fullness have we all received, grace upon grace.
John 1:15-16
(From the Gospel at the Divine Liturgy on Pascha)

Christ is Risen!

Back in the reflection on Holy Tuesday, I wrote about a cup, rocks and water and used these to illustrate the concepts of faith, works and grace. Faith is the cup, the structure of what we believe. Without rocks, the cup is empty, just like without works, our faith is empty. The rocks are the works, but done outside the structure of faith, the works become ends to themselves. So faith and works go hand in hand. Fill a cup with rocks and there are still empty spaces. This is where the water comes in. Pour water into the cup and it will fill all the empty spaces, and then the cup will be truly filled.

The water represents the grace of God. "Grace" is what fills the cup, however, we don't receive grace as a "flood" of water. We receive grace "spoonful by spoonful" in Holy Communion, and in small portions through daily prayer, meditation on scripture and acts of charity.

When I think of this verse, "grace upon grace," I think of how grace is not something we receive only one time, but something we receive on a continuous basis, grace upon grace upon grace upon grace. As we receive more of God's grace, we become more filled with Him and less affected by the emptiness that accompanies life's struggles. The empty spaces of our lives become filled. The more grace we seek, the more grace we receive. The more grace we receive, the more "refined" we become.

Let's go back to the example of the Grand Canyon. Why is the Grand Canyon so magnificent? It has been "refined" and reshaped by water. The Colorado River, which runs through the canyon, has continually shaped the massive rocks into the majestic landscape they have become. Glaciers did the same thing with Yosemite Valley, a deep valley in central California that is lined with massive and magnificent monoliths of granite, rising thousands of feet into the air. These natural wonders were not created in one moment, but refined bit by bit over a long period of time. Similarly, we as Christians are not transformed in one moment, but we are refined on a daily basis, as we receive "grace upon grace."

When I trim bushes at home, in order to make them look "perfect," it is a multi-step process. I pass by first with the hedge trimmer to take the majority of the branches off that I want to cut. Then I pass by a second time with the hedge trimmer and round the edges. Then I pass by a third time with a hand clipper and prune the bottom of the bushes to get them off of the ground. Then I pass by with a rake to collect the majority of the clippings. Then I bring a leaf-blower to blow out the excess leaves and blow them onto the lawn. Finally, I mow the lawn so that even the small pieces of the bush that were scattered on the lawn are no longer visible.

To become a Christian, to become "filled with grace and truth" (John 1:14), in order to truly see Christ as "ranking before" us (John 1:15), it takes a long time, and lots of "refining." We have to make "many passes" to prune our souls. We have to pass by in prayer, we have to pass by in scripture, we have to clean up through confession, we have to purify through Communion, and we have to renew ourselves on a daily basis.

I do not trim the bushes "one time for all time." They require regular maintenance. It is the same thing with our souls. "Grace upon grace" should be a daily pursuit, with a goal to partake in some way daily of the grace of God that is available to us in many ways.

Let the God-inspired Prophet Habakkuk keep with us the divine watch, and point out the light-bearing Angel, who with a vibrant voice declared: "Today, salvation comes to the world, for Christ has risen as Almighty." (From the Katavasias of the Paschal Season, Trans. by Fr. George Papadeas)

Experience God's grace in prayer today and every day!

Friday of the 5th Week of Pascha

Grace and Truth Supersede the Law

For the law was given through Moses; grace and truth came through Jesus Christ.
John 1:17
(From the Gospel at the Divine Liturgy on Pascha)

Christ is Risen!

I remember from my college days that I was a really good test-taker. I had this system that I called "read, retain, regurgitate, release." I would read the information, retain it in my brain, regurgitate it for the exam, and then it was released from my brain as the words were written by my pen. There were many times that I felt I held the information in my brain only long enough to take the test. If I took the exam three hours later, I might have failed it.

Now that I'm much older and have more life experience, I realize that while I was a good test-taker, I wasn't necessarily a good learner. I "learned" many times for the test and not for the love or desire to learn them. Now, well on the other side of college, I wish that I had been more focused on learning and retaining rather than just focused on the grade. (As an aside, this is not an indictment of our educational system, or my alma mater, so please do not read it that way).

It seems that the children of Israel had the same problem when it came to learning how to be God's people. God, through Moses, gave the Law to His people, a "syllabus" if you will on how to live. The Law had so many fine points, 613 of them to be exact, that no one could learn and live by all of them. Jesus would tell His followers in John 8:32, *"You will know the truth, and the truth shall set you free."* The Law, while certainly not false, did not set the people free. If anything, it imprisoned them. No one could remember, let alone keep, the 613 commandments.

Christ came in order to give us freedom. He brought grace and truth. He brought grace because grace fills what is lacking. He brought truth, because through Him, we are set free. The Law was focused on checking boxes—do this, don't do this. The Law was focused on the individual checking his own boxes. Grace and truth are focused on love, and love is not an individual thing. Love involves others. Love is taking from oneself and projecting onto someone else. Loving someone involves sharing time, offering help, offering forgiveness, offering patience, taking things that we have and offering them to someone else.

The Law was an important and necessary precursor to the grace and truth of Jesus Christ. Without the Law, there would have been no order. Without order, there would be chaos. Where there is chaos there is fear. Where there is fear there cannot be love (1 John 4:18). The purpose of order is not merely to have order, but to set the stage so that grace and truth could shine forth. The purpose of order is to cast out fear so that love can abide.

The purpose of law in modern society is to provide order and not promote chaos. The law says that I cannot harm my neighbor, or steal from my neighbor, or take over my neighbor's house or trespass at his table. The law doesn't tell me to love my neighbor. It only tells me not to hurt my neighbor. If I hurt my neighbor, I will be punished. There is no reward for loving my neighbor. However, many times when we are not hurting our neighbor, our motivation is self-serving. It is because we don't want to get in trouble.

With the Law as a foundation, Christ came to supersede the Law, to take us from a level of "goodness" to a level of "godliness." The motivation to do or not to do things, in the eyes of God, is no longer based on a fear of punishment, but a motivation to love one another.

College should foster a desire not only to test well, but also to learn. I should have, in hindsight, focused on being a better student (learning) than just being a great test taker. The focus of the Church and of the Christian message is not memorization of Bible verses and prayers. It is not avoidance of punishment and hell. The focus of the Christian message is on love for God, and love for one another. It is not on the avoidance of hell, but on the attainment of heaven. It is also not on the individual and his achievement, because our achievement as individuals is tied around our achievement as communities, and how much and how well we encourage love in our community. The law indeed makes communities safer, and makes for a good community. The grace and truth that came through Jesus Christ are what makes for a Godly community. There are differences between worshipping order and worshipping Christ. There is a crucial difference between a "good" life on earth and thriving in eternal life after our life on earth is over.

Jesus says in Matthew 5:17, *"Think not that I have come to abolish the law and the prophets; I have not come to abolish them but to fulfill them."* Saint Paul writes in Romans 13:10 *"Love does no wrong to a neighbor; therefore love is the fulfilling of the law."* In Galatians 5:14, he writes, *"For the whole law is fulfilled in one word, 'You shall love your neighbor as yourself.'"* As Christians, we follow the laws of our country, but in order to find Christ, we need to make sure that we are not only obedient to the law of man, but that we learn to love the grace and truth of Christ.

> *The feast according to the Law at its midpoint, O Christ our God, as the Creator and Master of everything, You said to all those who were present there, "Come that you might draw from Me the water of immortality." Hence with faith we cry to You as we prostrate before You. Your tender mercies grant to us, we pray. You are the fountain and source of our life, O Lord. (Kontakion, Feast of Mid-Pentecost, Trans. by Fr. Seraphim Dedes)*

Don't be content with being good today. Be Godly today!

Saturday of the 5th Week of Pascha

His Plans Don't Necessarily Match Our Plans

So when they had come together, they asked Him, "Lord, will you at this time restore the kingdom to Israel?" He said to them, "It is not for you to know times or seasons which the Father has fixed by His own authority.
Acts 1:6-7
(From the Epistle Lesson read at the Divine Liturgy on Pascha)

Christ is Risen!

Many reflections ago, I wrote about how in life I like to connect the dots. Sometimes in trying to connect the dots of life, things just don't make a lot of sense. Let's reflect on the comment of the Apostles in this scripture verse. These men had left their homes and businesses and followed Christ for three years. They had lots of moments to experience His glory—just add up all the miracles and what an awesome experience it must have been for them to witness the blind seeing, and the lame walking, and the dead coming to life, not just one time, but many times. Then there were the many comforting sayings and stories, and no doubt there were just the moments of friendship with this incredible man, sharing meals, taking walks, and sailing on the lake.

There were difficult moments. There were moments of doubt. There were moments of downright fear. How could a whole city turn against Christ? How could a bloodthirsty mob demand His crucifixion? How could He endure the pain of the beatings? There was the fear that they could be the next ones to die. There were moments of confusion when the tomb was empty and they didn't know where Christ was. There were moments of joy, as Jesus came and stood among them, risen indeed, just as He said He would be.

Now, with firm conviction that Christ really rose from the dead, that things happened just as He said they would, their minds naturally wandered to what was going to happen next, and they turned to a material concern, *"Lord, will you at this time restore the Kingdom to Israel?"* The Jews lived under the oppression of Rome for many years. The disciples were Jews and residents of the areas dominated by the Romans, victims of Roman oppression and over-taxation, just like everyone else. If Jesus had conquered death, it seemed like He would be able to conquer the Romans and restore the Kingdom to Israel, right? This was their way of thinking, and seemed logical, to them.

This is why the response of Christ must have come like a punch in the gut to them, *"It is not for you to know the times and the seasons which the Father has fixed by His own authority."* No doubt God had a plan, but that plan didn't necessarily match the ideas of the Disciples, that this new faith was going to bring political freedom to them as well. It must have been a hard, even bitter, pill for them to swallow—we've given up everything to follow You, where is the gain for us?

Following Christ does not necessarily bring material gain. In fact, in helping out the poor, it may even bring material loss. We may make grandiose plans for our lives and He may have other plans for us. There are times in my life when I am so busy that I seem to forget about God. How many times He puts His hand right on my shoulder and tells me "trust me, just let Me take care of this." Do I listen? If love is patient and kind and does not insist on its own way, (1 Cor. 13: 4-5), then my relationship with God will go even deeper when I am more patient and kind to others, and when I let go of some of my ideas and do it His way. Many times, God allows life to throw us curveballs, to tell us, "My will be done, not yours." Many times we plan things out and God has other plans. Many times things happen in His time and not ours.

I'm reminded of the story of the footprints in the sand, that in the tough moments of my life, when it seems like God has abandoned me, that He is really carrying me. He is carrying me to Him, to His glory, to His plan for my life.

Many times, it seems that things should happen in a certain season and then they don't. Someone thinks that "I should have been married by this time," or "I should have had children." or "I should have gotten a job promotion." We want these things in "our seasons" and not in God's seasons. There are certain things that perhaps God doesn't even want for our lives, because they are unhealthy for us. The message of Christ to the Disciples was not, "I do not love you and that's why I will not restore the Kingdom to Israel and give you political freedom." The message was, "I love you so much that I want you to focus on Me and on the eternal reward I am offering. Do not be satisfied with a temporal kingdom when you can have an eternal one." He offers the same message to us: "Do not be overly satisfied with life's successes, and don't be too disappointed with life's setbacks, or when things don't go the way that you envisioned them. For every victory gained in this life is temporary. I love you so much that if you stick by Me, throughout the seasons of your life, you will gain the eternal victory."

> *Christ the new Pascha, the living Sacrifice, the Lamb of God, Who takes away the sins of the world. Oh! Great and Holiest Pascha, Christ! Oh! Wisdom and Word, and Power of God! Grant us a clearer sign, that we may partake of You, in the unwaning Day of Your Kingdom. (From the 9th Ode of Pascha, Trans. by Fr. George Papadeas)*

Trust in God's plan for your life!

Sunday of the Blind Man

What is a Commission?

Then He said to them, "These are My words which I spoke to you, while I was still with you, that everything written about Me in the law of Moses and the prophets and the psalms must be fulfilled." Then He opened their minds to understand the scriptures, and said to them, "Thus it is written, that the Christ should suffer and on the third day rise from the dead, and that repentance and forgiveness of sins should be preached in His name to all nations, beginning from Jerusalem. You are witnesses of these things. And behold, I send the promise of My Father upon you; but stay in the city, until you are clothed with power from on high."
Luke 24:44-49
(From the Sixth Eothinon Gospel read at the Orthros Service)

Christ is Risen!

When I hear the word "commission" three things come to mind. The first is the "commissioning" of a ship. Many months and sometimes years are spent building a ship in "dry-dock." Ships are not built on the water, even very large ones like Navy warships. When a ship is finished, there is a "christening ceremony." Usually a bottle of champagne is broken over the bow of the ship and then the ship is "launched," meaning it slides down a ramp and into the water. After the commissioning, the ship sets off on whatever mission it was intended for—military service, transportation of freight, or sailing for fun. No "commissioned" ship just sits in the harbor. No ship is built just to sit around. They are all built to do something. The "commissioning" of the ship marks the end of the building process, but it begins the real work of the ship.

The second thing I think of when I hear the word "commission" is of graduates of one of the United States service academies throwing their hats into the air at graduation. These men and women who graduate from places like the U.S. Naval Academy, West Point and the Air Force Academy are now "commissioned" as military officers. Their training now complete, they are sent out as leaders of the United States military. As with the commissioning of the ship, their "commissioning" marks more of a beginning than an ending. The purpose of their "commissions" are to go out and *do* something, to be leaders. No commissioned officer is without a task to do. All are commissioned to do something.

The third thing that comes to mind when I hear the word "commission" is the way by which certain people get paid to do their jobs. There are jobs when one collects a salary. Let's say, for example, that a person works at a bank. On the 15th and 30th of each month, when everyone gets their paychecks, let's say that a lot of people run to the bank, and each worker at the bank has to work extremely hard and fast all day to keep up with all the customers. The next day, let's say that no one comes into the bank. Everyone did their banking the day before, so the workers do little. The workers at the bank make a salary. So, if everyone comes to the bank on one day and it is extremely busy, the workers make the same amount of money as on the day when no one comes to the bank and not much work needs to get done. A person who works for "commission," for example, a realtor, only gets paid when a house is bought or sold. If they don't work, they make no money.

This week's reflections are going to focus on our "commissions" as Christians. In each of the four Gospels, there was a "commissioning" of the Disciples by the Lord. We are the descendants of the Disciples, as we too are followers of Christ, and so these "commissions" extend to us as well. In each of the four Gospels, there is a call to action from Christ to the Disciples.

Like the commissioning of a ship, after a period of "building up" of the disciples through Jesus' teachings to them, they were sent out to preach to all the world. In the modern context we are the same. We are supposed to learn about the faith, to be "built" like strong ships, and then we are supposed to "sail out" in to the world and witness for the faith, to share the faith.

The commissioning of the Disciples was like their graduation day. As the Lord was about to ascend into heaven, He told the Disciples that their time of preparation was coming to an end and it was now going to be a time for action. In the Gospel of Luke, which is quoted today, the Disciples were going to be given "power from on high" which would sustain them in their work. This power is of course from the Holy Spirit, which would come into them on Pentecost.

Each military officer is given a specific commission. One commands a plane, another commands a ship, another commands a group of ground troops, and another works in intelligence. Likewise, each Disciple, and each of us as "disciples," has a specific "commission." We are all to spread the word of God in a different manner, giving a different witness. Some will do it as priests, others as teachers, others as builders, others as coaches, others as parents. But, we are each commissioned to DO something to spread the word of God in the world.

Like the realtor, we are not going to get a reward unless we work. Salvation in the Kingdom of God is not the result of sitting around. Merely receiving a commission is not enough either. The call to salvation is a call to action. The ship sails, the officer leads, and the realtor sells. All are called to action. So is each Christian, we are all "commissioned" in order to spread the Word of God in the world. We are all commissioned differently, in that we all will do our work in a different way. We are all commissioned the same in that we are supposed to be DO-ers.

Magnify, O My soul, Christ, the Life-giver, Who arose from the tomb on the third day. Oh! Divine! Oh! Beloved! Oh! Your most sweet voice! You, O Christ, have truly promised that You would be with us unto the end of all Ages. Wherefore, the faithful, rejoice, having Your words as an anchor of hope. (From the 9th ode of the Orthros of Pascha, Trans. by Fr. George Papadeas)

Live out your commission today!

Monday of the 6th Week of Pascha

We Are All Called to Be Disciples and Apostles

And Jesus said to the Disciples, "Go into all the world and preach the gospel to the whole creation. He who believes and is baptized will be saved; but he who does not believe will be condemned. And these signs will accompany those who believe: in My name they will cast out demons; they will speak in new tongues; they will pick up serpents, and if they drink any deadly thing, it will not hurt them; they will lay their hands on the sick, and they will recover."
Mark 16:15-18
(From the Third Eothinon Gospel read at Sunday Orthros)

Christ is Risen!

What is the difference between the word "Disciple" and the word "Apostle"? The word "disciple" means "student," and a student is one who learns. The word "apostle" means "one who is sent out" and the work of the apostle it to teach, in this case to spread the word of God. Just as a teacher was once a student, one who is going to be an apostle must first be a disciple. If God expects each of us to spread the Gospel, then He has called all of us to be apostles. Thus, we must first become good disciples, good students. It is interesting to note that in the Bible, the overwhelming majority (but not all) of the references to the twelve disciples that occur before their "commissioning" refer to them as "disciples." After the "commissioning and the Ascension, the overwhelming majority (though not all) references to them are as "apostles." Thus, the "commissioning" of the Disciples was to "commission" them as Apostles, for the students to go out and become the teachers of the Gospel.

In today's scripture passage from the Gospel of Mark, Jesus not only commissions the Disciples to, "Go into all the world and preach the Gospel to the whole creation," He mentions to them signs that will accompany them and those who they will spread the Gospel to. Those who believe, including the Apostles, will be able to cast out demons, they will "*speak in new tongues* (this foretells of Pentecost when the Apostles would speak in all the languages known to mankind), *they will pick up serpents, and if they drink any deadly thing, it will not hurt them; they will lay their hands on the sick and they will recover."*

There are two reasons for sharing these signs. First, it is to reiterate to the Apostles that they will be given great power from the Lord, to do extraordinary things, just as the Lord Himself did extraordinary and miraculous things. It served as a reminder to them that great power comes from God through us, His servants. With such great power would also come great responsibility.

The second reason is so that the Apostles would have a way to gauge God's grace at work in others. After all, if an Apostle was evangelizing people, how would the Apostle know who to appoint as a deacon, as a helper, or even who to ordain as a bishop (and later a priest). These "signs" were clues for the Apostles of a sense of holiness inside of someone being considered for leadership in the early church.

Most of us don't think of ourselves as "apostles." Many of us probably consider ourselves rather ordinary when it comes to faith, and certainly not extraordinary. The Lord, however, doesn't call us to be ordinary. He calls us each to be extraordinary. Just like He doesn't call us merely to be students, but to be teachers; He calls us to not only be servants, but to be leaders. He doesn't call us only to be Disciples, but to be Apostles.

Nowhere does it say that every apostle will be able to cast our demons or heal the sick, but the Lord gave each of us something of power and influence. There are many people whose "power" is in their humility, honesty, or work ethic. There are people who speak with powerful conviction about the faith. There are still others who give a powerful witness of their faith with their patience and perseverance. God has given each of us the ability to learn about the things of faith, to be a disciple. He has given each of us a way to lead others to Christ, giving each of us then the foundation to be good Apostles.

"Apostle" comes from the Greek "Apostello," which means sent forth. Christ sent forth simple fishermen to bring the world to Christ. These men were not educated and were rather pedestrian in their skill sets. However, the Gospel of Christ and the work of the Church is not so much about "brain work" as it is about "heart work." Christ has called each of us in some way, to be His Apostles. Before becoming an Apostle, however, one needs to be a Disciple. To be a Disciple, one needs devotion and interest. To be an Apostle, there also has to be continued interest in being a Disciple. For learning about the Lord is a lifelong endeavor, and speaking about Him with others should be as well.

> *Let no one doubt that Christ is risen, for He appeared to Mary and then was seen by those walking in the country. Again He appeared to the eleven initiates as they reclined, and sent them forth to baptize others. He then ascended to heaven from when He descended, confirming their preaching with a multitude of signs. (Exapostelarion of the Third Eothinon of Orthros, Trans. by Holy Cross Seminary Press)*

Be a disciple today! Be an apostle today!

Tuesday of the 6th Week of Pascha

He Works With Us Even When We Doubt

Now the eleven disciples went to Galilee, to the mountain to which Jesus had directed them. And when they saw Him they worshiped Him; but some doubted.
Matthew 28:16-17
(Gospel read at the Vesperal Liturgy on Holy Saturday morning)

Christ is Risen!

"Doubt" is a topic that comes up often not only in these reflections, but in any journey of faith. We wonder things like:

Is my faith strong enough?

Am I doing what God wants me to do with my life?

If God loves me, why does He allow me to struggle with certain things without success?

These thoughts can cause distraction at a minimum and can lead one to feel down and distraught at their worst. Today's scripture verse from the Gospel of Matthew is one that I take comfort in. Not only did the Disciples doubt in what they couldn't see (remember Thomas, "unless I see, I will not believe"), but they SAW Jesus and still some doubted. If these men could see and still doubt, then it makes me feel better about my moments of "unseen" doubt.

The Bible doesn't tell us exactly what these men were doubting. They saw Christ with their own eyes, so they weren't doubting His Resurrection. He had shown them so many proofs over forty days that they weren't questioning that. WE question that, because we haven't seen Jesus in body in front of us. By the time of the Ascension, the Disciples were not questioning this.

So, what then did they doubt? I would venture to say the same things that even devout Christians of today doubt the three questions I mentioned above, and a host of other questions that are associated with them. I consider myself a pretty devout Christian—I've centered not only my career, but also my life around Christ and the Church. Many times I still wonder is my faith really as strong as I think it is, or do I lead others to believe that it is. Many things in the world still don't make sense to me, whether it is my own shortcomings or the disappointing things that go on in society. I wonder about God's "master plan" and what role I play in it.

Sometimes I wonder if there really is a plan or if He allows things just to happen at random. In these ways, I can sometimes see myself in the place of the Disciples on the mountaintop. They are worshipping, beholding God's glory, and still having questions in their minds. From this I actually take great comfort—I can be a priest, a faithful worshipper, and I can experience God's glory and still have questions, and that's okay.

Why is that okay? The answer comes from Mark 16:20, *"And they went forth and preached everywhere, while the Lord worked with them and confirmed the message by the signs that attended it."* At the end of Mark's Gospel, just as the end of Matthew's, the Disciples are commissioned to preach the Gospel. Just like in Matthew's Gospel, doubts accompany them. Saint Mark is quick to point out in his Gospel account that "the Lord worked with *them*," meaning the disciples. He worked with them as they were, doubts and all. He worked with their shortcomings—remember they were mostly illiterate fishermen—and turned them into heralds of the Gospel. He worked with their doubts and helped them to become bold and confident preachers, who were ready to live and to die for their faith. No one is going to allow themselves to be killed without having conviction in what they are dying for. So, these men of sometimes-shaky faith quickly became men of "convicted" faith, because the Lord worked with them.

Today's message is one of hope for all of us: the Lord will work with us, even in our shortcomings, even in our doubts, just as He worked with the Disciples. The Lord meets us where we are—in our various states of brokenness, and then works with us to raise us to states of spiritual confidence. This happens because of two things—His faithfulness to us and our trust in Him. He is faithful to us—He desires us to be saved and to live in the knowledge of His truth, working our way to His everlasting Kingdom. If He didn't desire that, then why send Christ to redeem us to begin with? Why continue to shine His Light on the world each day if not to redeem the world? So, He is faithful to us. We show our faith in Him with confidence. On days when we don't have confidence, on days we have doubts, and we all have these kind of days, we show our faith by our presence—we show up in prayer, we show up to worship. The Disciples worshipped, and some doubted, but none left. Today's message is to stay present with God, keep worshipping, keep trusting, and allow Him to work with you. He knows what you need. He knows what I need. So, let us imitate the Disciples—let us continue to put our faith and trust in the Lord, and He will continue to work with us, in the ways that we need.

> *Let us go up with the Disciples into a mountain of Galilee to behold with faith Christ as He proclaims His power over things above and below. Let us learn how He teaches us to baptize all nations in the name of the Father and the Son and the Holy Spirit, and how we may be initiated in His mysteries as He promised, until the end of the world. (Exapostelarion of Eothinon One, Trans. by Holy Cross Seminary Press)*

Allow God to work with you and in you today!

Leave-Taking of Pascha

Recruiting Others is Part of the Deal

And Jesus came and said to them, "All authority in heaven and on earth has been given to Me. Go therefore and make disciples of all nations, baptizing them in the name of the Father and of the Son and of the Holy Spirit, teaching them to observe all that I have commanded you."
Matthew 28:18-20
(From the Gospel read at the Vesperal Liturgy on Holy Saturday morning)

Christ is Risen!

At every Baptism, the priest asks the person being baptized (when it is a baby, the sponsor answers this question on behalf of the child) a very important question, "Do you unite yourself to Christ?" This question is arguably the most important question that a person is asked in their lives. The answer to this question is what confirms that one is a Christian. Even though we are asked this question in a formal way only one time, it is a question that we must answer every day of our lives.

To be a Christian, there is only one possible answer: *yes*, I unite myself to Christ. If this is our answer, that yes, we are united with Christ and wish to be united with Him today and forever, then this answer comes with a "charge," presented as today's Scripture passage, which is also called, The Great Commission. Christ gave the Great Commission to His Disciples immediately prior to His Ascension. By extension, it is given to all of us when we are baptized and join the Body of Christ. This Gospel passage is read at every Baptism.

The Great Commission calls on everyone to go out and spread the Gospel. It is our collective responsibility to "baptize all nations." This is not the job of the priests only. Yes, the priests are the ones who conduct the baptisms. (Ironically, a baptism can be done by a layperson in the event of an extreme emergency, when an unbaptized child is likely to die before a priest can be reached. In this extremely rare instance, a layperson can baptize a child "in the air" by lifting up the child and saying "The servant of God [N] is baptized in the name of the Father and of the Son and of the Holy Spirit. Amen." This is a valid baptism. What makes a baptism a valid baptism is the invocation of the Holy Trinity—Father, Son and Holy Spirit—over a child. While this is normally done in the church by immersing an infant in water, if an adult is baptized and immersion is not possible, a lesser amount of water can be used. In the case of a child who is not baptized, but is severely ill, a baptism can be conducted in a hospital using a small amount of water, or in an extreme case, no water at all. Over the years of my ministry, I have conducted several "emergency" baptisms in hospitals, where I used a syringe filled with water and made "dots" of water over the child invoking the name of the Holy Trinity.) *All* people are called to recruit others for Christ. The "commandment" (not suggestion, it is a commandment!) to baptize all nations extends to all Christians. We are not to coerce or force people to be baptized, because the Christian faith is one of love, not of fear or compulsion. We are to "witness" for Christ in a way that encourages others to seek after Him as well. This means that each person's faith must be such that it is recognized by others as something to be emulated. If I know Christ and others can see what a great joy that brings to me, they will want that joy for themselves and they will seek after Christ as I have. If, however, I do not give a good witness for Christ, if I live a life that does reflect Christian joy or Christian values, then I can't be an effective "recruiter" for Christ and I cannot live out this commandment to baptize all nations.

Good news is supposed to travel fast. We all know how fast bad news travels. In our fallen condition, most of us enjoy sharing bad news through gossip. If we are eagerly gossiping, much more eagerly should we be sharing the Good News of Christ with one another. For this is what He has commanded us to do. We are to go and make disciples of all nations, baptizing them, and teaching them to observe all of the things that the Lord taught us.

Many times in our churches, this idea of recruiting others gets lost. We get involved in building programs and festivals, fundraisers and socials, and we forget the command to "grow" the Body of Christ. Indeed, spreading the faith must be a goal for every church community and every priest. That growth shouldn't be limited to capturing members of our culture or even members of our faith that have lapsed. It needs to extend to every soul who does not know Christ.

For the final time, I greet you with the Paschal greeting of "Christ is Risen!" Today is the final day of the Paschal celebration, as tomorrow is the feast of the Ascension. As we greet one another with these joyful words, let us do so with the prayer that we will greet each other with them again next year on Pascha, in health and in joy. As I tell my congregation each year on this day, there has never been a year where someone from the congregation did not pass away in between celebrations of Pascha. So, let us pray for those who will leave us that they will sing the beautiful hymn of "Christ is Risen" in the Kingdom of Heaven next year, as those of us who remain sing it here on earth.

It is the Day of the Resurrection! Let us shine forth in splendor for the Festival, and embrace one another. Let us say, "O brethren, even to those, who do not love us; let us forgive all things in the Resurrection, and thus let us exclaim: 'Christ is Risen from the dead, by death trampling down upon death, and to those in the tombs He has granted life.'" (Doxastikon of Orthros and Vespers of Bright Week, Trans. by Fr. George Papadeas; Christ is Risen, official version of the Greek Orthodox Archdiocese of America)

Christ is Risen! Truly He is Risen!

Feast of the Ascension of our Lord

He Ascended in Glory

So then the Lord Jesus, after He had spoken to them, was taken up into heaven, and sat down at the right hand of God.
Mark 16:19

(From the Third Eothinon Gospel of the Sunday Orthros)
"But you shall receive power when the Holy Spirit has come upon you; and you shall be My witnesses in Jerusalem and in all Judea and Samaria and to the end of the earth." And when He had said this, as they were looking on, He was lifted up, and a cloud took Him out of their sight.
Acts 1:8-9
(From the Epistle Lesson on the Feast of Ascension)

Before commenting on the Feast of the Ascension of the Lord, let's go back for a moment to His Nativity, His "descent" from heaven. Christ came down from heaven in a human way—He was "born" as a baby. He came in a private way, made known only to Mary and Joseph, to shepherds and Magi. There was a "cosmic" event, however, with the appearance of the star and the multitude of the angels. So, there was "glory" in Christ's descent to earth at the Nativity, but it was not made known to all.

The Ascension was different. Christ ascended in glory, in radiance. This occurred in the presence of His Disciples, the twelve and quite possibly even more than that. What a sight this must have been, to see Christ "lifting off" of the earth and ascending into the clouds and entering into the heavens.

It is not a stretch to say that the Ascension touches on all of the major events in the life of Christ. There was, at the Ascension, as described by hymnographers, a multitude of angels, with trumpets playing, reminiscent of the heavenly hosts at the Nativity. The heavens were opened, as they were at the Theophany/Epiphany. However, instead of the voice of the Father and the Spirit in the form of a dove alighting on Christ in the Jordan River, the heavens opened to receive Christ ascending to them. We are reminded of the brilliance of the Transfiguration, when Christ first appeared in the sky with Moses and Elijah. At the Crucifixion, Christ was lifted up on the Cross. At the Ascension He was lifted up on the clouds. At the Resurrection, He showed the fullness of His Glory, that He was Lord of life and death. In the Ascension, He showed His glory to all people.

Let's go back for a moment to the equation where God was on one side and man was on one side. At the time of the Creation, man was made to be like God, the equation was balanced. At the time of the Fall, man's side of the equation fell out of balance, because all of the human miseries entered on man's side, but were not on God's side. At the Nativity, the equation began to come into balance as Christ came to earth to experience our side of the equation. The equation was balanced at the time of the Crucifixion, as Christ died on the cross and experienced the human death that we will all experience.

The balance of the equation was short-lived. Because after the burial of Christ, He rose from the dead, something we have not done. Then He ascended into heaven and sat at the right hand of the Father. This is our future hope and the work of our salvation. We are to live in Christ, so that we can die like Christ. If we die like Christ, in perfect faith and trust in God, then we will be resurrected like Christ. We, too, will ascend to heaven. We, too, will be accounted worthy to sit at the right hand of the Father. This is the Last Judgment, where all will be judged either worthy to sit at the right hand of the Father (Paradise) or to be consigned to the left (condemnation). Because one cannot fall from heaven, if we are deemed worthy to sit at the right hand of God, the equation can be balanced for each of us for all time. For if we rise with Christ, ascend to heaven and sit at the right hand of the Father, then we will be with Christ and "like" Christ forever.

The Ascension was the last act of Christ's earthly ministry. It will be the last act of our earthly lives as well. This is the end point for our lives—it's either going to be an "ascension" in glory or a "descent" in condemnation. That's why we should pause and reflect on the Ascension, not only what it was like to witness that awesome event, but what it will be like for us to ascend to heaven and sit at the right hand of God. What a comfort to reflect on the journeys of our loved ones who have made this journey already ahead of us.

It's amazing how all of these events in the life of Christ tie together. The Resurrection wasn't the end of the story. Christ didn't rise from the dead so that we could rise from the dead, but so that we could rise from this earthly life and ascend in glory to heaven. This is why the Ascension is so important in our faith. For the Resurrection is not the end of the journey. The end of the journey is heaven. The Resurrection opened the path to Paradise. The Ascension opened the gates to heaven for Christ, and because of the Ascension, those gates can open for each of us as well.

With the disciples witnessing, You ascended O Christ, unto the Father, to sit beside Him. Angels ran before you and they cried aloud, "Lift up the gates, O lift them up, and Behold the King has ascended, to light-principled glory." (Exapostelarion, from the Orthros of Ascension. Trans. by Fr. Seraphim Dedes)

May we one day ascend in glory as well!

Friday after the Ascension

So, What Now?

And while staying with them He charged them not to depart from Jerusalem, but to wait for the promise of the Father, which He said, "You heard from me."
Acts 1:4
(From the Epistle Lesson read on the Feast of Ascension)

If you divide the history of the world into chapters, the first chapter would be, "The Creation of the world." The second chapter would be the period where mankind lived in total unity with God, "a period of Paradise." The third chapter would be, "The Fall of mankind," that moment when mankind chose to go away from God, which opened up a Pandora's box of negative consequences. The fourth chapter would be called, "The Period of Expectation." During this chapter, prophets foretold of the coming of the Messiah. Thus, this was an age of waiting, an age of expectation. The fifth chapter would be, "the earthly ministry of Christ," the thirty-three year period in which Christ walked the earth. All of the prophecies from, "The Period of Expectation" came true in His person. This chapter culminated in the crucifixion, the Resurrection, and lastly, the Ascension, the return of Christ to heaven, from which He had come.

With the Ascension begins the next chapter in the history of humanity, which could be entitled, "Living in the kingdom of God on earth, while waiting for the Kingdom of God in heaven." What does this mean? We are no longer "waiting" for the Messiah. He has come. He told us that the Kingdom of Heaven is not just a far off reality, but it is something we can live in during the present age. This is why in the Divine Liturgy in the Orthodox Church, the service begins with the words, *"Blessed is the Kingdom of the Father and of the Son and of the Holy Spirit,* now *and forever and to the ages of ages,"* to remind us that God's Kingdom is present in the *now*, as well as forever. We live *in* Christ by living as He taught us to live. He taught us how to love one another, how to forgive one another, how to have joy with one another, and how to serve one another. He taught us that if we live in Him in this life, that an even greater life awaits us. Yes, we can live in Christ in this life and experience His glory and His Kingdom in our life on earth. This sense of Godliness is constantly tempered by surrounding temptations and our continual succumbing to them. The Kingdom of Heaven will be a permanent glory, a permanent joy and a permanent perfection. While we get glimpses of these things in life on earth, they will be the normal and permanent lifestyle in the Kingdom of Heaven.

So, we live again in an age of expectation. We live in something great, but we await something even greater. In the first age of expectation, when God's people fell away from Him, He never abandoned them. He gave signs and promises through prophets and miracles so that the people would know that God still loved them and still had a plan for them.

In this new age of expectation, we see the same thing happening. Christ came, and then He left. He ascended into heaven, but He has left us signs and promises and daily miracles so that we know that He is God, that He loves us, and that He has a plan for us. The first promise of God to His people was the promise that the Holy Spirit would come to us as a "Comforter," to inspire, warm and sustain our faith through this life, into everlasting life. That promise was fulfilled on Pentecost, only ten days after the Ascension.

After Pentecost, God continues to work in the world on a daily basis. As I read today's brief scripture verse, I realize that like the Disciples, we are told *"not to depart"* but *"to wait for the promise of the Father."* We are to stay faithful to Christ, to "not depart" from His Commandments and to "wait" for His promises to be fulfilled.

There are many times in my life when I have been confronted with a task that seems undoable, or not advisable. Many times I have "heard God's voice" in my head saying "just trust me and do what seems impossible, and I will help you find a way." I think we've all had that experience. We come to a crossroads on a decision, even a small decision, and we wonder, "Should I?" One thing I can say for certain in my life, when I am faithful to God, He is always faithful to me. He is faithful to me even when I am not faithful to Him. This is what it means to, "wait for the promise of the Father." It means to stay faithful to God, even when things don't make sense, even when you are waiting "for a break."

Let's put ourselves in the position of the disciples for one moment—Christ "left" to ascend into heaven, but told them to wait for promises to be fulfilled. That was a moment of decision for them—stay and wait for the unseen to happen, or leave and go their own way. They elected to stay and wait—and their wait paid off in only a few days with the empowerment from the Holy Spirit. It continues to pay off to this day in ways large and small for just as God blessed them, He continually blesses us.

> *The Angels beholding the Master's Ascension were filled with great astonishment at how with glory He was lifted from the earth into heaven. To the sacred band of holy Disciples did the risen Lord command: Tarry in Jerusalem and I shall send you another Comforter, who shares the Father's throne and is of equal honor with Me, whom you see now into heaven taken up, being carried aloft on a cloud of light. (From the 9th Ode of Orthros of Ascension, Trans. by Fr. Seraphim Dedes)*

"Wait" with joy for the promises of God to be fulfilled in your life!

Saturday after the Ascension

Baptized by the Holy Spirit

"For John baptized with water, but before many days you shall be baptized with the Holy Spirit."
Acts 1:5
(Epistle read on the Feast of Ascension)

For the next couple of reflections, we are going to be discussing baptism as well as the Holy Spirit, as we move from the Feast of Ascension toward the Feast of Pentecost. One of the temptations in Christianity is to "check the boxes" while not really understanding what it is we are doing. One of the ways this happens is in the sacrament of Baptism. For many, unfortunately, baptism is just a ritual where we "check a box." Baptism is the necessary initiation into the Christian faith, but it is not an end point, it is just a beginning. If everyone who was baptized was in a church, our churches would be overflowing. Sadly, many just get the baptism done, but never really enter into the life of the church, or more importantly, the life of Christ.

Jesus was not the first person to be baptized. The concept of baptism pre-dated Him. "Baptism," before the time of Christ, was a ritual washing, similar to what the sacrament of confession is today. A person would go periodically (once a year) to be "baptized." This is why St. John had the title "the Baptist" or "the Baptizer" because he was one (of presumably a few) person who one could go to in order to receive the periodic ritual baptism with water.

So, when Jesus went to John to be baptized, He was following this custom of ritual washing, even though He had no sin to be washed of. When Jesus was "baptized," the Holy Trinity was revealed. We read in the Gospels, *"when He came out of the water, immediately He saw the heavens opened and the Spirit descending upon Him like a dove; and a voice from heaven, 'Thou art my beloved Son; with Thee I am well pleased.'"* (Mark 1:10-11). Thus was inaugurated a "new" baptism. We are baptized not merely as a ritual, but in the name of the Holy Trinity, imitating His example, and obeying the Great Commission imparted to the Disciples that all nations are to be baptized.

We are baptized not merely with water, but with the Holy Spirit. What does that mean? First, at a Baptism, the Holy Spirit is called to descend upon the water, as He did at the baptism of Christ, and to sanctify the water, to make it holy. We are then immersed in the now holy water. After coming out of the baptismal font, we are immediately anointed with the oil of chrismation, which represents the Holy Spirit. This fulfills what Christ said in John 3:5, *"Unless one is born of water and the Spirit, he cannot enter the Kingdom of God."* So, we receive the Holy Spirit in the sacrament of Chrismation.

To make a simple analogy, the way we do Baptism now is like washing a car—the Baptism is the washing away of the dirt. The Chrismation, or confirmation, is like waxing the car—it seals in the cleanliness and puts on a layer of protection from dirt and harm. The baptism "with water" that was done by John was like washing a car without waxing it. One had to come again and again to be washed clean. The baptism "with the Holy Spirit" is the added step of not only washing a person of sin, but also sealing them with the Holy Spirit, Who, through the sacrament of Chrismation comes to take permanent residence in someone.

The Old Testament, and the old baptism, was centered on rituals and "checking boxes" so to speak. This was good, in that it provided order and structure, but did not provide joy and hope, just order and structure. The New Testament and the baptism in the Holy Spirit, maintain order and structure (it is still a ritual initiation that we all have to do), but it provides more than that. The baptism "in the Holy Spirit" provides joy and hope and spiritual sustenance for the marathon journey through this life to everlasting life.

The Christian life is not one of checking boxes, but on living in a purposeful way. The purpose of our life is to glorify Christ. In turn, He shows us His glory, in ways large and small, each day. So, our expression of our faith shouldn't be worship of rituals, but being "alive" in our faith by loving God and loving one another in ways that are joyful and purposeful.

> *When the wellspring of the grace of the divine Spirit came down to those upon the earth and into fire-bearing streams parted poetically, it refreshed the Apostles and led them to the light. The fire became for them a dewy cloud and rainy flame illumining them. And we in turn through them received divine grace by means of fire and water. The holy light of the Holy Spirit has appeared and illumined the world. (Kathisma, Orthros of Pentecost, Trans. by Fr. Seraphim Dedes)*

Don't just "check boxes" today! Live with joy! Do whatever you do with purpose!

Sunday of the Holy Fathers of the First Ecumenical Council

Alive to God in Christ Jesus

Do you not know that all of us who have been baptized into Christ Jesus were baptized into His death? We were buried therefore with Him by baptism into death, so that as Christ was raised from the dead by the glory of the Father, we too might walk in newness of life. For if we have been united with Him in a death like His, we shall certainly be united with Him in a resurrection like His. We know that our old self was crucified with Him so that the sinful body might be destroyed, and we might no longer be enslaved to sin. For he who has died is freed from sin. But if we have died with Christ, we believe that we shall also live with Him. For we know that Christ being raised from the dead will never die again; death no longer has dominion over Him. The death He died He died to sin, once for all, but the life He lives He lives to God. So you also must consider yourselves dead to sin and alive to God in Christ Jesus.
Romans 6:3-11
(Epistle Lesson read at the Sacrament of Baptism)

The miracle of life is truly that—a miracle. We know that life is created with the biological matter of a male and female coming together, interwoven with a "soul" and this is what creates the miracle of life. In Orthodox Christian theology, we do not believe in the concept of "original sin," which is that the human being is born inherently sinful, having inherited the sin of Adam. (Believe me, I don't need Adam's sin, I have plenty of my own to answer for.) A person is not born "sinful." However, once they come out of the womb and take their first breath of imperfect air, they are united with the "sinful nature" of the world, a world of polluted air and imperfect, polluted people.

In the Sacrament of Baptism, the person being baptized "dies" to sin and puts on the new life, which is Christ. In the ancient church, when baptizing adults and not babies was the norm, this made more sense. After all, how does an infant "die to sin" when it isn't old enough to consciously commit sin? Even if a baby has lived only one minute, it has become united with the sinful nature, the sinful environment, which is why we "cleanse" our children through baptism and don't wait for them to get older and accumulate sins to be cleansed.

Before Christ, there was no concept of dying and living again. Death was finality. Christ raised people like Lazarus from the dead. He was raised from the dead. He can raise us from the dead after we die our earthly, physical death.

Dying, and living again, however, is not limited to physical death and eternal life. "Dying" is something we should do on a daily basis—we should "die" to sin, we should seek to "put to death" our sins, so that we can "live" in Christ. Now, this doesn't mean "sin more" so one can "die more" and then "live more." It means that we are to focus on living in Christ, and the more we live in Christ, the less we are spiritually dying from our sins. Christ, through prayer, scripture, worship, and charity, becomes the daily vitamin that keeps us healthy, that keeps us from falling spiritually sick. At those times when we are spiritually sick, Christ becomes the medicine that heals us from our spiritual sickness.

Every day, and in many moments of the day, there are choices to be made. We have a choice to choose good and a choice to choose evil. We can choose Christ or we can choose sin. Choosing Christ means to put aside the impulse to sin. It means putting sin to death, squashing it, and then choosing Christ. Of course, no one wins this battle every time. Some days, even with the best of people with the best of intentions, evil wins, we choose wrong. That is the human condition. The challenge, and it is a daily challenge, is to *die* to sin, to put sin away; and to *live* in Christ.

When a person loses weight, they shed pounds and are able to move faster and with more vitality. Dying to sin is like shedding the weight of sinful failures so that you can live with more Christian vitality. However, we know that "crash" diets don't work. The choice to live a healthy lifestyle is a daily choice to "die" to sinful eating habits and live with healthy ones. It's the same thing in the spiritual realm—we can't succeed as "crash" Christians, shedding lots of sinful baggage only to put it back on. The healthy Christian lifestyle is the one where we choose to "die" to sinful life habits on a daily basis and to live with Christ at the center. The more we die materially, and the more we die to our own sense of self (ego), the more we are alive spiritually! That is what it means to die to sin and be alive in Christ.

> *The magnificence of the One who in flesh became poor clearly was higher than the heavens raised. Our fallen nature has now been honored by its session with the Father. Therefore let us celebrate and with one voice jubilantly cry aloud, and with gladness of heart let us clap our hands. (From the 9th Ode of Orthros of Ascension, Trans. by Fr. Seraphim Dedes)*

Die to sin and live in Christ today!

Monday after the Ascension

John's End—The Purpose of the "Book"

Now Jesus did many other signs in the presence of the disciples, which are not written in this book; but these are written that you may believe that Jesus is the Christ, the Son of God, and that believing you may have life in His name.
John 20:30-31

But there are also many other things which Jesus did; were every one of them to be written, I suppose that the world itself could not contain the books that would be written.
John 21:25
(From the Eleventh Eothinon Gospel of Sunday Orthros)

Each of the four Evangelists ends his Gospel in a different way. A few days ago, we read in the Gospel of St. Mark how, *"They (the Apostles) went forth and preached everywhere while the Lord worked with them and confirmed the message by the signs that attended it. Amen."* (Mark 16:20) Today we examine not only the purpose of John's Gospel, but also the purpose of the Bible altogether.

John's Gospel actually has two "endings." Both are quoted above. Both verses agree that John's Gospel is not an exhaustive record of Christ's ministry, that there are other things He did that are not recorded in the Gospel. This recognizes the possibility of other written accounts of Jesus' earthly life and ministry, which strengthens the truth of Christ's ministry, since it is confirmed in other writings.

John 20:31 gives the "mission statement" for the Gospel. The purpose of the Gospel is for us to *"believe that Jesus is the Christ, the Son of God, and that believing you (we) may have life in His name."* This statement is significant. Why? Because it reveals what the Gospel is, and what it should be for our lives.

The Gospel is a history book, because it tells the history of Christ's earthly ministry, but it is more than that.

The Gospel is a guidebook to good and moral living, because following its precepts will help lead to a good life, but it is more than that.

The Gospel is the roadmap to God's Kingdom. It is God's Word speaking to us today. In Greek, the Gospel is called the, "Evangelion," which means, "The Good News." The Gospel is indeed the best news, because it not only tells us God's plans, but also reassures us that we are part of those plans. I once heard the Bible called, "God's love letter to each of us."

Because Jesus is the Christ, the promised Messiah, the time for our salvation is at hand. We are not wondering if we can ever attain salvation, but when. Having life in His name is not just our destination, but is part of the journey of life right here and right now. There is enough information in the Gospel for us to believe. There is enough knowledge in the Gospel for it to bring power to our lives. There is enough power that speaks to us through its words—the words of Christ, recounted by His followers, inspired by the Holy Spirit and preserved in these words—that studying the Bible, specifically the Holy Gospels, changes lives.

In prayer, we speak to God. In the Scriptures, God speaks to us. Yes, there are many ways to hear God's voice, but the best way is through reading the Scriptures. One doesn't have to read a lot to take away inspiration. A chapter or even a few verses a day provide direction and inspiration. We are to read the Bible repeatedly and constantly. To read the same passages over and over again only serves to bring deeper meaning as more layers of the message are uncovered and revealed to us.

A prayerful reading of the Bible leads to the revelation of the secrets of a Godly life. Why do I say "secrets," as if to say "hidden messages"? Because for the one who does not read the Bible, or the one who does not read it carefully, or for the one who "reads" and does not allow it's words to penetrate his soul and affect his life, then the Gospel is just words on paper. For the one who reads it carefully, for the one who reads it prayerfully, allowing the words of the Gospel to touch his soul and affect his life, the Gospel is a powerful tool, a holy "book" and the "best news" one can ever hope to hear.

There is a purpose to the message and there is a reason why the evangelists wrote the Gospels and why we are to read them. That purpose is to strengthen our belief that Jesus is the Christ, the Son of God, and with confidence in this, that we may have life in His name, both in our daily life and for eternal life.

> *You were born, as You Yourself willed; You appeared, as You Yourself wished; You suffered in the flesh, O our God; You rose from the dead, having trampled death; You were taken up in glory, Who fills the universe, and You sent us the Divine Spirit, that we might hymn and glorify Your Divinity. (Doxastikon, Orthros of Ascension, Trans. by Fr. Seraphim Dedes)*

Read the Bible today, and every day!

Tuesday after the Ascension

The Most Important Thing in Life Is the Only Non-Seasonal Thing We Do

Then He led them out as far as Bethany, and lifting up His hands He blessed them. While He blessed them, He parted from them, and was carried up into heaven. And they returned to Jerusalem with great joy, and were continually in the temple blessing God.
Luke 24:50-53

There are many "seasons" in life, seasons that are anticipated, seasons that are endured, seasons that are enjoyed, seasons that end, sometimes even seasons that come again. There are childhood years, then teenage years, high school, college, young adult life, single life, married life, child-rearing years, working years, retired years, perhaps years of sickness and decline, until finally the years end. As I look back at my life today, besides a mother and brother whom I've known all my life, everything else can be classified under the umbrella of a season. Even the season of parent and sibling could end at some point.

The only thing in my life that is not seasonal is this—"continually in the temple blessing God." That's the only thing I've done my entire life. I used to take piano lessons, be part of the Boy Scouts, play soccer and go to college. I used to live in California, Massachusetts, Connecticut and North Carolina. I currently live in Florida, serve a church in Tampa, direct a summer camp, and enjoy mowing the lawn. I may one day travel to Europe, have a grandchild or retire. The *only* thing that is going to be part of every season of my life is "continually in the temple blessing God."

I admire people who are really old who come to church. People who are in the sunset of their lives, who walk a little slower, who have fought all their battles, and have all their scars and who are still "continually in the temple blessing God." Because it means that even their seasons of disappointment and frustration haven't shaken their faith or their hope in God. Sometimes the dissatisfactions in life cause people to stop coming to the temple to bless God. However, it is important to maintain "vigil" in the temple, even when the seasons of life disappoint us.

The ultimate hope for the Christian life is to be in heaven, where we will continually be blessing God. This is why it is so important to be in the temple blessing God in this life, because it prepares us to do it in heaven for everlasting life.

There are three distinct phrases in this verse that merit acknowledgement. First, the word *continually*. Continually means constantly. It doesn't mean once in a while or when we feel like it, or twice a year on Christmas and Easter. Continually means all the time. Worship of God and living the Christian life is something we are to strive to do continuously, not only when it is convenient, and not only when life is good. In fact, when life is challenging that's when we want to go to God even more. When life is good, we want to go to God in gratitude. Prayer and worship, scripture and charity should be constants in our lives.

In the temple means coming to the Lord in both a corporate and sacramental context. Many people joke that they are "continually with God" on the golf course or while fishing. I'm glad that people think about God while relaxing—that is a great thing. We know that God is not only in the temple. He is everywhere. We can connect with God and encounter God anywhere. However, it is critical that we connect with Him *in the temple.* For the temple gives us two things—it gives us fellowship with others who are making the same journey. It gives us Christ Himself in a way that we can only experience Him in the temple, in the sacrament of Holy Communion. So, it is important to be *in the temple* continuously.

Finally, *blessing God* is what we are to be doing when we come to the temple. It really saddens me when people come to church habitually late, or when they never receive Holy Communion, or when they come to turn on the coffee machine or sell tickets to the dinner dance in the hall, but never actually worship in the church and think that somehow passes for worship. When we come to the temple, the purpose in doing so is to bless God and for God to bless us. We come to church to *give* blessing to *God*. If we are not coming to glorify God in our worship, why come? We come to receive something from God, His blessings. So if we come late, or come distracted, or come angry, or even come just to check the box, we're really not receiving the blessing God intends for us to have.

The ending of Luke's Gospel, which is today's verse, shows us that as the Disciples saw the Lord ascending in glory, they knew that the season of His earthly ministry was over. They also knew that a new season was beginning, and it was going to be the first "season" that had no end for them, the season of continually being in the temple blessing God, in preparation for receiving His blessings forever, in the heaven to which Christ ascended. He showed us the way to the Kingdom—an important component of which is continually blessing God—so that He will continually and eternally bless us.

> *The unoriginated and pre-eternal God, having in mystical manner now deified the human nature He assumed, has on this day ascended. AS He was proceeding up into heaven with glory great, Angels who had run ahead pointed Him out to the Apostles; and worshipping before Him, they cried aloud, Glory to you, O God, who has ascended. (Kathisma, Orthros of the Ascension, Trans. by Fr. Seraphim Dedes)*

Make sure you get to "the temple" this Sunday!

Wednesday after the Ascension

I Am with You Always!

"And lo, I am with you always, to the close of the age."
Matthew 28:20

Before Christ, there was a mistaken notion that God resided in the temple in Jerusalem. People had to go to the temple to pray. When Jerusalem fell and the people of Israel were exiled to Babylon, not only did they mourn the loss of their city, they even mourned the loss of their God. For they thought the destruction of the temple was the death of God.

God *is* in the temple, and we are to continually worship Him there, as we read in the last reflection. God is also everywhere outside of the temple as well. Not only should we continually be in the temple blessing God, but also we should be blessing Him outside of the temple.

In Orthodox worship, we relive the life of Christ at each Divine Liturgy. The preparation of the Holy Gifts is the Nativity. The prayers, petitions and scriptures remind us of the teachings of Christ. The Great Entrance and placing of the Gifts on the altar is the journey to Golgotha. We hear the "words of institution" from the Last Supper. The Holy Spirit descends on the Gifts in a way reminiscent of Pentecost. Our receiving of Holy Communion is a foretaste of our personal Resurrection in Christ. The receiving of Holy Communion is not only the climax of the service, but also the pinnacle of human experience. Because what moment can be of greater joy than partaking of Christ?

If Holy Communion is the climax of the service and the pinnacle of our worship experience, and if worship is a "break" from the challenges of life outside of worship, then the person who has just received Holy Communion might actually walk away with bittersweet feelings. The joy of receiving Christ might be tempered with the "now I have to go back out into the world" feeling. So, in the Orthodox worship experience, there is a moment that represents the Ascension, with the comforting words of Christ, "Lo I am with you always." After Holy Communion, the priest will hold the chalice in front of the congregation one more time, and say the words, *"Now and forever and to the ages of ages,"* reminding us that as we conclude our worship and depart into the world, that Christ will be with us at all times.

This is a reminder of two things—first, that Christ is always with us. He walks with us every day, in every decision, in every conversation, in every challenge. He is there to provide guidance, wisdom, comfort, patience—whatever is needed. Second, our Christianity does not fit into a compartment. Christ should not be compartmentalized. Worship isn't just "checking a box." Worship is the pinnacle, the crowning jewel, in a life that is supposed to be all about Christ. If Christ is "always" walking with us, then we should "always" be walking with Him.

We should have a sense of Christ at all times. I should sense Christ sitting with me at the computer as I'm typing, because He is there. I should sense Christ in every conversation I have, because He is there. Because Christ is there at all times, that should affect what I write, what I say, what I do. The hymn quoted below speaks of Christ being with us and therefore no one can be against us. With Christ there is no need to fear, because He guards, guides and protects all those who place their hope in Him.

"*I am with you always,*" provides us comfort, but also provides us accountability. If Christ is with us always, then we have to honor Him at all times, we have to strive to behave in a Christ-like manner at all times. We all put Christ in a compartment, so to speak, because we can't be actively thinking about Him when we are sinning. I cannot honor Christ while gossiping, as an example. Or while cursing, or cheating, or getting angry. Impossible. Christ is none of those things. Christ personifies love and love isn't present in any of these things.

"*I am with you always,*" calls us to put away temptations and continually focus on Him. It reminds us that today is a day to rejoice because the Lord made the day, and will be with us in it. It is a reminder that if we go with the Lord, then who can be against us, what can anyone really do to us?

People can try to take our possessions, they can take our reputations, and they can try to take our dignity, but no one can take away our faith. No one can take away our potential for eternal life. No one can take away Christ from us. "*I am with you always,*" is a reminder that Christ is the only thing we have always, and that if we always have Him, that provides joy and comfort for today, direction for tomorrow, purpose for life, and destination for eternal life.

> *When You had fulfilled the dispensation for our sake, and united things on earth with the things in heaven, You were taken up thither in glory, O Christ our God, going not away from any place, but continuing inseparable, and to them that love You crying out, "I am with you, and there is, therefore, none against you." (Kontakion of the Ascension, Trans. by Fr. Seraphim Dedes)*

Go with Christ today!

Thursday after the Ascension

Don't Just Stand Around

And while they were gazing into heaven as He went, behold, two men stood by them in white robes, and said, "Men of Galilee, why do you stand looking into heaven? This Jesus, who was taken up from you into heaven, will come in the same way as you saw Him go into heaven."
Acts 1:10-11

As we wind down these reflections that took us through Lent, Holy Week, the Paschal Season and now the Ascension, pointing us toward Pentecost and beyond, let's review a few of the topics we've covered in the journey, that today's scripture reminds us of.

First, moments of uncertainty are part of any Christian journey. In today's verses, we see the Disciples gazing up toward heaven, wondering what the Ascension meant. In fact, they were probably wondering, "What just happened?"

Secondly, in our moments of uncertainty, God speaks to us. Sometimes it is in ways that are obvious, like two men standing in white robes who spoke to the Disciples. Sometimes God speaks through people or through other means, signs, etc. Sometimes God speaks in ways that are not so obvious, but He does speak, and in order to hear Him, we have to be listening. We have to have eyes that are open to seeing messages, ears that are open to receiving them, minds that are open to understanding them, and most especially hearts that are open to accepting them. God most definitely speaks. It is often us who fail to listen.

Third, the two men questioned the Disciples and asked, "Why do you stand looking into heaven?" I read this to mean, "Why are you standing there looking confused? There is work to do, so stop standing around and go do it."

Fourth, we are told that Jesus will come back again the same way that the Disciples saw Him go. He will come in glory. In the Creed we say, "He will come again in glory to judge the living and the dead." In Matthew 25:31-46, we read that the Lord will come again and judge all the nations.

The message for today is: "Don't just stand around staring and wondering. Go and do something. Because Jesus is Lord, and He is coming back and when He does, He will judge each of us on what we have done with our lives." So, we better get busy using our talents in a way that honors Him and helps one another out. This takes us back to the message of the two great commandments—that we are to love God and one another. We are to do this using the unique talents He gave each of us, knowing that we will one day stand before Him as our judge when He returns in glory to judge us all.

Staring at the heavens is not an entirely useless thing either though. While I don't stare up at the skies looking perplexed very often, I do gaze on them in awe, because God created the skies and everything that is under them. My place in the universe is very insignificant in the magnitude of God, yet in the eyes of God, my place is as important as anyone else's place, since I, and each of us, are of infinite value in His eyes.

Staring at the heavens reminds me that I am not the center of the universe, that One who is much greater than me made me, and that my purpose in life is to honor my Creator, so that one day, just as Christ ascended into heaven, that the clouds of the skies will part and the gates of heaven will be open. So that as Christ entered and sat at the right hand of the Father, I may one day as well.

So, stare and ponder, but *do* as well!

> *The men of Galilee, watching as You were taken up from the Mount of Olives with Your Body, O Logos, heard the voice of Angels who cried out to them, saying "Why do you stand and look? This Jesus, henceforth incarnate, will come again, in the same way as you saw Him go. (From the Praises of Ascension, Trans. by Fr. Seraphim Dedes)*

Ponder on the things of God today. Serve God and serve others today!

Leave-Taking of the Ascension

The Holy Spirit Comes Down as Fire on All People

When the day of Pentecost had come, they were all together in one place. And suddenly a sound came from heaven like the rush of a mighty wind, and it filled all the house where they were sitting. And there appeared to them tongues as of fire, distributed and resting on each one of them. And they were all filled with the Holy Spirit and began to speak in other tongues, as the Spirit gave them utterance.
Acts 2:1-4

Many of us are familiar with the Old Testament story of the Tower of Babel, as told in Genesis 11. We read in that account that all of the people of the earth had one language and few words. They decided to come together to build a tower to the heavens. So, God descended on Babel and created languages, in order to confuse the people so that they could not build a tower to heaven. Because the way to heaven was not going to be a man-made tower, it was going to be our Lord Jesus Christ. The Tower of Babel marked the creation of all the languages of the world, and with the diversity of languages also came a division of peoples, for people only associated with those who spoke the same language.

In the time of Christ, there was a great division of languages and cultures. Jews and Samaritans did not like one another. No one liked the Romans, and the Jews considered Gentiles barbarians. So, when the Holy Spirit descended upon the Disciples on Pentecost, He gave them the ability to speak in all the languages of the earth. All those who were gathered in Jerusalem heard the Good News of Christ in their own language.

At the time of the Ascension, when Jesus "commissioned" the Disciples to "baptize all nations" (Matt. 28:16-20) they must have felt very inadequate when thinking about this daunting task. For not only would they need to travel to foreign lands and encounter foreign customs, but they would also have to be able to articulate the Gospel in foreign languages. The grace of the Holy Spirit, again defined as that which heals what is infirm and completes what is lacking; the Godly quality that makes ordinary extraordinary, empowered the simple fishermen to be able to speak in all the languages known to men. Not only were they able to utter words in these languages, they were able to speak with eloquence and conviction. Think about that. These men who had doubts and fears throughout the earthly ministry of Christ, were not only enabled to speak in all the languages, but spoke with such boldness and confidence that three thousand people converted to the faith on that very first day (Acts 2:41). The Lord, who had once divided the nations at Babel, now through the Holy Spirit, united the world by allowing every person of every nation to hear the Gospel in his or her own language.

The Holy Spirit comes into each of us, as He did for each of the disciples. As the flames came on each disciple, bringing them a specific language to speak and eloquence with which to speak it, the Holy Spirit comes into each of us. He gives to each of us a talent by which to glorify Him and to serve one another. Some are doctors, some are farmers, some are mechanics and others are teachers. There are thousands upon thousands of different and unique talents, all of which are needed for our world to work.

The other thing that the Spirit does is that it gives each of us a unique and special way to proclaim the Gospel. A few are called to be priests and serve the church as their life's work, but it is not just the priests who are called to share the Gospel. Each of us has a talent to proclaim the Gospel. Some can do it as Sunday School teachers, others can sing in the choir, some can be greeters, and others can visit the sick. Any and all of us should cultivate the ability to pray for others and to pray with them. There are hundreds of ways to express the Gospel.

As important as it is to cultivate our talents so that we can maintain a vocation, it is equally as important to cultivate our unique talent by which we further the message of the Gospel. It is really important that we remember this as we prepare for our careers and as we advance in them. It is important that we also continually advance in our knowledge of the Gospel and of spiritual things, and it is important that we strive continually in ways large and small to advance the Gospel of Jesus Christ, guided by the Holy Spirit. None of us are likely to see tongues of fire on our heads, the way that the Holy Spirit came on the Apostles. All of us have tongues of fire in our hearts, the light of the Holy Spirit burning in us. It is up to us to stoke the fire and spread the message. Come back tomorrow to learn the various languages of the Gospel and how to speak them.

> *When the Most High God came down and confused the tongues, He divided the nations. When He distributed the tongues of fire, He called all to unity. And with one voice we glorify the all-Holy Spirit. (Kontakion, Pentecost, Trans. by Fr. Seraphim Dedes)*

Let the "fire" of the Holy Spirit burn in your heart and inspire your life today!

Saturday of the Souls before Pentecost

How Many Languages Can You Speak?

Now there were dwelling in Jerusalem Jews, devout men from every nation under heaven. And at this sound the multitude came together, and they were bewildered, because each one heard them speaking in his own language. And they were amazed and wondered, saying, "Are not all these who are speaking Galileans? And how is it that we hear, each of us in his own native language? Parthians and Medes and Elamites and residents of Mesopotamia, Judea and Cappadocia, Pontus and Asia, Phrygia and Pamphylia, Egypt and the parts of Libya belonging to Cyrene, and visitors from Rome, both Jews and proselytes, Cretans and Arabians, we hear them telling in our own tongues the mighty works of God."
Acts 2:5-11

"We hear them telling in our own tongues the mighty works of God." What an amazing feeling that must have been for the people in Jerusalem on that first Pentecost to hear the Gospel of Jesus Christ in their own language! People who didn't speak Hebrew, or Aramaic or Greek, the predominant languages of the Jewish world at that time, heard the message of salvation in a language that they could understand.

One of the greatest challenges in the church is getting the message into a language that people understand. For those who are Greek Orthodox, this is not the perennial battle of do we offer the services in Greek or English? In fact, today's message is not about the spoken language of worship, but the unspoken languages, many of them, that are needed, in order to spread the message of Christ to everyone.

It is important for the church, and for each member of the church, to be "multi-lingual," to be able to speak more than one language. Here are some examples of the various languages of the church:

The language of prayer. This is perhaps the toughest language to learn. It involves speaking to an unseen God. Do we "think" prayer? Do we "pray out loud?" Do we know how to pray with others? Do we pray from a book or from the heart? Or a combination? The language of prayer includes all of these things.

The language of worship. There is a certain "language" needed in order to worship. This language includes singing, and not feeling self-conscious about it. It includes making gestures, like the sign of the cross, lifting up hands, bowing heads. This is the language in which we praise God, and we do it in the context of community. The language of worship is a language we share collectively.

The languages of community. There are many languages that are spoken in a "community." There are many communities to which we belong. There are communities of marriage, family, friendships, work environments and churches. In these communities, there are many languages: there is a language of teaching, a language of listening, the language of presence (just "being" with someone), and the language of "empathy."

In a church community, there are many languages used to present the Gospel. The language of summer camp is a lot different than the language spoken at the seniors' group. Kids at summer camp learn the Gospel through water balloons and canoes, while at a Bible study, the Gospel is communicated through devotion and discussion. There are many languages within Sunday School, as the three year-old will learn the Gospel differently than the high school student.

The language of love. This is one of the most beautiful yet complex languages because people give and receive love in different ways and with different preferences. For those who are married, I encourage you to read the book, *"The Five Love Languages"* by Gary Chapman. It will give you great insight on how two people might really love each other, but speak a different language of love. There are different versions for single people and for children and teenagers.

The language at the end of life. This is perhaps the most difficult language to speak and very few of us speak it well. Many people at the end of life speak a language about squeezing every minute out of life and cheating death, rather than speaking about and encouraging the entrance into eternal life. Those who speak this language poorly are sometimes judged as having no faith. Those who do speak it well are sometimes judged as fatalistic. This language in particular is one that we all need to speak better.

The Church is supposed to speak all the languages—that's why a thriving church community has not only a good liturgical (or worship) life, but has a vibrant Sunday School, an effective young adult program, a strong youth group, a good Bible study groups, a solid choir, a group for seniors and a group that specializes in outreach. This is because everyone speaks a different language and needs to hear the Gospel in "their own" language. If this church is supposed to speak all the languages, then it is important that the members of the church each learn a few of these languages, because *these* are the languages in which the Gospel is heard. Thus, we must translate the Gospel into these languages, so that it can be heard by all.

> *Now the Apostles of Christ are clothed with power from on high; for the Comforter renews them and is renewed in them, by a mystical renewal of knowledge. And preaching in those strange and exalted words, they instruct us to worship the eternal and simple nature in three hypostases of God the benefactor of all. Therefore, since*

we have been illumined by their teachings, let us worship Father, Son and Spirit, and let us earnestly pray for the salvation of our souls. (From the Aposticha of the Vespers of the Descent of the Holy Spirit on Pentecost, Trans. by Fr. Seraphim Dedes)

Make it a goal to learn many "languages," so that you are in the best position to spread the Gospel to the most people in the diverse ways that they will "hear" it.

Pentecost

A Little Pentecost at Every Liturgy

And all were amazed and perplexed, saying to one another, "What does this mean?" But others mocking said, "They are filled with new wine." But Peter, standing with the eleven, lifted up his voice and addressed them, "Men of Judea and all who dwell in Jerusalem, let this be known to you, and give ear to my words. For these men are not drunk, as you suppose, since it is only the third hour of the day."
Acts 2:12-15

Have you ever wondered why the Divine Liturgy is celebrated on Sunday morning, and not on Sunday afternoon or evening? It has to do with the "Hours" of the day that we mentioned previously. Remember that the "hours" correspond to the hours of sunlight. So the first hour is sunrise, the third hour is mid-morning, the sixth hour is mid-day, the ninth hour is mid-afternoon and the twelfth hour is sunset. Now, because the hours of the sun vary based on if it is summer or winter, in modern times, we consider the first hour around 6:00 A.M., the third hour at 9:00 A.M., the sixth hour at noon, the ninth hour at 3:00 P.M. and the twelfth hour at 6:00 P.M.

In Acts 2:15, in Peter's address to the crowd, we know that the Pentecost event, the descent of the Holy Spirit, occurred about the third hour of the day. We know that the miracle of Pentecost was that the Holy Spirit came down on simple men and endowed them with the gift to speak the Gospel in all the languages known to man. In other words, ordinary men were given the gift to become extraordinary in their ability to proclaim the Gospel, and all of this was made possible by the gift of the Holy Spirit.

When we celebrate the Divine Liturgy in the Orthodox Church, we bring gifts that are rather ordinary, bread and wine, and during the service, we ask for the Holy Spirit to come down, *"upon us and on the gifts here presented, and make this bread the precious Body of Your Christ, and that which is in this cup to be the precious Blood of Your Christ, changing them by Your Holy Spirit, Amen, Amen, Amen."* (Divine Liturgy of St. John Chrysostom, trans. by Holy Cross Seminary Press) In this sense, every celebration of the Divine Liturgy is like a little Pentecost, because not only do we call the Holy Spirit to come down upon the Gifts we are presenting, to make ordinary things into the extraordinary Body and Blood of Christ, but before we ask the Holy Spirit to consecrate our Gifts, we ask for Him to come "*upon US,*" to make us extraordinary as well.

The Divine Liturgy is celebrated mid-morning, between the "third" and "sixth" hours of the day (between 9:00 A.M. and noon) because this is the time of day when Pentecost happened. (There are, of course, certain exceptions to this, including prescribed Vesperal Liturgies on Christmas Eve and the Eve of Epiphany, when we are supposed to celebrate the Divine Liturgy in the evening. The Paschal Divine Liturgy was moved in recent years to the midnight hour. By "economia" or dispensation, Bishops of the church allow priests to celebrate the Divine Liturgy in the evening on certain occasions. The Pre-Sanctified Liturgy during Lent has no consecration, no descent of the Holy Spirit, so it is held in the late afternoon or evening. The Sunday Divine Liturgy, the Liturgy observed on the Lord's Day, with the exception of Pascha, is always offered between the third and sixth hours of the morning.)

After the Divine Liturgy in most Orthodox churches today, there will be three special prayers offered in the context of a Vespers service. (Vespers is normally celebrated in the evening hours, but because this Vespers is so important, and because the church recognizes that many people won't come back for this service if it were held tonight, it is appended to the morning's Liturgy). This service is many times called, "The Vespers of the Descent of the Holy Spirit." These three prayers offer us a glimpse into history—they recall the saving work of Christ, as well as the historical event of Pentecost. They ask the Holy Spirit to come into us with a continual infusion of His grace. They ask the Holy Spirit to help sustain us through our lives. they reference the Kingdom of Heaven, praying for loved ones who have already passed away, and asking that we be reunited with them in Heaven.

Many people think that the church is an heirloom or a relic that has become outdated and is stagnant. Nothing could be farther from the truth. The church doesn't call on us to merely "remember" these important days of Pascha and Pentecost. It calls on us to continually live in them. We are supposed to live in the state of joy that the Apostles had at the Resurrection. We have the opportunity to be "graced" by the Holy Spirit at every Divine Liturgy. Each week we experience Pentecost anew. We not only remember it. We experience it. We ask for the Holy Spirit to descend on each of us each week and to give us the strength and the grace to be extraordinary in our lives. We do not only ask for the extraordinary to come down on the Gifts, but upon us as well.

> *Let us celebrate with joy this final post-festal feast, O believers; for it is the feast of Pentecost today, and the fulfillment of the promise and the appointed time. For on this day the fire of the Paraclete descended on the earth immediately, as in the form of tongues, and illumined the Disciples and made them initiates of heaven. The holy light of the Holy Spirit has appeared and illumined the world. (Kathisma, Orthros of Pentecost, Trans. by Fr. Seraphim Dedes)*

Receive the Holy Spirit (again) today!

EPILOGUE—THE MISSION OF THE CHURCH

The Great Commission and the Ascension of Christ
Thru the hand of Fr. Anthony Salzman, www.imageandlikeness.com

Feast of the Holy Spirit

Life in the Early Church

Now when they heard this they were cut to the heart, and said to Peter and the rest of the apostles, "Brethren, what shall we do?" And Peter said to them, "Repent, and be baptized every one of you in the name of Jesus Christ for the forgiveness of your sins; and you shall receive the gift of the Holy Spirit."
Acts 2:37-38

For the last week of these reflections that have brought us through Triodion, Lent, Pascha, the Ascension and now Pentecost, we are going to focus on "life in the early church" which should serve as a blueprint for life in the modern church. The Pentecost event was transformative for the whole world. Why? First, the Apostles were able to communicate the Gospel in all the languages known to man. Everyone heard the Gospel in his or her own language. Second, people who did not know the Christian message saw, before their own eyes, simple men become extraordinary speakers. They saw the power of God at work, and it captivated their hearts; they wanted to know more.

When people heard all of the amazing things that Peter and the rest of the Apostles were saying, they approached them and asked how their own hearts could be transformed as well. The zeal of the Apostles made for a compelling witness and people were very attracted to what they were seeing.

Peter told the people that coming to Christ was a three-step process. First, they had to repent. They had to change the orientation of their lives from their previous life toward their Christian life, believing and acting appropriately. Second, they needed to be baptized for the "remission" of their sins. (In the Greek translation of Acts 2:38, the word, "afesin," meaning, "remission" is used. As occurs many times in the English translations of the Bible, this word is mistranslated as "forgiveness." "Remission" means complete wiping out of sin, which is what Christ did on the Cross, thus it is the more correct translation.) If they did these two things—come to Christ in repentance, and accept Him through baptism—then they would receive the gift of the Holy Spirit.

In the Orthodox Church, immediately after one is baptized, he or she receives the Holy Spirit through the sacrament of Chrismation. Holy Chrism is made from many oils taken from all corners of the world and consecrated approximately every ten years at the Ecumenical Patriarchate in Constantinople (Istanbul, Turkey). The Holy Chrism is then distributed to all the Orthodox Churches in the world and all those who are baptized are then anointed with the Holy Chrism, sealing them with the Holy Spirit.

The Holy Spirit is continuously bestowed on the faithful through the sacramental life of the church. The Holy Spirit descends at each Divine Liturgy, consecrating the bread and wine into the Body and Blood of Christ. The faithful are to partake of the Eucharist often. Even if someone does not receive Holy Communion at the Divine Liturgy, they still stand in the presence of the Holy Spirit as was mentioned in the last reflection.

The Holy Spirit "effects" all of the sacraments in the church. We have mentioned the Divine Liturgy. We have mentioned the Sacrament of Chrismation, which is the Holy Spirit coming into someone. At the Sacrament of Baptism, we call upon the Holy Spirit to come down and bless the water, so that the person who is baptized is "changed," putting away the old person and living for Christ, because the water is no longer ordinary water, but the saving water of baptism.

When we receive the Sacrament of Holy Unction during Holy Week (or other times of the year), we ask for the Holy Spirit to descend on the oil we bring, a rather common commodity, and we ask that the oil be transformed with healing power, to heal the physical and spiritual wounds of those who are anointed with it. In the Sacrament of Confession, we ask for the grace of the Holy Spirit to come down on the person who is repenting of their sins, to loose the sins that they have confessed. In fact, the final prayer of the sacrament offers, "*The grace of the Holy Spirit, through my (the priest's) unworthy person, has loosened and forgiven your sins.*" The priest doesn't forgive the sins. The person confessing doesn't loosen his or her own sins. Rather, it is the grace of the Holy Spirit that loosens the sins of the faithful, allowing them to recommit themselves to Christ and be loosened of their former guilt.

The Sacraments of Baptism and Chrismation are required sacraments of initiation. In order to come into the life of the church, one has to receive these two sacraments. They are offered one time in a lifetime. The Sacraments of Holy Communion, Holy Unction and Confession are to be done on a more frequent basis. Holy Communion should be received, ideally, on a weekly basis. Holy Unction is received at a minimum of once a year, during Holy Week. The faithful should partake in the Sacrament of Confession at least once a year.

There are two other sacraments that are "optional," meaning that they are not needed in order to experience a full life and a successful journey to salvation. The Holy Spirit "effects" these as well. In the Sacrament of Marriage, we ask for God's heavenly grace, the Holy Spirit, to come down on a man and a woman and unite them into a family. Again, ordinary made extraordinary through the grace of the Holy Spirit. In the Sacrament of Ordination, ordinary men are endowed with the Holy Spirit to be the celebrants of the sacraments and leaders of the church. I can tell you from experience, celebrating the sacraments is an extraordinary, otherworldly experience.

Thus, life in the church is a continual experience of receiving the Holy Spirit. As Peter said, "repent and be baptized and then receive the Holy Spirit." Baptism is a one-time event. Repentance is something we all must strive to do on a regular basis. We are aided in this by receiving the Holy Spirit on a continual basis as well.

As many of you as were baptized into Christ have put on Christ. Alleluia. (From the Divine Liturgy on Pentecost, Trans. by Fr. Seraphim Dedes)

Live with "grace" today!

Tuesday after Pentecost

The Shortest Distance Between Two Points is a Straight Line

For the promise is to you and to your children and to all that are far off, every one whom the Lord our God calls to Him." And he testified with many other words and exhorted them, saying, "Save yourselves from this crooked generation."
Acts 2:39-40

There is no question that the shortest distance between two points is a straight line. That's one of the reasons why the interstate freeway system was created, to get people from place to place across our country in the most efficient way possible. Taking "back roads" not only takes longer, but if these roads are not well traveled, if they don't have "services" like gas stations, restaurants and hotels, then they might not be the safest roads by which to travel.

There is no question that we live in a "crooked" society. It seems that we have a hard time arriving at any destinations because we can't pick the right roads. For instance, to have a good marriage requires honesty, patience and forgiveness. If these drop out of a marriage, then the marriage becomes "crooked." This is because instead of driving straight on the interstate to a happy marriage, a couple is taking the "back roads" and "hoping" they find their destination. Yes, it is still possible to find the destination, but it takes more time and there is more risk that one is not going to make it. This is why marriages are not making it—because they are going off of the straight path and trying to make it without a road map.

There were certain "rules" and "standards" that made society "upwardly mobile." When people saved money, they put a sizeable down payment on a house, the houses grew in value, and people "flipped" houses and bought larger houses. When banks were deregulated and all of a sudden anyone could have a house, the dream of home ownership actually declined, because now the route was "crooked" and not the "straight" route it had been.

These days, hardly anyone spends four years in college. They either rush through in two or three, or drag out a four-year program into five or six years. Neither really works.

I read somewhere that God made the day twenty four hours long—eight hours to work, eight hours to rest, and eight hours for family, house, relaxation, hobbies, exercise, and spirituality. We've tinkered with that formula so that now many people work more than eight hours, sleep much less than eight hours and family time, relaxation, exercise, hobbies, and spirituality are getting squeezed out. God also "commanded" us to remember the Sabbath, to have a day of rest, to worship and to be with our families. It is one of the Ten Commandments. Again, we have tinkered with that as well, which no doubt has contributed to the continued decline of the family unit, and increase in personal stress.

The best way to a happy marriage is *not* to live together before getting married. The best way to raise a child is in the context of a marriage. We've messed with those formulas as well. Again, if the goal of life is to get from where we are to where God is, then the best way to do that is to get off the "back roads" and get on God's highway for us; to stop walking the crooked path and get on the straight one.

In traveling circles, there are many who will tell you that the journey is more interesting if you take the back roads; to stay on the interstate is just boring. I might agree with this if I didn't have a destination in mind, or an urgency to get there. We have a destination in mind—heaven. We have feel urgency—no one knows how long he or she has to live. So, it is best to take the safe path that will take us in the most efficient way to our glorious destination.

Finally, sad to say, there are people who don't believe in the destination. They have no use for the map. They live on the back-roads of society, and just like the person who travels the back roads with no map, they become lost. They have no sense of direction. As the years of life go by, they wonder whether they even have a purpose.

Echoing the words of St. Peter, let us save ourselves from the crooked generation we live in, and get on the straight path that God has laid for us, the one that doesn't get us lost on the back roads, but the one that leads us to His Kingdom.

> *Your Church is arrayed in the holy blood of Your Martyrs who witness throughout the world, as though in purple and fine linen. Through them she cried to You, Christ our God, "Send down to Your people Your tender love, grant peace from above to Your commonwealth, and to our souls Your great mercy. (Apolytikion from the Feast of All Saints, Trans. by Fr. Seraphim Dedes)*

Walk the straight path today!

Wednesday after Pentecost

Three Thousand Souls in One Day!

*So those who received his word were baptized,
and there were added that day about three thousand souls.*
Acts 2:41

That oration of St. Peter must have been pretty incredible, if it converted three thousand souls in one day! I often think about church growth—it is part of my "ministry" as a priest and part of my "job" as an administrator of a parish. Why is it that some churches are growing and others are in decline? Why is it that overall in America, at this time, churches in general are in decline? At the outset, on the day of Pentecost, three thousand people, who woke up that morning, not knowing what Christianity was about, were converted and gave their lives to Christ. How did that happen?

There are two actions that took place that led to this mass conversion of people. The first action was a "witness" on the part of St. Peter and the other Apostles. This witness included "preaching." The Apostles taught about Christ, using all the languages that they were empowered to speak in. The Apostles not only imparted words, but they imparted these words with zeal, confidence, conviction and boldness. There is a critical difference between the words that are spoken and how they are said. There is a big difference between the "ouch" someone says when they stub their toe on a piece of furniture, and the harrowing cry of pain when someone has broken an arm or leg. Likewise, there is a difference in the message of Christ when it is offered "to check a box" and when it is offered with great feeling, inspiration, and conviction.

Very few people actually talk about Christ. We do a lot of talking about the church, and what the church should do better. We do not do enough talking about Christ. We don't give a lot of witness for how the power of Christ can change lives. When is the last time you spoke to someone about how Christ has changed your life? In order for the message of salvation to be spread, there need to be people who can spread it. Imagine St. Peter and the other Apostles, if they had received the Holy Spirit on Pentecost, and they just rejoiced by themselves, didn't say anything to anyone? The Church would have been short-lived. They recognized that they had been imbued with an ability to preach the message of Christ and they did. Each of us has been given the same ability to spread the Gospel in some language. The challenge is do we have enough knowledge in order to speak credibly about Christ, and do we have enough confidence, zeal, conviction and boldness to step out and actually do that?

The second thing that was needed on the day of Pentecost was people to "receive" the words of St. Peter and the other Apostles. Scream out a message in a forest where there is no one to hear it and the message goes nowhere. Scream out a message to a crowd of people who are wearing headphones and it doesn't go anywhere either. Listen to a message with a heart that is closed and the message is quickly forgotten. So, there need to be hearers for the message to spread and those hearers must come with open hearts. Before one can share the message, one has to understand and accept the message, and that can only happen when we have a heart that is ready to receive the message.

Many people look at the message of Christianity like a buffet at a restaurant. They want to pick and choose which parts to follow. This dilutes the message because when we pick and choose only which parts we want to follow, we are not equipping ourselves to spread the genuine message, just part of it. For instance, one can't just speak of the joy of the Lord without speaking of our need for repentance. Joy is easy, repentance is hard. One cannot rejoice in the sacrifice of Christ without making his or her own sacrifices.

The reason that hearts aren't open to Christ is that our society doesn't encourage that. In fact, it discourages and slanders the Christian message at almost every turn. Additionally, we, the messengers, are at times giving a diluted message.

There are two things I can say for certain regarding growing the church. First, it is a commandment of Christ to grow the church, not merely a suggestion. So, if a church community, or any individual Christian, does not understand the need to grow the church, there is something fundamentally lacking in that community or individual. Second, we can't force people to come to Christ. We can work hard to model Christian behavior, share the joy of the Lord and work on our own salvation. These are things we can do. In modeling these things, we encourage others by example.

If we see ourselves like the Apostles, as "fishers of men," then it is important that we have the tools (in their case the boats and the nets, in our case the knowledge of the faith) and the persistence (in their case, remember the fish didn't always bite right away, and in our case, those who hear the message don't always receive it, or receive it right away) to keep casting the net again and again, with joyful anticipation of catching fish. Remember when the disciples cast the net on the "right" side; this is when they caught the fish. When we cast the net in the right way, we will catch (Christians) as well.

Blessed are You, O Christ our God. You made the fishermen all-wise, by sending down upon them the Holy Spirit, and so through them you drew the world into Your net. O Lover of mankind, glory to You. (Apolytikion, Feast of Pentecost, Trans. by Fr. Seraphim Dedes)

Think of ways that you can help spread the faith and grow the Church.

Note: There is no fasting the week after Pentecost, so no fasting today or Friday.

Thursday after Pentecost

The Purpose of the Church

*And they devoted themselves to the apostles' teaching and fellowship,
to the breaking of bread and the prayers.*
Acts 2:42

Many times, even those who are very involved in the church (this includes priests, Parish Council members, Sunday School teachers and others in church leadership) forget about the true purpose of the church. As we continue to discuss the life of the early church, today's verse mentions the main activities of the early church, activities that should form the purpose and the core of church life in every church community today.

Those involved in the early church, we are told in Acts 2:42, had four purposes: Teaching/learning about the faith, fellowship, breaking of the Bread (the Eucharist) and prayers. A fifth was soon added, which was the "daily distribution," serving food to the poor and the widows. (Acts 6:1) These were the purposes of the church, the anchors of community life in the early church. Churches that want to be successful today would do well to make these five activities the core of their ministry.

Teaching/Learning—Knowledge is power. There is no power for someone in something they have no knowledge of. For example, I do not know much about the periodic table in chemistry. So, when someone starts talking about the elements and their properties, I quickly tune out and move on. If our knowledge of Christianity is like my knowledge of chemistry, then we will quickly lose interest in the things of God. Teaching and learning about the faith is also not confined to Sunday School, or to children. We should strive to continually learn about our faith, and we should see opportunities to teach others about the faith throughout our adult life. We must become lifelong students who at the same time are lifelong teachers.

Fellowship—A Christian does not live in isolation. Being a Christian is about being "in communion" with the Lord and with one another, following the two great commandments which are to love God and to love our neighbor. St. Paul tells us in Galatians 6:2 that we are to "bear one another's burdens" and this is done in the context of fellowship.

Breaking of the Bread—The central act of the church is the celebration of the Eucharist. One can learn about the faith in a Bible study in a home. One can have fellowship with other Christians outside the church. The central act of the church community is the Eucharist because that is what is unique to the church community. It is the one thing that the church community does that cannot be done outside of the church community. Every church is, in reality, a Eucharistic assembly. So, the church where I serve in Tampa is really the Eucharistic assembly of Tampa, because this is where the Orthodox Christian faithful of Tampa gather to celebrate the Eucharist.

Prayer—The most basic function of the church is prayer. Prayer is done constantly. Individual members pray to the Lord. Members pray for one another. Gatherings open and close with prayer. The priest prays with and for his parishioners. Prayer is something that should be done daily by all Christians, multiple times per day.

Daily distribution—From the get-go, there was a sense that the church needed to minister to the poor, and to those outside of the church. Community outreach, both ministering to one's own church community and the community outside of the church, was important in the life of the early church. The church had a great desire to serve the poor, the widows, those afflicted in any way, so that no one would go hungry, no one would go without prayer, and no one would be excluded from fellowship.

The early church was not a social club. It didn't have a food or cultural festival to sustain itself. It wasn't concerned with putting up beautiful buildings. It didn't single out people for awards or recognition. The Church had a narrow focus—teaching, fellowship, the Eucharist, prayer, and charity. It did these five things constantly and it did them well.

Remember that the early church was growing at a rate of 40% per decade. And it did that by sticking to the "basics." If we want to recover the spirit of the early church, and enjoy the growth and the vibrancy of the early church, it is found in teaching, fellowship, the Eucharist, prayer and charity. Yes, there is a need to build a church complex to establish a home base for church activities, yet it is necessary for Parish Councils and budgets to administer the church. The church exists for us to learn about Christ, to enjoy fellowship with one another, to receive the Eucharist, to pray and to give/help/serve others who are in need. So, whatever our role is in the church, whether we are the priest, the Parish Council member, the Sunday School teacher, or the parishioner, we have to remember that we each play an important role in fulfilling the true mission of the church.

> *Christ the Lord has made wondrous all of His Saints that were on the earth, for as the Apostles declared, they bore His marks and in their flesh shared His sufferings, adorning themselves therewith, and distinguishing themselves in the beauty that is divine. Let us therefore praise and acclaim them as never-fading flowers and as voluntary victims, and as the Church's unerring stars. (From the Praises of the Feast of All Saints, Trans. by Fr. Seraphim Dedes)*

Make sure you stay involved in learning, teaching, fellowship, the Eucharist, prayer and charitable outreach on a regular basis.

Friday after Pentecost

"Common" is the Root of "Community"

And fear came upon every soul; and many wonders and signs were done through the apostles. And all who believed were together and had all things in common; and they sold their possessions and goods and distributed them to all, as any had need.
Acts 2:43-45

In the Old Testament, we were introduced to the concept of the tithe, which is that ten percent of everything a person had was given to the temple, in order to contribute to the welfare of all. For those who complain that the Old Testament has been superseded by the New, that nothing in the Old Testament applies today, and that the concept of the "tithe" is an archaic idea of an age gone by, the book of Acts seems to imply that all possessions are to be given to the church community. Given the choice between giving 100% or giving 10%, it seems that ten percent is the easier choice.

While someone could use these verses to debate the merits of "communism" as a Godly political system (it isn't), as I reflect on these verses, I want to focus on the word "common." "Common" is the root word of both "Community" and "Communion." The Church is the Body of Christ, a "community" of believers who come together to partake of "Holy Communion." Without "community" and without "Communion," there is no Church. Without points in "common," among the worshippers, there is neither of these.

The ideal church community strives for the common good, the good of all people. The greatest "good" is Holy Communion, which is why this is the centerpiece of any Church. People coming together on a regular basis to partake of Divine Nature is what the Church is all about. Communion is not enjoyed privately. In fact, there cannot be a celebration of the Divine Liturgy unless there is at least one person besides the priest present. Every time Holy Communion is administered, it is in the context of community. So that even when the priest gives Communion to someone who is in the hospital, it is the priest and patient who are present, a "community" of two people.

Partaking of Holy Communion is the central act that Christians experience in community. This is why it is perplexing that some members of the "community" rarely partake of Communion, or even worse, rarely participate in worship. Worship and the Eucharist is central to the community and all members in it. How can one consider himself a member of the community, if he does not engage in worship, or receive Holy Communion?

Any "community" is set up based on things held in "common." This is why the center of the church community cannot be "culture." In the Greek Orthodox Church as an example, not all members are of Greek ancestry. If "Greek" is the center of the community, then members who are not of Greek ancestry cannot truly be part of the community. The youth group is not the center, neither is the senior's group, neither is the Parish Council, or the community outreach groups. The most "common" denominators of all Christians are Christ and our need for Him to save us from our sins. That's why humility and repentance should be at the center of "community" life, second only to the Eucharist. This is why prayer is at the heart of every activity, and worship is the most important activity in the community, because these are the two things that unite us in Christ, and that unite us with each other.

"As any had need" means that in the ideal church community, everyone bears the burdens of the others, as we read in Galatians 6:2. If someone has two coats, as Jesus says in Luke 3:11, *"let him share with him who has none; and he who has food, let him do likewise."* If we are looking out for one another, there ideally should be no one who is hungry, no one who is without a home, and no one who is without a friend. There should be a sense of the "common good" in each community. That means that if I'm sharing the pew with someone sitting next to me, ideally I should know his or her name and even his or her need, so that I can help carry the burden.

In a book I read once about church work, I read the terms "worship circle" and "fellowship circle." The "worship circle" is defined as all those who worship. The "fellowship circle" is defined as those who share in the community life outside of worship. There are many people who are part of the "worship circle," but not part of the "fellowship circle." Their experience of church consists of worshipping and nothing else. Sad to say, there are a few people who are part of the "fellowship circle," who participate in the various aspects of community life who are not part of the "worship circle." Ideally, there are not two circles—everyone worships, and everyone is part of the community life outside of worship as well.

I will always believe that if everyone gave ten percent of their income to the church, and if every church gave ten percent to social welfare programs, that we wouldn't need government to provide welfare, nor would we be constantly solicited by various charities. Because the church, to a large extent, has not followed this teaching of giving *"as any had need,"* government and other organizations have taken over this domain, which is not necessarily a good thing. It is certainly not consistent with the verses above. Finally, a person's choice to contribute to the life of community or to the general welfare of others should be just that, a choice. Contributing to the general community because it is required, is not the same as doing out of love. The choice to give should be done out of a sense of compassion and love for others and should be a matter of conscience. When our lives are examined at the Judgment Seat of Christ, He will know what is in each of our hearts, in the conscience of each, so we have ample incentive to give and to love.

In the ideal life, participation in church becomes one of our primary, if not the primary thing that we do. For what is more primary than the Eucharist, "Communion," and what is more of an incentive or encouragement to participate in the Eucharist, than to do so in the context of a loving, supportive and encouraging "community"!

> *By their virtues' effulgent light, they made the earth to be heaven-like and they imitated the death of Jesus Christ. These are the ones who have walked the way that leads to immortal life. By the surgery of grace, they removed human passions as healers of mankind. And united throughout the world the Martyrs have courageously contested. Let us extol all the Saints today. (From the Praises of the Feast of All Saints, Trans. by Fr. Seraphim Dedes)*

Help someone who "has a need" today!

Leave-Taking of Pentecost

Do What Pleases God

And day by day, attending the temple together and breaking bread in their homes, they partook of food with glad and generous hearts, praising God and having favor with all the people. And the Lord added to their number day by day those who were being saved.
Acts 2:46-47

There are lots of things to read concerning the Christian life. First and foremost, there is the Bible, which we should all be reading on a regular basis. There are books on theology and church history. There are self-help books, daily meditations and reflections like these. There are lots and lots of them, beautiful and inspiring and unique messages crafted by very devout Christian authors. The amount of information that is out there about living the Christian life is astounding. In this age of mass information, just about all of it is only a few clicks of the mouse away.

Sometimes we are victims of information overload. We take in a lot, and sometimes it is hard to retain a lot of it. How can we boil down all the information into useful mantras that we can use to guide our daily lives?

One of the simplest mantras I use in my life is, "Do what pleases God." If I use this mantra as a guide in every decision I make, I am going to make many more good decisions than bad ones. Think about this mantra and hold it up to the various decisions you make each day. Does your driving please God? How about your effort at work? Does your marriage please God? Does your parenting please God? Does your obedience to the commandments please God? You could hold up dozens, if not hundreds of things you do on a daily basis to this litmus test. Is what I am doing pleasing to God?

In today's scripture verse, we read that Christians were attending the temple together on a daily basis. In the early church, it was the practice to receive the Eucharist on a daily basis. Emphasis is placed on the gladness and generosity that was felt in the hearts of the people. This seems to be a far cry from the disposition of the hearts of many today. The people were continually praising God. Having favor with those around them was important as well. For having the favor of God and the favor of others go hand in hand. Just like loving God and loving one's neighbor are the two greatest commandments. In doing one, the other follows. If we do what pleases God, we will find favor with our neighbor. If we extend our love toward our neighbor, this will be pleasing to God.

The net result of all of this was the growth of the church, because people saw a faith that people were not only willing to die for, but that people were willing to live for on a daily basis. The genuine love and joy that was lived in the lives of the early Christians was contagious. In modern society, our collective state of angst and mistrust, cynicism and ego make it hard to present a church that is attractive to the one who doesn't know Christ.

Doing what pleases God is a great way to recapture the joy of those early Christians, who, while not well learned in the faith, still lived with a contagious zeal. We are much more educated than they; we have an ability to read and to acquire information for ourselves that they didn't have, yet, by and large, the church is not growing. It's not for lack of information. It is for lack of gratitude toward God.

One goal that each Christian should set is to recruit at least one more Christian. It pleases God when more are added to the number of those being saved. That was true in the book of Acts and it is still true today. So, as we set spiritual goals for ourselves, we should set a goal to recruit other people to join the Body of Christ. We should set goals for how many people we will talk to about Christ, how many conversations a week that we want Him to be a part of.

We should set goals to pray on a daily basis, to read scripture on a daily basis, and to do what pleases God on a daily basis. Certainly our prayers and study of the scriptures are pleasing to God, because these things bring us closer to Him. We need to set as a *daily* goal to minister to those around us. For finding favor with others, by serving them, is how one finds favor with God. So, evaluate each conversation, each action, and each interaction by this barometer—does this please God?

> *O Planter of creation, Lord, to You does the entire world bring as an offering the God-bearing martyr Saints, as being nature's first fruits. At their earnest entreaty, keep Your Church in a state of profoundest peace, through the Theotokos, O Lord abundantly merciful.* (Kontakion, Feast of All Saints, Trans. by Fr. Seraphim Dedes)

Do what pleases God today!

Feast of All Saints

The End Goal for Everyone—Numbered Among the Saints

Jesus said: "Everyone who acknowledges Me before men, I also will acknowledge before My Father who is in heaven; but whoever denies Me before men, I also will deny before My Father who is in heaven.
Matthew 10:32-33

He who loves father or mother more than Me is not worthy of Me; and he who loves son or daughter more than Me is not worthy of Me; and he who does not take his cross and follow Me is not worthy of Me.
Matthew 10: 37-38

Then Peter said in reply, "Lo, we have left everything and followed You. What then shall we have?" Jesus said to them, "Truly, I say to you, in the new world, when the Son of Man shall sit on His glorious throne, you who have followed Me will also sit on twelve thrones, judging the twelve tribes of Israel. And every one who has left houses or brothers or sisters or father or mother or children or lands, for My Name's sake, will receive a hundredfold, and inherit eternal life. But many that are first will be last, and the last first.
Matthew 19:27-30
(Gospel read at the Liturgy on All Saints Day)

Today ends the Paschal cycle that began 18 weeks ago. We had the period of the Triodion, the time when we evaluated the changes needing to be made in our spiritual lives. Great Lent gave us an opportunity to make modifications and start new habits. Holy Week was a time to remember and relive the Passion and Resurrection of Jesus Christ. The Paschal season has been a time of celebration and renewal. Now with the Paschal season coming to an end, it's time to stay focused on doing the things we've learned on this journey.

The last feast of the Paschal cycle is the feast of All Saints. While other Christian denominations celebrate this day on November 1, the Orthodox Christian Church places it after Pentecost, as the end to the Paschal cycle, to remind us that this is the end goal of all Christians, to achieve the blessedness of the saints in the Kingdom of Heaven.

Jesus tells us in the Gospel lesson those who have lived for God and not for the world will be rewarded in the Kingdom of Heaven. They *"will receive a hundredfold and inherit eternal life."* Those who were first with everything, but didn't live a Christian life will be counted as last for eternal life. Those who have lived a Christian life, those who have put Christ first (and anyone who does that is going to suffer in some way, some will even suffer greatly), those who were accounted as "last" in this life, will be accounted as "first" by being accepted into the Kingdom of Heaven.

As Christians, we are called to holiness. We are called to be like Christ in every way—we are to be obedient to the commandments. We are to help others. We are to preach, to teach, and to help heal our fellow man. We are to help carry one another's burdens. We are to stay faithful even to death. A death like Christ's, one that is experienced with faith in God, with forgiveness toward others, will lead to a Resurrection like Christ's, Ascension into heaven, and an enthronement at the right hand of the Father. In 1 Peter 1:13-16, we read:

> *Therefore gird up your minds, be sober, set your hope fully upon the grace that is coming to you at the revelation of Jesus Christ. As obedient children, do not be conformed to the passions of your former ignorance, but as He who called you is holy, be holy yourselves in all your conduct; since it is written, "You shall be holy, for I am holy."*

The end goal of life, the purpose of our life, is to "graduate" to eternal life. The Paschal journey is a yearly "course" designed to keep us focused on that goal. It is the same cycle we experience every year. As every year goes by we become both older in life experience and closer to our judgment before God, which will determine if we inherit eternal life. As we leave this journey, let us do so with focus on the overall goal—eternal life. How do we reach that goal? The answer is in the verses above—*Be Holy, as He is Holy*. How do we do that? Set God as the source and center of your life. Start each day off with prayer and with gratitude. Live each day with purpose. Strive to help someone each day. Learn how to have empathy. Strive to forgive. Work to improve. Trust that God has a plan. Have faith even when you don't understand. Choose joy.

The goal of the Church is to help people find their way to Paradise. The goal of the people in the Church is to help one another in realizing this goal. The purpose of this Lenten and Paschal journey has been reminding, relearning and renewing our commitment to this goal. The ending of the Paschal season this year is not the end of the journey. It is the end of this year's chapter. It is time to practice what we've learned. Next year, in early spring, we'll get another refresher and reminder, and make the journey again, a year older, a year wiser, and a year closer to the destination.

Many of the prayers in the services of the church end with the phrase *"through the intercessions of the Holy Theotokos and ever-Virgin Mary and all the saints who have pleased You (God) throughout the ages."* Many of us are concerned with our legacy. What will people remember of us when we are no longer here? I have a long way to go in my journey to salvation, but one thing I know I've learned already, it doesn't matter how people remember me when I'm no longer here. It matters what the Lord thinks of me when I'm no longer here. Our number one goal, as far as legacy goes, is to be numbered among the saints, to be living eternally with those who have pleased God. The word "Saint" in Greek is "Agios," which means "set apart." If God is going to set us apart and honor us with eternal life, then the goal of this life is a journey to holiness that starts by striving to set ourselves apart every day. We don't have to wait for Lent or Pascha to do this. We don't even have to wait until tomorrow. Holiness is something we can pursue at any moment. So pursue it today, tomorrow, and every day, until we attain the glory of God, in His everlasting Kingdom!

The Baptist John the Forerunner, the Apostles and Prophets, Martyrs and holy Hierarchs, the Devout and Ascetics, and the divine Hieromartyrs, and the God-loving women, and all the Righteous men of old, and the Angelic orders, let us extol dutifully honoring them with praises, while entreating our Savior Christ, that we attain their glory. (Exapostelarion, Feast of All Saints, Trans. by Fr. Seraphim Dedes)

Be holy, as He is holy!

To Him be the glory to the ages of ages. Amen.

CPSIA information can be obtained
at www.ICGtesting.com
Printed in the USA
BVHW062338240221
600655BV00002B/5